ROGER VOSS'
GUIDE TO

PORT
AND
SHERRY
AND OTHER
FORTIFIED WINES

ROGER VOSS'

GUIDE TO

PORT

AND

SHERRY

AND OTHER
FORTIFIED WINES

Mitchell Beazley

Published in Great Britain in 1993
by Mitchell Beazley International,
an imprint of Reed Consumer Books Limited,
Michelin House, 81 Fulham Road
London SW3 6RB
and Auckland, Melbourne, Singapore and Toronto

Part of this text was first published in 1989 as part of *The Mitchell Beazley Pocket Guide to Fortified & Dessert Wines.*

ISBN 1857321804

The author and publishers will be grateful for any information which will assist them in keeping future editions up to date. Although all reasonable care has been taken in the preparation of this book, neither the author nor the publishers can accept liability for any consequences arising from the information contained herein, or from the use thereof.

A CIP catalogue record for this book is available from the British Library

Editor: Anthea Snow
Art Editor: Paul Tilby
Illustrations: Madeleine David
Maps: Sue Sharples
Production: Fiona Wright

Executive Editor: Anne Ryland
Art Director: Tim Foster

Typeset in Bembo
Produced by Mandarin Offset, Hong Kong
Printed and bound in China

Contents

How to Use this Book   6

Introduction   7

Port   15

Madeira   67

Sherry   84

Málaga   126

Montilla-Moriles   134

Vins Doux Naturels   141

Pineau des Charentes   150

Marsala and Other
Sicilian Fortified Wines   152

California and Other
US Fortified Wines   163

Australian Fortified Wines   178

Fortified Wines from Other Countries   210

How to Use this Book

The guide is organized geographically, first covering the principal European and New World fortified wines, then a group of other fortified wine-producing countries for whom these wines represent a much less significant proportion of the total wine production.

Each chapter gives a comprehensive introduction to the country or region and its fortified wine. This includes information on the vineyard areas, the grapes grown, the various styles of wine and how they are made. There is also a brief history of the wine, a discussion of how best to serve and enjoy it, and, where relevant, information on visiting the producers.

The introductory sections are followed by profiles of selected producers and an assessment of their wines in which star ratings are awarded on the following basis:

★	Below average quality
★★	Average quality
★★★	Good in their class and category
★★★★	Supreme examples of a particular style
→	Represents finer gradations within this framework

For the major fortified wines, the profiles of producers are in the form of an A–Z listing giving the address and telephone number, and, where available, the following information: the year the company was founded, the amount of vineyard land owned, ★ the stock held (for port, madeira, sherry, Málaga and Marsala), additional brand names the company sells under (brands other than the company name itself) and details of visiting times. The names of producers which can be cross-referenced elsewhere in the same chapter are shown in small capital letters.

★ The amount of vineyard land owned is expressed in hectares (ha) (1 hectare is equivalent to 2.47 acres) and gives, wherever possible, only the land planted with vines for the production of fortified wines.

Introduction

Defining a fortified wine is easy: it is a wine to which brandy or neutral spirit has been added. But I suspect that for many people this definition does not help a great deal. The question that should be asked is not 'What is a fortified wine?', but rather 'What are fortified wines?'.

We all know, and have almost certainly drunk, sherry and port. But what of the many other fortified wines from around the world – some of purely local interest, such as Floc de Gascogne from Armagnac or *ratafia* from Champagne, others of much wider renown (even if often, sadly, only in the kitchen), such as madeira and Marsala. What of the *vins doux naturels* of the south of France, the chocolate-brown wine of Málaga in southern Spain or the liqueur Muscats and Tokays of Australia. All are fortified – but what an immense variety of tastes and sensations.

Wines were first fortified for convenience. In the days when transportation of wines by sea was a hazardous affair and there was no guarantee that the quality of what arrived on foreign shores would be the same as that which left the producer, adding a little brandy was found to be a very good preservative of what was often a pretty rough and ready sort of wine. Port, madeira and Marsala developed in this way, and sherry too, probably, although the wines of the Jerez region seem to be have been fortified since far back into the mists of Moorish Spain.

One of the curiosities of the traditional, Old World fortified wines is the influence the British had on nearly all of them. Being an island nation, the British suffered from the problems of transportation by sea more than most. Once a bright spark had discovered that a spot of brandy did wonders to prevent the wine from turning into vinegar when travelling, it was not long before its addition was seen in Britain as a positive benefit and not simply a necessity.

British traders and merchants were also prominent in the development of most of the major fortifieds. In port, Marsala and madeira they dominated the trade for centuries, while, in the case of sherry, there was a partnership on a more equal footing with local merchants. In Australia, Cyprus and South Africa, it was

British demand for cheap fortifieds that created the wine industry, although in South Africa and Australia the production of table wines has now taken over.

But why should what are in effect hybrid wines survive when the reasons for their existence have gone? After all, it is perfectly possible now to transport acceptable table wine from the Douro Valley in Portugal, or from Marsala in Sicily. But the fact that you cannot say the same for table wine from the sherry region of Spain (despite valiant efforts by some producers to make an exciting table wine from the Palomino grape), gives a clue to the survival of fortified wines.

It does seem that the base wine for fortifieds is often better fortified than unfortified. But then, one could perhaps argue that producers make a table wine designed to be fortified – so in the Douro Valley, for example, the wine for port tends to be tougher, more tannic and more alcoholic than that intended for use as table wine. On the whole, it seems, the best base wines for fortifieds are, for whites, a fairly neutral but not acid wine, with decent fruitiness but not too much character, and, for reds, a pretty tannic creature which needs time to soften.

Despite the considerable differences between, say, a *fino* sherry and a tawny port, they do have factors in common besides the addition of brandy. One is the importance of wood in their production, another the importance of ageing, and a third the importance of blending. Any fortified wine producer making a quality product uses wood in considerable quantities. It is there (in the form of barrels) because a fortified needs to breathe, to undergo a degree of oxidization. Keeping a fortified under stainless steel simply locks the wine into a state of suspension, in which no development is possible.

So it needs to mature. A fine tawny port will have spent at least ten years in wood; a *fino* sherry may have been in a *solera* which dated back 100 years. And the same is true of any of the other great fortifieds – the array of casks in an Australian winery making liqueur Muscat or tawny port-style wines will be just the same as the array in Marsala or Jerez de la Frontera.

Apart from the *vins doux naturels* and Pineau des Charentes of France, which are not designed to be aged, there is only one great fortified wine style which breaks the mould: vintage port. Here the ageing is done in bottle, and some would argue (I do not agree) that the wine is the worse for it and that the vintage ports are not as fine as the great tawnies.

The argument centres around the spirit in the wine. Maturation in wood over a long period not only ages the wine and makes it more complex, it also brings about a marriage between wine and spirit that some find lacking in vintage ports. It is a question of taste, of course, rather than rules: those who like vintage port will not care one jot whether the spirit is married to the liking of others.

Fortified wines in general have had a hard time in the last 15 years. They have been hit by a general move away from heavy, alcoholic drinks to much lighter ones, and by the overproduction of poor quality wines. The first problem is a matter of public perception – many fortifieds have acquired a frumpy image at a time when every drink must be seen to be glamorous, to represent a certain lifestyle. All the major fortifieds have gained this poor image: port as the drink to mix with lemonade; sherry as the drink for maiden aunts once a year at Christmas; madeira and Marsala as bottles for the kitchen rather than the drawing room.

I suspect the solution to problem number one lies in the solution to problem number two, because this negative image arrived just as Marsala producers seemed fixated by strange flavourings: chocolate, coffee, fruit, egg – anything but straight wine. It arrived as madeira producers were churning out wines that were not even made from the grapes named on the labels. It arrived as the sherry industry was rocked by a scandal of overproduction and the dumping overseas of poor quality wines.

Port seemed to be less affected by low standard wines than the other major fortifieds, and it is not surprising therefore that it has bounced back from the doldrums much more quickly and positively than the others. It has shed its 'port and lemon' image and gained a firm, high quality image in its place.

Although examples of poor standard fortified wines are still available, producers do seem to have realized that the future does not lie in making huge quantities of the 'cheap and cheerfuls'. Indeed, with the world in general drinking less, but better, wine, fortified producers will have to follow suit. Then, fortifieds will find their niche not as the only possible source of wholesome wine – as they were, for the British at least, in the days of sailing ships –

but as great wines in their own right.

Time moves slowly in the world of fortified wines – the very nature of the wines sees to that, but changes do take place and in the past five years have done so not so much in production methods as in politics and organization.

This is particularly true of port and sherry, which today continue to be the two major fortifieds, in terms of both prestige and volume. Port is currently in the middle of a serious political row involving one of its regulatory bodies, the Casa do Douro, which has taken an interest in one of the largest port shippers. For other shippers this is tantamount to the gamekeeper turning poacher, and considerable fury has been vented, much I suspect to the bemusement of politicians in Lisbon, against whom many of the arguments have been directed.

In the sherry industry, circumstances are changing by consensus. There has been general agreement that sherry needs a new image, and similar general agreement that there is too much sherry around. The result has been a significant drop in the size of vineyard area and in production. For some companies this has led to an upgrading in quality, and it is perhaps significant that those companies who emphasize quality are the ones who are currently doing well. It may be that, at last, sherry is moving in the right direction.

Here, then, are fortified wines. For me, they are some of the most fascinating wines to be found – fascinating partly because of the traditions that created them, and for the stimulating company of those who make them, but also, of course, because of the sheer pleasure they give me as drinks.

Acknowledgments

In preparing this guide, I have found the wine world, as always, to be more than helpful and generous. In particular I would like to thank many friends in the port trade: James and Paul Symington of the Symington group; Bruce Guimaraens of Fonseca Guimaraens and Alastair and Gillyanne Robertson of Taylor, Fladgate & Yeatman; João Nicolau de Almeida, whose work at Ramos-Pinto helped me understand grape varieties in port; Jeremy Bull and the Cálem family and Peter Cobb of Cockburn Smithes. Cristiano van Zeller of Quinta do Noval checked through the port introduction and answered questions. John Cossart was meticulous in making sure I was up to date on the rules and regulations. For the sherry chapter, assistance, advice and help with arranging visits to Jerez, came from Graham Hines of the Sherry Institute of Spain in London and from Bartolomeo Vergara in Jerez; both made sure I had the latest news on the plans for this wine.

The Wine Institute of California, gave me immense help for the section on California's fortified wines. Further afield, all the people I visited in Australia were overwhelming in their hospitality, but I must single out the Brown family of Brown Brothers in Victoria and Bill Chambers of Chambers of Rutherglen, as well as Englishman-turned-true-Aussie Stephen Walker of Gullin & Co in South Australia. Hazel Murphy of Wines of Australia in London made the superbly coordinated arrangements for my initial stay, and it was the Rutherglen Agricultural Society and Chris Pfeiffer who gave me the chance to revisit the historical heartland of Australian fortifieds.

To all these, and to the many people in the British wine trade who have been so generous with their assistance and advice, and to all the producers who have let me taste their wines and have filled in questionnaires, my grateful thanks.

Fortified Wines and Food

Wines	Aperitifs	Soups and Starters	Fish and Shellfish
Port	White port, tawny	Tawny: pâtés, fruit starters, meat soups	
Madeira	Sercial	Sercial, Bual: cold consommé melon, pâtés	Sercial: crab lobster
Sherry and Montilla-Moriles	*Fino, manzanilla,* dry *amontillado*	*Fino, manzanilla*: salads with olives or salamis, asparagus. Dry *amontillado*: cold or light soups, smoked salmon	*Fino, manzanilla*: all shellfish, fried fish. *Amontillado*: sardines, herring
Málaga			
Marsala	*Vergine, vergine stravecchio*	*Vergine, vergine stravecchio*: shellfish, pâtés	*Vergine, vergine stravecchio*: lobster
Liqueur Muscats and Tokays			
Moscatel de Sétubal			
Vins Doux Naturels, Pineau des Charentes	Pineau des Charentes		

Poultry, Meat and Game	Desserts Fruits, Cakes	Cheeses	Digestifs
	Tawny: apricots, treacle tart, sponge puddings	Vintage, vintage styles: Cheddar, goat's milk cheese	Vintage and vintage styles, tawny
	Bual: fruit pies. Bual, Malmsey: sponge cakes	Bual: Cheddar, Emmental	Malmsey
Amontillado: duck, pheasant, roast meats, esp lamb	Sweet oloroso: tarts, cakes Amontillado, palo cortado nut-based puddings	Dry Oloroso Roquefort, Stilton	Sweet oloroso, cream sherries
Hare	Moscatel: most sweet fruits. Dulce: chocolate	Drier styles: Cheddar	Dulce
Cold meats	Superiore: egg-based desserts (zabaglione)	Vergine: blue cheeses	Superiore
	Sweet puddings, ginger (just), rich cakes, Christmas pudding	Liqueur Tokays (Muscadelles): blue cheeses	Yes
	Almond-based puddings, pastries		Yes
	VDNs: summer fruits, fruit cakes, meringue, chocolate cake		VDNs

Serving Fortified Wines

An all-purpose glass for fortified wines. The standard round-bowled Paris goblet can also be used: the 6 oz size is best for fortifieds rather than the larger table wine size. Fill it only two-thirds full (no more) so that the bouquet of the wine can be appreciated.

The copita, the glass used in Spain for drinking sherry. It allows the bouquet of the wine to concentrate in the narrow opening before being released, and has a neat stem to hold so that a chilled *fino* does not lose its cool in the warmth of your hand. Only fill the glass two-thirds full.

Port

The grandeur of port is a reflection of the land from which it comes. The rugged, dramatic, wild splendour of the Douro Valley of northern Portugal is a fitting home for a wine that has so imbued a way of life. Even today, despite the construction of new roads, the Douro is still one of the most remote – as well as one of the poorest – regions of Europe, and its wine has the same raw power as the schist mountains on which its grapes are grown and where it is produced.

The Port Vineyards

The port vineyards are in the Douro Valley, due east of Porto. They stretch from just west of the town of Peso da Régua (or simply Régua) to the Spanish border, and take in a number of side valleys. There are about 250,000 hectares in the area, of which about 10–12 percent is planted with vines. The region is divided into three: the Baixo Corgo (the area around Régua, to which the Corgo, a tributary of the Douro, acts as a convenient boundary), the Cima Corgo (the area surrounding Pinhão) and the Alto Douro (the region up river from the Valeira Dam, above Tua). The further east, the lower the rainfall, and it is generally accepted that the finest vineyards are in the more easterly zones: the Cima Corgo and the Alto Douro.

Port, until recently, was unique among the world's wines in that its vineyards were 150 miles (94 km) from all its main storage cellars. There are historical reasons for this (*see* The History of Port), but there is also a climatic one. The Douro is an inhospitable place even today: baking hot in summer, freezing cold in winter, and still relatively inaccessible. It was not, until the advent of air-conditioned cellars, considered suitable for maturing port. Far better were the wet, humid conditions of coastal Porto, where the wine could mature slowly in a climate with a narrower temperature range.

Even 25 years ago, the visitor to the Douro vineyards would have seen rugged mountainsides terraced with rows of vines,

The Port Quintas

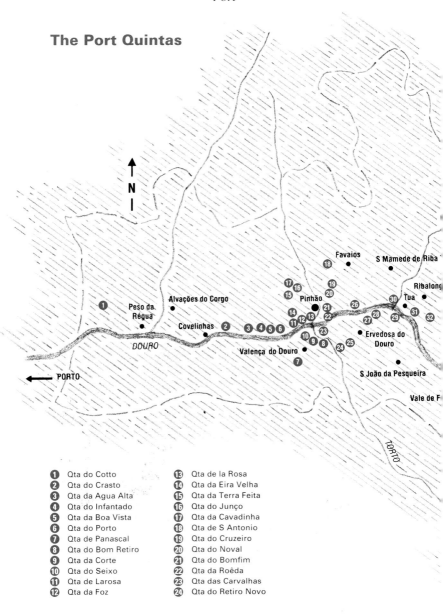

❶	Qta do Cotto	⑬	Qta de la Rosa
❷	Qta do Crasto	⑭	Qta da Eira Velha
❸	Qta da Agua Alta	⑮	Qta da Terra Feita
❹	Qta do Infantado	⑯	Qta do Junço
❺	Qta da Boa Vista	⑰	Qta da Cavadinha
❻	Qta do Porto	⑱	Qta de S Antonio
❼	Qta de Panascal	⑲	Qta do Cruzeiro
❽	Qta do Bom Retiro	⑳	Qta do Noval
❾	Qta da Corte	㉑	Qta do Bomfim
❿	Qta do Seixo	㉒	Qta da Roêda
⓫	Qta de Larosa	㉓	Qta das Carvalhas
⓬	Qta da Foz	㉔	Qta do Retiro Novo

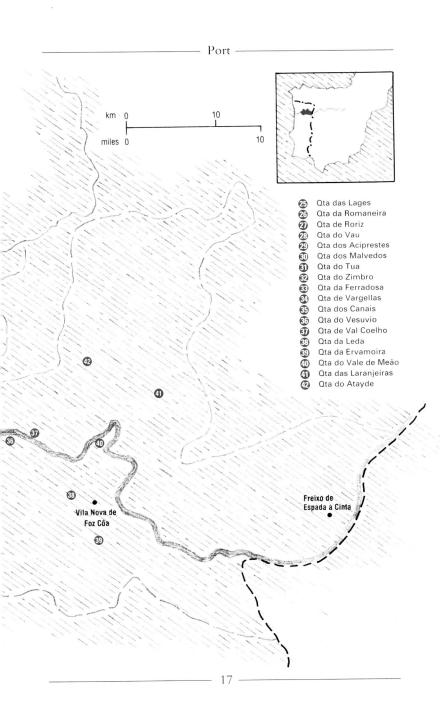

25 Qta das Lages
26 Qta da Romaneira
27 Qta de Roriz
28 Qta do Vau
29 Qta dos Aciprestes
30 Qta dos Malvedos
31 Qta do Tua
32 Qta do Zimbro
33 Qta da Ferradosa
34 Qta de Vargellas
35 Qta dos Canais
36 Qta do Vesuvio
37 Qta de Val Coelho
38 Qta da Leda
39 Qta da Ervamoira
40 Qta do Vale de Meão
41 Qta das Laranjeiras
42 Qta do Atayde

Vila Nova de Foz Côa

Freixo de Espada à Cinta

miniature in the distance, and, below, a fast-moving river forcing its way through rapids and rocks, treacherous but beautiful.

Today, although the splendid mountain scenery remains, much has changed. The river has been dammed to provide water for hydroelectricity, and become a series of huge, sinuous lakes. In many areas, the narrow, stone terraces (of perhaps two rows of vines) have given way to wider, earth-buttressed terraces, called *patamares*, along which tractors can move for ploughing and spraying. In some vineyards, there have been experiments with running the vines in rows up and down the hillsides, rather than along them. And although an argument continues to rage about the benefits of this, it is generally agreed that on less precipitous slopes there are practical advantages to this method of planting.

In recent years, there has been a huge amount of new planting, as well as the re-planting of existing vineyards, which has increased production by 3–4 percent. This work has been funded partly by loans from the World Bank, partly by investment from the multinational companies who now control so much of port and see demand growing, and partly by individual companies striving to improve the quality of what they produce. The task of planting has been divided equally between enterprising growers and the port shippers, who would like to have greater control over the origin of their wines through owning vineyards.

Certainly the quality of wine being produced in the Douro has increased dramatically in the past 15 years. Previously, any of the 48 permitted grape varieties could be planted in any order and taken to be pressed together. There was no question of picking grapes at their optimum ripeness – indeed there could be only an average degree of ripeness with the many different varieties ripening at such different rates. Equally, there was no attempt to study which varieties produced the best wines, and to which vineyards they were most suited. The fact that in this comparative chaos so much good wine was produced, is a testament to the skill of the blenders at the port shippers and to the virtues of maturation in cool, dark lodges.

While many peasant farmers (and there are 25,000 who are authorized to make wine for port, with an average holding of a quarter of a hectare) still cling to the old, mixed vineyards, an increasing number of shipper-owned vineyards are being changed

A *barco rabelo*, the traditional means of transporting wine to the lodges at Vila Nova de Gaia.

to a new method of planting, by type, in which each area of the vineyard is planted with the variety most suited to it. Vinification, too, is now taking place by grape variety.

In addition, the original array of 48 approved – out of more than 80 recognized – varieties, or *castas*, has been whittled down to nine, which are now regarded as the principal varieties and are the only ones permitted to be planted. Of these, six are seen as the most important. They each give their own character to the final blend of port:

Grape Varieties

Mourisco Tinto Producing a light-coloured wine, but one with good, tannic structure, this variety is less favoured than the other five.

Tinta Barroca The variety which provides the tannin and firmness needed for port to mature and to live to a good age.

Tinta Roriz This variety provides a full-bodied wine, soft and smooth, adding breadth to the blend.

Tinto Cão Due to its low yields, this grape variety almost became extinct, but the elegance, the complexity and above all the colour of the wine it produces make it a refined ingredient in port blends and have led to its revival.

Touriga Francesa This was, until recently, believed to be related to the Pinot Noir. It produces intense fruit flavours, good acidity and high alcohol.

Touriga Nacional A low-yielding vine, producing a spicy wine, but one that lacks enough of the tannin necessary to port. It is however considered to be the region's finest variety and there is talk of using it to produce single variety ports.

The other three varieties are **Bastardo**, **Sousão** and **Tinta Amarella**. For white port, the preferred varieties are **Malvasia Fina** and **Malvasia Grossa**.

How Port is Made

The harvest usually takes place between September 15 and October 15. There are two reasons for this spread of dates: the differing aspects of the vineyards and the capacity of the wineries.

Most farmers still make the wine themselves and then sell it to the port shippers, but there is always close supervision by the shippers, who buy regularly from the same vineyards. At harvest time they can be seen charging along the hillsides' dusty tracks, checking that the grapes are ready for picking, that the quality is right and that the farmers are controlling the fermentation.

Grapes from the shippers' vineyards and sometimes from their principal farmers, are taken to the shippers' wineries in Pinhão and Régua, in Tua or other smaller villages, or to the shippers' own *quintas* (farms). Other grapes find their way to the cooperatives, which make about 40 percent of the base wine for port.

Fermentation used to be carried out entirely in huge stone *lagares*, where the grapes were crushed by foot. It still is in some traditional *quintas*, but modern technology is increasingly taking over. Stainless steel auto-vinificators are used widely, and these keep the grape must turning over automatically to extract the maximum colour from the skins.

At a critical point, brandy is added to stop the fermentation. This is done when the winemaker thinks that the wine has reached the right levels of alcohol and sugar – in other words, it is strong enough and yet still sweet enough. The wine is then run off the auto-vinificators into barrels, called *tonnels*, and grape brandy (*aguardente*) is added at the rate of 100 litres of brandy to 450 litres of wine. It is now port.

The spring following the vintage has traditionally seen the removal of the wine from the Douro Valley down to the port lodges at the mouth of the river in Vila Nova de Gaia, the town across the Douro from Porto and the controlled zone (the *entreposto*) in which all port shippers were, until 1987, required by the Portuguese government to mature their wine. But changes to the regulations mean that the wine can now be shipped direct from the Douro Valley rather than having to go first to Vila Nova de Gaia, and as a result some single-*quinta* ports are being matured in the Douro and shipped direct from there. Such wine, apart from its own individual characteristics, is also supposed to exhibit the Douro Bake – the result of being matured in much higher temperatures than those of Vila Nova de Gaia.

Most port however is still matured in, and shipped from, Vila Nova de Gaia. In the port lodges, the wine is decanted from the tanker lorries used to transport it from the Douro (replacing the romantic, single-sailed *barco rabelo* boats which used to bring the wine down-river until the advent of the dams). It is then put into wooden barrels, called 'pipes' (after the Portuguese for 'barrel', *uma pipa*). Each shipping pipe contains 534.2 litres, while a lodge pipe (in which the wine is stored in the lodge) holds 555 litres.

At this point, the shipper's laboratory and tasters set to work on the new port to determine its quality and what style it will eventually take: whether it will become a basic ruby or tawny, whether it is more suitable for ageing and should become an old tawny, or indeed whether the wine has the potential to make a vintage port. All port is a blend in some form or other, either using wine from a number of years or – as with vintage port – using different lots from a single year.

Styles of Port

Although the only styles of port which have to be bottled in Portugal are those with a vintage date or age indication (that is, vintage port, late-bottled vintage port, aged tawnies and *colheitas*), most firms do in fact carry out all their bottling in their lodges at Vila Nova de Gaia. A seal over the cork from the Instituto do Vinho do Porto indicates the genuine character of the wine and that it has been bottled in Portugal. Port bottles without a seal will have been filled outside Portugal.

While every shipper makes most of the following styles of port, each will also have a 'house character' which seems to be retained whatever the style of wine. In the directory section I have given some indication of that character for each producer. There is also a general division in port houses between those which follow a 'British' style – often quite tannic and tending to dryness – and those which follow a 'Portuguese' style – soft, sweeter, more mellow and faster maturing. British-named houses tend towards the former (but not exclusively so), while Portuguese-named houses aim towards the latter (again this is not exclusive). The division is most obvious in vintage wines.

Except for white port, every port starts life as a ruby. As it matures in the pipes, it loses colour and gradually becomes tawny. There are, within the basic split between ruby and tawny, many categories, some of which can seem quite confusing.

White Port

An aperitif style, made either quite dry or sweet. It is popular in Portugal and France but is seen only occasionally elsewhere. It first appeared in the 1930s, when Taylors launched Chip Dry.

Ruby Categories

Ruby This is the basic port, fortified with brandy, given three years' maturation and then sold. It is, in essence, the original port – red Portugal.

Late-bottled vintage (LBV) A post-Second World War creation, this is a wine from one year which has been held in cask for a longer time than a true vintage port – in this case for between four and six years – and which is regarded as ready to drink once bottled. LBVs are intended as a substitute for the, pricier, vintage ports, but most are only a pale imitation of the real thing, enjoyable as they can be. LBVs may have the same vintage as true vintage ports – a potential source of confusion.

Vintage character This is an LBV port, but one which is a blend of a number of years. Quite what the phrase means is, it seems, up to the shipper – yet another labelling confusion.

Crusted An anomalous category for which no legal definition exists. This port is blended from a number of vintages and then matured for four years in bottle. Unlike LBV and vintage character wines, it is not filtered before bottling and it throws a deposit (a crust). To my mind, crusted ports are closer than the LBV wines to vintage port, and shippers should be encouraged by all port drinkers to sort out the current confusion over this category. Because of this anomalous situation, crusted ports have to be exported from Portugal in bulk and bottled elsewhere.

Single-*quinta* This is a vintage port, usually made in a year that is not generally 'declared' and for which all the wine, in almost every case, comes from one vineyard. Some confusion has crept into this category because certain wines have been sold under the name of a *quinta* which are in fact blended wines from a number of different vineyards. Discussions are still being held about this category, and a proposal has been put that single-*quinta* ports must be vinified and bottled on the *quinta* – something that is not yet possible because of the lack of facilities on the farms. Yet more confusion is now being added to port labelling, with some shippers selling single-*quinta* wines from 'declared' years. While most single-*quinta* wines are produced in the vintage ruby style, others appear as aged tawnies.

Vintage The top category of ruby port, made from wine from a single year and bottled between two and three years after the harvest. Only the very finest wines are put aside for vintage port – and those only in good years – but it is not until the two years are up that a vintage is 'declared'. Usually a number of shippers – and even, occasionally, all of them – will declare a vintage in the same year. These are the ports that keep for ever and need many years in bottle to mature: all other ports are ready to drink once bottled.

Tawny Categories

Tawny The basic tawny is a wine that has been matured in wood until its colour has begun to fade and it has acquired a certain nutty character. Most basic tawnies are bottled when two years old. Since it is impossible to achieve a true tawny colour after two years, these wines are essentially heavily filtered young rubies which were light in colour to begin with. A certain amount of blending of young ruby and white ports together also takes place to create a finished wine that is tawny-coloured.

Aged tawny This is a much superior style of tawny. The finest wines, destined for long maturation, can lie in casks for anything up to 40 years. They will then be sold as aged tawnies and have an age indication on the label: 10-year-old, 20-year-old, 30-year-old, 40-year-old etc. One of the many confusions of port labelling stems from the fact that these wines are re-blended when necessary to keep to the style approved by the Instituto do Vinho do Porto as being 'like a 10-year-old' etc.

Colheita This is a tawny port which is sold with a vintage date on it – often as many as 20 or 30 years after that vintage, although it may be sold after a minimum of seven years. In order to preserve its freshness, a *colheita* port is lightly filtered every five years, and then returned to the pipes. *Colheita* ports are not bottled until the shipper receives an order for the wine.

There is obviously considerable confusion in the labelling of port, especially regarding the LBV, vintage character, crusted and vintage styles. Indeed, there seems to be a tendency to try to pass off the first three as true vintage port. Further regulations are obviously required.

Controls on Port

In contrast to the contradictory and feeble controls on port labelling, the port vineyards are some of the most tightly controlled in the world. The Douro vineyards have been divided into categories of quality by the Casa do Douro. The classification system awards points based on the type of soil, the gradient of the land, its altitude, the direction it faces, the local climatic conditions and the type and age of the vines planted. Each vineyard is graded and then allocated to one of the categories below, from F up to A. The higher the grading, the greater the proportion of grapes which may be made into port (more grapes may be produced, but they must be sold for use in table wine). Also, of course, the higher the grading, the higher the price a farmer will get for his or her grapes.

The classification criteria are set out in the table overleaf, and the classes are awarded as follows: Class F, 400 points and below; Class E, 401–600 points; Class D, 601–800 points; Class C, 801–1,000 points; Class B, 1,001–1,199 points; Class A, 1,200 points or more.

Vineyards graded F are not allowed to make port, although in exceptional years this ruling may be waived. Class E vineyards are permitted in an average year to make 500 litres of port per 1,000 vines; Classes D and C may make 550 litres per 1,000 vines; Classes A and B may make 600 litres per 1,000 vines. These amounts change according to the vintage and are set each year by the Casa do Douro. As an indication of the difference in yield between the best and worst vineyards, it is estimated that a Class E vineyard can produce three pipes of port per 1,000 vines, while a Class A vineyard will only manage one pipe.

But the controls on port do not stop short at the vineyards. Each year representatives of the Associacão dos Exportadores

Classification of the Port Vineyards

Category	Minimum points subtracted	Maximum points awarded
Location	- 50	+ 600
Aspect	- 1,000	+ 250
Altitude (lowest best, grapes grown above 600m not permitted for port)	- 900	+ 150
Gradient (steepest best)	- 100	+ 100
Soil	- 350	+ 100
Schist (best type)	N/A	+ 100
Granite (worst type)	- 350	N/A
Mixture of schist and granite	- 150	N/A
Microclimate (sheltered land best)	0	+ 60
Vine varieties (recommended varieties best)	- 300	+ 150
Age of vines (oldest best)	0	+ 60
Vine density (lowest best)	- 50	+ 50
Productivity (lowest best)	- 900	+ 120
Vineyard maintenance	- 500	+ 100
Total	**- 3,150**	**+ 1.490**

do Vinho do Porto (Port Wine Shippers' Association), the Casa do Douro and the Instituto do Vinho do Porto meet to decide how much port is to be made. The amount will depend on the export figures of the previous year and the calculation is designed to avoid an excessive build up of stocks. Just under half the wine produced in the Douro is made into port – the rest is sold as table wine or is sent for distillation (some of which then goes into port as *aguardente*) The Instituto do Vinho do Porto lays down the rules and regulations regarding maturation and shipping and issues guarantee seals for bottles so that only the agreed quantity may be bottled or shipped.

The control system, which is fine in theory, has been thrown into confusion in recent years. The Casa do Douro, supposedly an independent arbiter among the growers and shippers, has taken a financial stake in the largest of them all, the Royal Oporto Wine Company. This, for many shippers, has been seen as a conflict of interests, and heated discussions are going on to determine whether the Casa do Douro should continue in its current role. Until this is sorted out, it is unlikely that any of the questions about port labelling will be settled.

The Major Quintas

While many *quintas* are tiny, peasant-owned properties, there are also some fine, large estates in the Douro. Many belong to the shippers, but others are owned by farmers who sell, often under a very long-term contract, to the shippers. Because of the remoteness of the Douro, many *quintas* are miniature worlds, with large, comfortable estate houses, reminiscent in some cases of planters' villas in the West Indies, with a kitchen garden, chickens, plenty of dogs, and estate workers who are there for much of the year – certainly from spring to the end of the harvest. In the same complex will be the winery, traditionally consisting of huge stone *lagares* in a vast, cavernous room, but now more often containing stainless steel auto-vinificators surrounded by all the equipment of a modern winery. A list of the major *quintas*, their vineyard size and class is set out overleaf.

Name of Quinta	Owner	Size	Class	
Quinta dos Aciprestes	Real Companhia Velha	120 ha	A	
Quinta da Agua Alta	Borges de Souza	40 ha	A	*(1)*
Quinta do Atayde	Cockburn Smithes	150 ha	A	
Quinta da Boa Vista	Offley Forrester	50 ha	A	
Quinta do Bomfim	Silva & Cosens (Dow's)	35 ha	A	
Quinta do Bom Retiro	Adriano Ramos-Pinto	60 ha	A	
Quinta dos Canais	Cockburn Smithes	50 ha	A	
Quinta das Carvalhas	Real Companhia Velha	150 ha	A	
Quinta da Cavadinha	Warre	29 ha	A	
Quinta da Corte	Pacheco & Irmãos	35 ha	A	*(2)*
Quinta do Cotto	Montez Champalimaud	52 ha	C	
Quinta do Crasto	Quinta do Crasto	42 ha	A	
Quinta do Cruzeiro	Fonseca Guimaraens	18 ha	A	
Quinta da Eira Velha	Newman family	25 ha	A	*(3)*
Quinta da Ervamoira	Adriano Ramos-Pinto	75 ha	A	
Quinta da Ferradosa	A A Cálem & Filho	300 ha	A	
Quinta da Foz	A A Cálem & Filho	50 ha	A	
Quinta do Infantado	Herederos de João &			
	Lopes Roseira	55 ha	A	
Quinta do Junço	Borges e Irmão	46 ha	A	
Quinta das Lages	Moureira da Fonseca	80 ha	A	*(4)*
Quinta das Laranjeiras	Sandeman	14 ha	B	
Quinta da Leda	A A Ferreira Sucrs	37 ha	B	
Quinta dos Malvedos	W & J Graham	70 ha	A	
Quinta do Noval	Quinta do Noval	106 ha	A	
Quinta de Panascal	Fonseca Guimaraens	39 ha	A	
Quinta do Porto	A A Ferreira Sucrs	24 ha	A	
Quinta do Retiro Novo	Wiese & Krohn	9 ha	A	
Quinta da Roêda	Croft	120 ha	A	
Quinta da Romaneira	Romaneira	47 ha	A, C	
Quinta de Roriz	van Zeller family	50 ha	A	*(5)*
Quinta de la Rosa	Bergqvist family	40 ha	A, B	
Quinta de S Antonio	Fonseca Guimaraens	12 ha	A	
Quinta do Seixo	A A Ferreira Sucrs	75 ha	A	
Quinta da Terra Feita	Taylor, Fladgate & Yeatman	48 ha	A	
Quinta do Tua	Cockburn Smithes	25 ha	A	
Quinta de Val Coelho	Cockburn Smithes	25 ha	A	
Quinta do Vale de Meão	Olazabal family	50 ha	B	*(6)*
Quinta de Vargellas	Taylor, Fladgate & Yeatman	44 ha	A	
Quinta do Vau	Sandeman	74 ha	A	
Quinta do Vesuvio	Symington family	67 ha	A	*(7)*
Quinta do Zimbro	Sampaio family	10 ha	A	*(8)*

Notes: *(1)* wine sold to Churchill Graham; *(2)* wine sold to Delaforce; *(3)* wine sold to Cockburn Smithes; *(4)* wine sold to W & J Graham; *(5)* wine sold to van Zellers; *(6)* wine sold to Ferreira; *(7)* the wine from this *quinta* is not sold under a Symington house name, but bottled and sold separately; *(8)* wine sold to Silva & Cosens for Dow's Ports.

The History of Port

Port was certainly, like so many other fortified wines, largely the creation of the English. But, again as for other fortifieds, the practice of fortification came about almost by accident. The wine was originally considered simply to be a red from Portugal – red Portugal, as it was known in its earliest days.

Those days date back at least to the 16th century, when wine from the north of Portugal was one of many commodities, such as oil and fruit, shipped by English traders. They brought in English woollen cloth and cotton as well as the cod that the Portuguese needed for their national dish of salted cod, *bacalhau*.

Originally, the wine they were shipping was from the Minho area of northern Portugal, the region stretching north of the Douro Valley to the Spanish border. Then, as today, the region made thin, high-acid red and white wines (*vinhos verdes*). It was only when demand for these wines outstripped supply that the English merchants ventured into the Douro Valley to buy fresh supplies of wine. This happened during the reign of William III, at the end of the 17th century, when French wines were difficult to obtain in Britain not only because of war, but also because of the broader political situation.

At that time the Douro Valley region, 150 miles (94 km) up-river from Porto, the second city of Portugal, was almost impenetrable. The only access was by mule on atrocious tracks over the mountains of the Sierra de Marão. There was nowhere to stay or sleep and the countryside when reached was deeply inhospitable. Yet these imperturbable English merchants, full of thoughts of how much money could be made selling Douro wines, journeyed to this strange region, bargained for the wines in their extremely rudimentary Portuguese (or, equally likely, simply shouted at the peasants in English) and started the tradition of shipping Douro wines to England.

The centre of English trade with Portugal was then Viana do Castelo, north of Porto and near the source of the Minho wines. As the Douro wines grew in importance, so the centre of activity shifted to the city of Porto, at the mouth of the Douro. It was then that some of the families whose names still appear on bottles of port arrived to trade: from England came the Warres and the Crofts;

from Holland came the Kopkes and a little later the van Zellers; from Germany came the Burmesters.

The English traders formed by far the largest colony. They operated under the benefit of a number of treaties between England and Portugal, starting with the treaty of alliance in 1386 (still formally in existence today), continuing with the treaty of 1654, which made England 'most favoured nation' in Portugal, and culminating in the Methuen Treaty of 1703, which gave permanent preferential treatment to Portuguese wines in England. By 1666 a Factory House had been established in Porto, which acted as an association for the English merchants. This, in the form of the British Association, survives to the present day.

The Douro wine being shipped at this time was hard, tannic stuff, untouched as yet by brandy. It was over the next 150 years that, little-by-little, port wine was transformed from a clumsy, unyielding drink into the smooth, sweet product we know today. Fortifying with brandy was originally carried out to stabilize the wine during its transportation from the Douro to Porto and thence to England. It was only after the upheavals of the Napoleonic wars, in the early 19th century, that the beneficial effects of stopping fermentation with brandy truly came to be appreciated.

Even then, there was a strong rearguard action from those who regarded the addition of brandy as adulteration of the wine. Joseph James Forrester – one of the great characters in the history of a wine that has bred characters in profusion – attacked the practice in 1844, believing that port should be a natural wine and not a fortified one. The cry 'adulteration' was by that time a familiar one. In the 18th century, the practice of adulterating Douro wines with substances as strange as elderberry juice (to give colour) was so widespread, and the quality of the resulting wines so poor, that the Portuguese government stepped in to create a state monopoly, which brought all the Douro wines under strict control before they were sold to the merchants.

Control was kept by the Companhia Geral da Agricultura dos Vinhos do Alto Douro, known variously as the Old Wine Company and, later, as the Royal Oporto Wine Company (under which name it trades today as one of the largest port shippers). It was the creation of the Portuguese Prime Minister of the day, Sebastian Carvalho e Melo, Marquês of Pombal. By the time of

Forrester, its activities were being corrupted by venal officials, who apparently never even tasted the wines they were supposed to be controlling.

Although, luckily for us, Forrester never succeeded in turning the clock back to a time of natural, unfortified, wines, his attacks on adulteration did clean up the quality of port, and for the next 30 years this wine enjoyed a golden period. In the minds of many British patriots, port was the glue that held the Empire together. It was the source of many strange drinking customs and the cause of innumerable paragraphs in the etiquette books. This was the time when vintage port really became what we know today, and when all the most famous port shippers, both British and Portuguese, were firmly established.

Forrester's name is inextricably linked with the 'wine widow' of port, Dona Antónia Adelaide Ferreira, widow of the owner of the company of that name. It was she who put the high Douro region (the region furthest east in the Douro Valley) firmly on the map and created some of the magnificent *quinta* houses, such as Quinta do Vesuvio and Quinta do Vale de Meão. She died a multi-millionairess. Forrester himself died when his boat capsized at the rapids of Cachão da Valeira. He was drowned, but his companions – Dona Antónia and Baroness Fladgate (of the family which is a partner in Taylor, Fladgate & Yeatman) – were saved by their crinolines, and by the lack of a heavy money belt.

The golden age of port was rudely interrupted in the 1870s by the arrival of the phylloxera louse, which was already busy destroying the rest of Europe's vineyards by attacking the vine roots. By 1881 it looked as though the port vineyards were finished, but the introduction of American root stocks saved the day.

Port had by now become not simply the drink of the English middle and upper classes. It was the beginning of the age of port and lemon, the 'ladies' drink', and of a time when countries other than Britain began to take more of an interest in port, when the French started to drink ruby and tawny port as an aperitif.

In 1929 the port trade felt the impact of the Wall Street Crash. A number of firms failed, and, as the market slumped, there was an overproduction of wine. The Portuguese government stepped in to set up regulatory bodies: the Casa do Douro, the Port Wine Shippers' Association and the Instituto do Vinho do Porto (*see* Controls on Port). After the Second World War, port began to lose its popularity to that other great fortified wine, sherry. Sherry parties became the fashion and it was discovered that by the time sherry and wine had been consumed at dinner, there was less inclination to hit the port bottle afterwards. The port shippers, who had assumed they had a captive market, and had done no advertising, found themselves losing customers.

This crisis during the late 1940s and the 1950s led to the disappearance of many firms, to the amalgamation of others, and to yet others being swallowed up by multinationals – a process which continued right up to the 1980s. But in the 1980s, port saw a revival of interest in its better products – its vintage and aged tawny wines – as distinct from the cheaper styles used for port and lemon. (The biggest market, however, is still for the aperitif ports which are drunk in France.)

The early 1990s have seen a return of structural problems in the port industry as well as falling shipments and prices. The situation of one of the main regulatory bodies – the Casa do Douro (*see* page 27) – means that the existing controls on port are being questioned, and sometimes ignored. In addition, falling demand has led to some dumping of cheap port and to price undercutting between shippers, especially in the bulk markets such as France and Belgium. The quality of some of this port is dubious to say the least, and there is a risk that the whole range of ports may suffer. At the upper end of the market, there is currently a glut of maturing vintage port, which has caused prices to fall. For this reason, when the '91 vintage was declared in 1993, only small quantities of wine were bottled.

The Factory House

The first records of this association of British shippers date from 1666, but it was at the end of the 18th century that it came into its own, with the building of a splendid edifice in what was then the Rua Nova dos Ingleses (English Street), but has since been renamed by patriotic Portuguese the Rua do Infante Dom Henrique. This granite-faced building was constructed between

1786 and 1790, and is still the home of the British Association. It brings together the 13 British port shippers: Churchill Graham, Cockburn Smithes, Croft, Delaforce, Fonseca Guimaraens, W & J Graham, Martinez Gassiot, Morgan Brothers, Robertson Brothers, Sandeman, Silva & Cosens (Dow's), Taylor Fladgate & Yeatman, and Warre. Regular lunches (for men only) are held on Wednesdays and the building is also used for dinners held by one or other member house.

Storing and Serving Port

Most port is sold ready to drink, so you can keep bottles in your cellar or in a reasonably cool, dark place (under the stairs or in a cupboard) for as long or as short a time as you like. The bottles should be left on their sides to stop the corks drying out. Only vintage port needs to mature in bottle – how long depends on the vintage, and the producer, but few vintage ports are ready to drink before ten years, and many not before 20 years. Vintage port bottles should be kept in the wooden box in which they came (if you have bought a case) or laid in racks on their side. Try not to disturb them because that will simply shake the deposit, which every bottle will have. As a guide, keep the white spot, traditionally painted on the bottle, uppermost.

Vintage port and crusted port are the two styles that need decanting. Once a bottle of port is open it begins to deteriorate, but not as fast as wine, and provided the bottle is not almost empty, a vintage or LBV will last a few weeks if properly corked. The lighter tawnies begin to fade after a week.

White port is the aperitif wine and should be drunk chilled. A twist of lemon and a dash of tonic or soda make it an extremely refreshing drink. Like any other white wine, it deteriorates fast once opened. Tawny ports, too, can be chilled if the day is warm, and are good either as aperitif wines or after a meal, when a vintage or LBV style would be too heavy. In Portugal, at the end of a meal, perhaps after a glass of vintage port, the shippers will tuck into tawny as an easier wine to drink in quantity.

Vintage ports need to be drunk with more reverence than other styles. They have aged longer – they are more expensive as well – and they are great wines. Drink them at room temperature (but not at centrally heated room temperature) from glasses sufficiently large to allow you to smell the bouquet (a requirement when drinking any wine).

When to Drink Vintage Port

Vintage port, bottled after only two years in wood, needs many years in bottle before it is ready to drink. A minimum of ten years is needed for any quality vintage port – from whatever producer. After that, it begins to be a question of producer, personal taste and the quality of the vintage itself.

On the whole, vintage ports from producers with Portuguese names tend to mature more quickly than those from producers with British names. It is not necessarily a question of one being better than another, simply a general difference in the house styles. Firms which cross the boundary are Quinta do Noval (which makes long-lasting ports) and smaller firms such as Smith Woodhouse and Gould Campbell (whose ports mature relatively quickly). Firms whose ports take longest to develop – up to 20 years – include Taylor, Fladgate & Yeatman, W & J Graham, Warre, Dow's and Fonseca Guimaraens. Other firms fit somewhere in between; their styles are discussed in the directory of producers that follows.

The great vintages since 1945 (which was one of the best vintages this century) were: '47 '48 '55 '60 '63 '70 '77 '83 and '85. Lesser years were: '50 '58 '66 '69 '75 '80 and '82. It is too early to say which category the most recent declaration – '91 – falls into. Not every shipper declares a vintage port each time there is a vintage year, but most do declare in vintage years. (The exceptions were '82 '83 and '91, when the port world was split into two camps.) Wines from lesser years obviously mature more quickly, but it would be a mistake to drink anything younger than a '75 vintage at present.

Great pre-Second World War vintages include the superb '27 and the '34 (which was declared by only a few houses).

Port Customs

Passing the port Port is passed clockwise round the table (that is, from right to left) once the host has served his (or her) principal guest seated on the right. The custom probably has the simplest of explanations – it is easier for most people to pass a heavy decanter of port with the right hand than with the left, since most people are right-handed.

Today the custom is less rigidly adhered to. A much greater crime than passing the port the wrong way is not passing it at all. The traditional words used to nudge a slow-moving guest were 'Do you know Dr Wright of Norwich?' or 'Bishop of Norwich', phrases recalling a clergyman of the 1850s who became notorious for talking too much at table and not passing the decanter.

Toasting with port Toasts with port were once a traditional conclusion to formal banquets. Like all toasts they were made standing, except, that is, for toasts in the Royal Navy, where diners remain seated. The reason for this peculiarity dates from the time when King George IVth was dining aboard a naval ship, stood to make a toast and promptly hit his head on the low ceiling.

Port and gout A fallacy this one. Medical evidence has shown no link between port consumption and gout. Gout is hereditary and caused by excessive uric acid in the blood, not by the excessive intake of alcohol.

Visiting Port Shippers

Many of the port shippers' lodges in Vila Nova de Gaia are open to the public. You will usually be given a guided tour through the lodge, an explanation of how port is made, and a tasting of the company's main products – with a chance to buy afterwards. Some shippers require an appointment to be made, in which case an introduction from a wine merchant back home can be useful. Arranging an appointment will probably allow you to have a personalized visit.

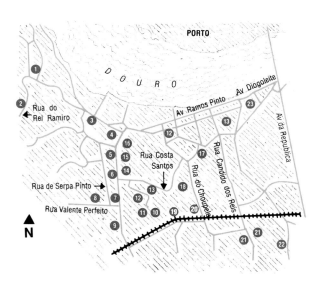

Vila Nova de Gaia: The Port Shippers

1. Fonseca Guimareans
2. W & J Graham
3. A A Ferreira Sucrs
4. Royal Oporto Wine Company
5. Delaforce Sons
6. Niepoort
7. Martinez Gassiot
8. Cockburn Smithes
9. Barros, Almeida
10. Dow's
11. J W Burmester
12. Adriano Ramos-Pinto
13. Sandeman
14. Rozès
15. C N Kopke
16. Wiese & Krohn Sucrs
17. Croft
18. Taylor, Fladgate & Yeatman
19. Warre
20. Offley Forrester
21. Quinta do Noval
22. Borges e Irmão
23. A A Cálem & Filho

How the Directory of Producers is Organized

Each shipper (the name given to a port house, which buys in wine or grapes, makes port, stores and then sells it) has a standard entry. The name, address and telephone number are given, and then the following details where available: the date the firm was founded; the amount of vineyard owned that is used for fortified wine (most shippers own only a small proportion of the vineyards from which they obtain grapes), and information about any special *quintas* (farms) owned. These may also be listed as single-*quinta* wines under 'Additional brands'. An indication of the size of the shipper is then given, expressed as the number of pipes held in the lodge. Additional brand names, other than the company name, that the firm's ports may be sold under are then listed, followed by the hours at which the lodge is open to the public. At the end of each entry is a list of vintages declared since 1945 (still the greatest post-War port vintage).

Producers

Barros, Almeida   ★→
PO Box 39, Rua D Leonor de Freitas 182, 4400 Vila Nova de Gaia. Tel (2) 302320. Founded 1913. V'yds: 95 ha incl Quinta da Matilde. Additional brands: Barros Port; Porto Barros. Visits: weekdays 9–12.30, 2–4.30.
Although relatively new in port trade terms, this is one of the largest shippers. Much of what it produces is young rubies and tawnies, which go to the French and Portuguese markets. It also owns H & C J Feist, FEUERHEERD BROS, Hutcheson, C N KOPKE and VIEIRA DE SOUZA, as well as the Douro Wine Shippers' Association. The firm's style is very much in the Portuguese house tradition of lightish wines; it makes a speciality of vintage *colheitas*. Of its standard range, I have enjoyed the 10-year-old tawnies and 20-year-old tawny, which is exceptional, but have found the LBV to be much too sweet and heavy. Of the vintage ports

produced, those under the Barros and Kopke brands are the best, but these tend to develop quickly and the oldest worth drinking now is the '77, which is definitely mature. However, with the '83 and '85 there has been a move to a more long-lasting, drier style of wine.

Vintages declared since 1945: '45 '48 '51 '55 '57 '60 '63 '65 '66 '70 '74 '75 '77 '78 '80 '82 '83 '85 '87 '89 '91.

Borges e Irmão   →★
Avenida da Republica 796, 4401 Vila Nova de Gaia. Tel (2) 305002. Founded 1884. V'yds: 1,029 ha incl Quinta do Junço, Quinta da Soalheira. Stock: 13,100 pipes. Additional brands: Cocktail (white); Estrela de Ouro; Quinta do Junço; Quinta do Ronção; Quinta da Soalheira; Tribuno. Visits: weekdays 9–6.

This is one of the few port houses traditionally to have had a substantial involvement in table wines – the Vinho Verde Gatão, Trovador Rosé and Meia Encosta Dão are its brands. The firm was founded by the Borges brothers as part of a wide-ranging business that also included what is now one of Portugal's major banks (Banco Borges e Irmão). Today, there are two large vinification plants – one in the Minho for *vinho verde* and one in the Douro for port. Although the firm has had considerable involvement in the port business for some time, the quality of these wines is always average, and sometimes rather poor. Its best wines are single-*quinta colheitas*, such as those from *quintas* do Junço, Soalheira and Ronção. The basic ruby and tawny are just that, while the vintage wines tend to a light, quick-maturing style, although unlike some houses it is careful about which vintages it declares. It is strong in the bulk port markets, such as Holland, Belgium and France.

Vintages declared since 1945: '45 '55 '58 '60 '63 '70 '79 '80 '82 '83 '85 '88 '89 '91.

J W Burmester   ★★ →★★★
Rua de Belomonte 39, 4000 Porto. Tel (2) 321274/321299. Founded 1730. V'yds: 40 ha incl Quinta Nova de Nostra Senhora do Carmo. Stock: 4,600 pipes. Visits by appt.

This is a family-owned firm, with the founding family still in charge – a rare occurrence even in such a tradition-ridden business as port. The Burmesters came originally from Germany, but reached Portugal after having taken refuge in England during the religious wars of the 17th century. Despite the indignity of being expelled during the First World War as enemy aliens, the family returned and after considerable legal proceedings recovered its property and returned to the business – which continues to this day in a fairly traditional manner, despite the arrival of modern bottling lines in the Vila Nova de Gaia lodge.

Burmester's finest wines are its *colheita* ports and aged tawnies – up to 40-year-old wines. It has an extraordinary stock of old *colheitas* still available, which date back to the last century. (Although, naturally, these have been refreshed with new wines in the intervening years, the basis of some of them dates back to the 1890s.) This was one of the first firms to produce a late-bottled vintage (in 1964). These wines are able to age in bottle because, before bottling, they are neither filtered nor fined (a process in which the sediment is induced to fall to the bottom of the barrel).

Vintages since 1945: '50 '54 '55 '58 '60 '63 '70 '77 '80 '84 '85 '89 '91.

A A Cálem & Filho   ★★★→

Rua da Roboleira 7, 4000 Porto. Tel (2) 2004867. Founded 1859. V'yds: 417 ha incl Quinta da Ferradosa and Quinta da Foz. Stock: 15,900 pipes. Additional brands: Beira-Rio; Fine Ruby, Tawny, White; Old Friends Fine Tawny; Quinta da Foz; Quinta do Sagrado; Secofino (extra dry white); Tres Velhotes. Visits: weekdays 9–5.

This is one of the few family-owned port houses whose wines bear the name of the owners. It is certainly the largest, and is currently in an expansionist mood, with new vineyards coming on stream at Quinta da Foz and Quinta do Sagrado (both in the Pinhão region), the purchase in 1992 of Quinta da Ferradosa in the Alto Douro, and a new vinification plant at Barroca. And yet, like many port firms, it started up by accident. The original business of shipping wine to Brazil was expanded to enable the firm to bring back wood for making casks, on what would otherwise have been empty ships. Owning casks quickly developed into owning wine to fill them. Cálem's lodges in Gaia have a tangible memory of these origins in the huge cask staves which make up the floors. (The lodges are right by the huge double-decker bridge that links Gaia to Porto and are frequently devastated by flooding from the river.)

The quality of the firm's wines has improved dramatically in recent years. They tend towards sweetness and a dark colouring but, increasingly, also have a firm backbone and a concentration which have pushed them up high in the quality league. Tres Velhotes, the biggest-selling wine, is a fresh-tasting young tawny. The vintage character has a good touch of maturity, as have the LBVs, and the aged tawnies and vintage *colheitas* have been making their mark. The Quinta da Foz is now made as a single-*quinta* vintage port ('82 '84 and '87). The firm's '85 vintage port was acclaimed as one of the best of that year, but like all Cálem's vintages it will mature over 10–12 years rather than the 15–20 needed by wines from some other houses.

Vintages since 1945: '55 '58 '60 '63 '66 '70 '75 '77 '80 '83 '85 '91.

Champalimaud
See Quinta do Cotto

Churchill Graham   ★★★→
Rua da Fonte Nova 5, 4400 Vila Nova de Gaia. Tel (2) 3703641. Founded 1981. V'yds: none. Additional brands: Dry White; Finest Vintage Character; Quinta da Agua Alta. Visits: weekdays 9.30–12.30, 2.30–5.30.

There was great excitement in the trade when John Graham (of the family which used to own Graham's port) announced he was setting up a shipping company: it was the first independent port shipper to be established for 50 years. John Graham had worked for COCKBURN SMITHES and TAYLOR, FLADGATE & YEATMAN before going solo. On doing so, he was not allowed to name his ports 'Churchill Graham' (the W & J GRAHAM company, now owned by Symingtons, felt its own name came too close to it) so he settled for 'Churchill' (his wife's maiden name). The company's policy has always been to aim for the premium end of the market. Its wines are very concentrated and full, and created an instant success with the '82 vintage, which was sourced from *quintas* Agua Alta (in the Douro Valley, west of Pinhão), Manuela and Fojo (in the Pinhão Valley), all owned by Jorges Borges. Churchill's subsequent business has been built on a first-rate crusted, and the, more prosaic, vintage character. The '85 vintage was less successful than the '82 and the '91 is potentially outstanding, while the '87 Agua Alta is a wine that will mature relatively quickly. It is still early days for this firm, but it is already a firmly-established part of the port scene.

Vintages since 1945: '82 '85 '91.

Cockburn Smithes ★★★→★★★★
Rua das Coradas 13, 4400 Vila Nova de Gaia. Tel (2) 3794031. Founded 1815. V'yds: 255 ha incl Quinta do Atayde, Quinta dos Canais, Quinta da Sta Maria, Quinta do Tua, Quinta de Val Coelho. Stock: 30,000 pipes. Additional brands: Fine White, Ruby and Tawny; Harveys Directors Bin; Light White; Quinta da Eira Velha; Special Reserve. Visits: weekdays 9–12, 2–4.

One of the most famous names in port and certainly one of the most familiar (partly due to Cockburn's Special Reserve ruby-style port, which is the brand leader in the UK market). Founded in the year of Waterloo by Robert Cockburn, the firm was joined by Henry and John Smithes in 1848, becoming Cockburn Smithes. Much later, in 1961, it took over MARTINEZ GASSIOT and then, in 1962, was itself taken over by HARVEYS OF BRISTOL. It is now part of the Hiram Walker group. In recent years, Cockburn has expanded its vineyard interests with the purchase of a large area of land at Vilariça, in a side valley of the Douro, almost on the Spanish border. This new land is on comparatively flat ground, in contrast to the steep-sloping, traditional port vineyards, and is just coming into full production. The firm has three major lodges in the Douro, at Régua, Tua and Foz Côa. In the pink-walled lodge in Gaia is one of the few working cooperages in the wine trade.

Out of all this accumulation of property, there comes a range of commercial wines which never falls below a good standard. The famous Special Reserve is in a category all of its own – a soft, comparatively sweet, aged ruby, full and with good fruitiness, very easy to drink. The firm's new aged tawnies are some of the best available, quite full, nutty, spirity wines. The Harveys Directors Bin, which Cockburn also makes, is a tawny with full, mature, sweet fruit. Light White and the, sweeter, Fine White are good examples of white ports. The LBV is firmly in the commercial mould. Due to demand on its stocks (needed for the Special Reserve) Cockburn has not declared vintage wines as regularly as some other houses, but when it does, they are very much in the upper middle rank. The '85 and the '91 are the best from recent decades.

Vintages since 1945: '45 '47 '50 '55 '60 '63 '67 '70 '75 '77 '83 '85 '91.

Croft ★★★
Largo Joaquim Magalhães 23, 4401 Vila Nova de Gaia. Tel (2) 305514. Founded 1678. V'yds: 120 ha at Quinta da Roêda. Additional brands: Distinction Finest Reserve, Tawny Reserve; Fine Tawny, Ruby, White; Morgan ports; Quinta da Roêda; Triple Crown Fine Ruby. Visits: no.

This is one of the two oldest port firms (the other being Warre). It was founded by John Croft, who married into a Yorkshire wine family, the Thompsons. Subsequent Crofts were pillars of the port trade: Thomas Croft founded the Anglican Church in Porto, and another John Croft helped Wellington during the Peninsular War and was created Baron da Estrella by the Portuguese government by way of thanks. By 1827, Croft was the fourth largest port house and it remained in family hands until it was sold to W & A Gilbey in 1911. Both firms went on to form International Distillers and Vintners, part of the Grand Metropolitan Group. Croft in Portugal is managed jointly with Croft in Jerez. The firm also owns Morgan ports (acquired in 1952) and DELAFORCE ports. Its vineyard interests include the beautiful Quinta da Roêda at Pinhão, bought by the Croft family in the last century and regarded as one of the showpiece *quintas* of the Douro.

Croft's ports never seem quite to achieve the reputation they deserve. But, while much of the firm's output is of straightforward, commercial wines (the basic Fine Ruby and Tawny are in this category), and the Distinction Finest Reserve is in the soft, ill-defined style of COCKBURN's Special Reserve (Croft's main competitor), the firm also makes some very good aged tawnies (especially the 10-year-old) and its vintage wines can compete with the best. The single-*quinta* wine, Quinta da Roêda, has been produced in non-general vintages. The first was the '67, followed by the '78 '80 and '83. These and the vintage wines proper exhibit a flowery quality which comes from the Roêda vineyard. The '82 was one of the few acceptable vintage ports from a year that saw a declaration by only a minority of shippers, while the '85 will be very fine, and the '75, now very mature, was one of the best from that year.

Morgan ports are generally sold under buyers' own labels, but there have been vintage declarations of a small number of cases.

Croft vintages since 1945: '45 '50 '55 '60 '63 '66 '70 '75 '77 '82 '85 '91. Morgan vintages since 1945: '45 '48 '55 '60 '63 '66 '70 '77 '82 '85.

Delaforce Sons ★★
Largo Joaquim Magalhães 23, 4401 Vila Nova de Gaia. Tel (2) 302212. Founded 1868. V'yds: none owned, but exclusivity of Quinta da Corte. Additional brands: Dry White; His Eminence's Choice Superb Old Tawny, 10 Years Old Tawny; Paramount Full Ruby, Medium Tawny; Quinta da Corte; Special White. Visits: no.

Although this firm is now part of CROFT, it still operates at a separate lodge and has its own, individual brands. Members of the Delaforce family are still involved in the business. The family, originally Huguenots who fled from France to England in the 17th century, came to Portugal in 1834 and set up shop independently in the port trade in 1868. Delaforce was sold to International Distillers and Vintners exactly 100 years later. The lodges in Gaia are some of the most interesting to visit for their traditional aspect, with their perpetually uneven floors and relics of past port practices. The Quinta da Corte, just down river from Pinhão, is operated exclusively by Delaforce although not owned by the firm.

The Delaforce ports are divided firmly into three categories: the rather dull, standard range, exported mainly to Germany and France; the usually soft His Eminence's Choice tawny, and the vintage wines. The single-*quinta* vintage, Quinta da Corte (first release '78), showed some delicate character in the '80. The best vintage since 1966 is the '85, which has an excellent, ripe fruit taste.

Vintages since 1945: '45 '47 '50 '55 '58 '60 '63 '66 '70 '75 '77 '82 '85.

Dow's ★★★→★★★★
Silva & Cosens, Travessa Barão de Forrester, 4400 Vila Nova de Gaia. Tel (2) 3796063. Founded 1798. V'yds: 35 ha

at Quinta do Bomfim. Stock: 24,100 pipes. Additional brands: AJS Finest Vintage Character; Boardroom Old Tawny; Fine Ruby; Quinta do Bomfim. Visits by appt.

Silva & Cosens was founded by Bruno da Silva, an enterprising Portuguese who evaded French warships to ship port to England during the Napoleonic wars. Silva & Cosens merged with Dow & Co in 1877 and from then on the brand name of the company's ports has been Dow's. The Symington family acquired Silva & Cosens in the early years of this century, and now runs it in conjunction with its other port houses, W & J GRAHAM and WARRE. The Quinta do Bomfim at Pinhão was bought by Silva & Cosens towards the end of the 19th century, and there the firm pioneered the replanting of the Douro vineyards after they were devastated – as were all European vineyards – by phylloxera. Since then, it has been one of the first companies to use auto-vinification techniques – on the Quinta do Bomfim estate, where all the wines are made.

The quality of Dow's ports is of an all-round top standard. The firm seems to succeed both at vintage wines and at aged tawnies. The best of the tawnies are the 10-year-old and the Boardroom Old Tawny, a softly nutty 15-year-old wine. The crusted port has great character and is an admirable alternative to pricier vintage wines. Even the LBV, so often seen as a highly commercial, rather bland style of wine, is full of the quite dry, but big and powerful style characteristic of Dow's. The single-*quinta* port here is Quinta do Bomfim. Of the vintages, the '63, '77, '83 and '85 are very great wines, with '66, '80 and '91 following closely behind.

Vintages since 1945: '45 '47 '50 '55 '60 '63 '66 '70 '72 '75 '77 '80 '83 '85 '91.

A A Ferreira Sucrs ★★★
Rua da Carvalhosa 19/103, 4400 Vila Nova de Gaia. Tel (2) 300866. Founded 1751. V'yds: 125 ha incl company vineyards at Quinta do Porto, Quinta do Seixo, Quinta da Leda; family-owned vineyards at Quinta do Vale de Meão. Stock: 20,000 pipes. Additional brands: Dona Antónia Personal Reserve; Duque de Bragança 20-year-old; Quintado Porto 10-year-old; Quinta do Seixo; Superior Ruby, Tawny, White. Visits: weekdays 9–5, Sat 9–12.

This firm possesses, in its history, one of the greatest names in the port trade. Although it was founded in 1751 by a vineyard owner, José Ferreira, it was not until his grandson, António, died and António's widow, Dona Antónia, took over that it made its mark in the port trade. Dona Antónia was one of those truly formidable widows that the wine trade produced in numbers during the 19th century (La Veuve Clicquot in Champagne is another example). She pioneered vineyard holdings up river from Régua that are now seen as the finest port vineyards; she built magnificent houses (*quintas* Vale de Meão and Vesuvio have superb buildings) – and she was there at the tragic drowning in the Douro of Baron James FORRESTER, in 1862, where her own life was saved only by her buoyant crinolines. She was known popularly as Ferreirinha, for her charitable work, a name that is still attached to the company products. Her daughter narrowly escaped the clutches of the King of Portugal – in the end she married the Count of Azambuja, the king's nephew.

Today the Ferreira family still owns many of the vineyards that supply the wine for its ports. But in 1987 it sold the company to Sogrape, the producer of Mateus Rosé, which has been prepared to invest heavily to maintain the quality of Ferreira ports. Ferreira is also involved in the table wine trade, making what is possibly Portugal's greatest red wine, Barca Velha, and Esteva, both from Douro vineyards.

The style of port here (known as the 'port the Portuguese drink' on account of its massive sales on the home market) is soft, sweet and raisiny. While the Superior range is the most popular, the firm rises to the greatest heights with its aged tawnies, both the Quinta do Porto 10-year-old and the superb Duque de Bragança 20-year-old, which is almost like a fruity, nutty Christmas pudding in its richness. The vintage wines, often underrated and, before the '91, not released until ready for drinking, are marked by sweetness and a comparatively rapid maturation. The firm makes a single-*quinta* vintage port from Quinta do Seixo.

Vintages since 1945: '45 '47 '50 '58 '60 '63 '66 '70 '75 '77 '78 '80 '82 '83 '85 '87 '91.

Feuerheerd Bros ★→
PO Box 39, Rua Serpa Pinto 534, 4401 Vila Nova de Gaia. Tel (2) 302320. Founded 1815. V'yds: 95 ha. Additional

brands: Anchor; Commendador; Marquês de Soveral; Royal Banquet. Visits: weekdays 9–2.30, 2–4.30.

This firm, now part of BARROS, ALMEIDA, was founded by the Hamburg-born Dietrich Feuerheerd as a general merchant company (like so many port firms). It began shipping port in 1881 and became an important brand in France, the ports being served at banquets given by the President for various visiting British monarchs. Like many of the non-British port shippers, it specializes in *colheita* ports and aged tawnies. Its vintage wines are generally on the extremely light side.

Vintages since 1945: '55 '57 '58 '60 '63 '65 '66 '70 '74 '75 '77 '78 '80 '82 '83 '85.

Fonseca Guimaraens   ★★★★
Travessa Barão de Forrester 404, 4401 Vila Nova de Gaia. Tel (2) 304505. Founded 1822. V'yds: 69 ha incl Quinta do Cruzeiro, Quinta de Panascal, Quinta de S António. Additional brands: Bin 27; Quinta de Panascal; Siroco (white). Visits: May to end Sept, weekdays 10–6; Quinta de Panascal, all year, weekdays 10–6.

For many years, until 1988, this firm was called simply Guimaraens Vinhos, while Fonseca was its brand name. Now the confusion has been eased by attaching Fonseca to the company name, and Guimaraens to the brand name. This is as it should be for there is still a Guimaraens running the business. In fact the company operates in tandem with TAYLOR, FLADGATE & YEATMAN, the two having merged in 1948.

The firm started life as Fonseca in the 18th century, but it really got going in 1822, when Manuel Pedro Guimaraens acquired the business. The Guimaraens family comes from Braga, but has, over the past century or so, become completely anglicized.

Fonseca Guimaraens ports are some of the greats in the trade. From the famous vintage character Bin 27 right up to the top quality vintages, they manage to retain a house style: plummy, rounded, rich, jammy and very weighty. The firm has recently introduced an LBV and the '83, the first, was one of the best of its type: elegant and with a definite vintage character, due to very slight filtration before bottling. The aged tawnies maintain the house style, emphasizing fruit. There are two styles of vintage wine: the Fonseca Guimaraens wines, which are produced in lesser years but nonetheless seem to achieve a standard many other port houses would envy, and the great Fonseca vintage wines, which get better and better. Of the latter, the '70 is soft, rich and full of intense fruit, more advanced than some great wines of this vintage. The '80 is one of the best of an underrated vintage, and the '85 will be superb in 15 years' time. A recent release is the single-*quinta* Quinta de Panascal, the '78 being light, quite straightforward but still with the Fonseca plumminess.

Fonseca vintages since 1945: '45 '48 '55 '60 '63 '66 '70 '75 '77 '80 '83 '85.

Gould Campbell ★★→★★★
PO Box 26, 4401 Vila Nova de Gaia. Tel (2) 3796063.
Founded 1797. V'yds: none owned; buy regularly from
Quinta dos Entre Caminhos and Quinta dos Lagares.
Stock: drawn from stock of Smith Woodhouse. Additional
brands: Fine Ruby, Tawny, White. Visits by appt.

Like many port firms, this one originated in a merger between an English importer and a Portugal-based shipper. In this case it was George Clode, who set up in London in 1797, and Garrett Gould, who started his business in Lisbon and Porto at about the same time. Mergers brought James Campbell into the Gould business and later George Clode bought what had by then become Gould, James Campbell & Co. In 1970, the Symington family bought the house and the name. The ports are now made and shipped by SMITH WOODHOUSE, another Symington company.

The ports shipped under the Gould Campbell label are generally middle-weight wines. The vintage ports are never designed to last for ever, but can be pleasant drinking after ten or 12 years. The '80, one of the lighter vintages, had plenty of raisiny fruit but was already within sight of maturity in 1988. Both the '83 and the '91 are richer and fuller but not particularly complex. I prefer the vintage character to the LBV, and there is an excellent crusted port, while both the 10-year-old and the 20-year-old tawnies are very true to type.

Vintages since 1945: '45 '47 '50 '55 '60 '70 '75 '77 '80 '83 '85 '91.

W & J Graham ★★★→★★★★
PO Box 19, 4401 Vila Nova de Gaia. Tel (2) 3796065.
Founded 1820. V'yds: 70 ha at Quinta dos Malvedos.
Stock: 11,000 pipes. Additional brands: Fine Ruby,
Tawny,White; Six Grapes; Quinta dos Malvedos.
Visits by appt.

One of the three principal companies to make up the group run by the Symington family (*see* Dow's and Warre), Graham is one of the major names in the port trade. Yet it was set up almost by accident, when a shipload of port was used to pay off a bad debt in the textile trade, in which the Graham family was originally engaged. The firm was family-run until 1970, when it was sold to the Symingtons.

Although originally part of the Graham company, the show estate at Tua, Quinta dos Malvedos, was bought by the Symingtons at a later stage. The lodge in Gaia is in a spectacular position, looking up river to the two-deck bridge, and out over all the other port lodges. The stars from this house are its vintage wines. Their style is rich and quite sweet, but always with a pleasing freshness. Of recent vintages, the '70 '77 '83 and '85 are the finest, with the '83 and '85 ranking in the top two or three of those years, and the '91 perhaps being the very best of that vintage. The '63 was another great Graham port. Until recently, the Malvedos vintage port, produced in lesser years, did not come entirely from the *quinta* itself, but new plantings mean that it is now a true single-*quinta* wine. The LBV continues the house style of sweetness, and the aged tawnies also tend in this direction. They are less impressive than the vintage wines. The Six Grapes is an old-style, rich, beefy ruby.

Vintages declared since since 1945: '45 '48 '55 '60 '63 '66 '70 '75 '77 '80 '83 '85 '91.

Gran Cruz Porto →★
Rua Visconde das Devesas 360, 4400 Vila Nova de Gaia. Tel (2) 304762. V'yds: none.

Almost unknown in Anglo-Saxon markets, Gran Cruz Porto is the biggest selling brand in France, where its light tawnies are especially popular as aperitifs. Unusually for a port firm, it holds few stocks and owns no vineyards, preferring to buy its wine from other shippers.

C N Kopke ★★→

PO Box 42, Rua Serpa Pinto 183/191, 4401 Vila Nova de Gaia. Tel (2) 302420. Founded 1638. V'yds: 95 ha incl Quinta São Luiz. Stock: 3,700 pipes. Additional brands: Aperitivo (dry white); Bridge (ruby); Old World (tawny); Quinta São Luiz; Victoria (tawny). Visits: weekdays 9–12.30, 2–4.30.

This is the oldest port house, founded by Cristiano Kopke, son of the consul for the German Hanseatic towns in Lisbon. At one point, the firm had links with the van Zeller family of QUINTA DO NOVAL, but it is now owned by BARROS, ALMEIDA.

The best wines from this firm are the *colheita* vintage tawnies, which are in a soft, rounded style and tend towards sweetness. The '75, matured in wood for nine years, is soft and elegant. Other wines are less memorable. The standard range is sweet, while the 10-year-old tawny is rather too soft. The Quinta São Luiz vintage wines, rich and with plenty of fruit, mature at around ten years of age, and are generally less expensive than vintage wines from the major houses.

Vintages since 1945: '45 '52 '55 '58 '60 '63 '66 '70 '74 '75 '77 '78 '79 '80 '82 '83 '85.

Martinez Gassiot ★★→★★★

Rua das Coradas 13, 4401 Vila Nova de Gaia. Tel (2) 394031. Founded 1790. V'yds: owned jointly with Cockburn Smithes. Additional brands: Fine Ruby, Tawny, White; Selected Tawny; Old House 10-year-old Tawny; Directors 20-year-old Tawny. Visits: weekdays 10–12, 2–4.

The firm was founded by a Spaniard, Sebastian González Martinez, who was based in London's Mincing Lane, from where he sold port, cigars and sherry. He was joined in 1822 by John Peter Gassiot and they acquired a lodge in Vila Nova de Gaia in 1834. One of their first managers was John Delaforce, whose younger son founded his own port firm. Martinez left the firm to the Gassiots, who became great City of London benefactors (appropriately, after the Second World War, they acquired cellars under the house that once belonged to Dick Whittington). The firm was floated on the Stock Exchange in 1902. In 1961 it was bought by HARVEYS OF BRISTOL and its production is now run jointly with

COCKBURN's, although stocks are kept separate.

Unusually, a considerable proportion of Martinez stocks is kept at Régua in the Douro Valley, and the higher temperatures there (compared with Vila Nova de Gaia) give a distinctive baked character – known as the Douro Bake – to the firm's ports. This is particularly apparent in its wood-aged wines, such as the Directors 20-year-old Tawny and the 10-year-old Old House Tawny (the current Directors is still quite sweet and warm and exhibits no signs of drying out). The LBV, which stays in wood for five years, is almost tawny in colour. The crusted port (bottled 1985) is smooth, rich and mature, a good example of this underrated style, but some other wines – the vintage character and Selected Tawny – show too much spirit and not enough fruit. The firm's vintage wines are not as important, although some from the 1960s were exceptional; I prefer the style of Gassiot's 1970s vintage wines (especially the '70) to those of the 1980s.

Vintages since 1945: '45 '48 '50 '55 '60 '63 '67 '70 '75 '82 '85 '87 '91.

Messias   →★
PO Box 1, 3050 Mealhada. Tel (31) 22027. Founded 1923.
V'yds: 260 ha at Quinta do Cachão and Quinta do Rei.
Stock: 8,400 pipes. Additional brand: Quinta do Cachão.
Visits: weekdays 9–12.30, 2.30–5.

This independent, family company is equally involved in the table wine business in the Bairrada (hence the Mealhada address), Dão and Douro. The port part of the firm was started in 1930, a few years after Baptista Messias set up as a wine merchant and shipper. The firm makes a range of commercial ports, which are mainly exported to western Europe and Latin America, as well as to ex-Portuguese colonies in Africa. The vintage wines here are very much in the soft, quick-maturing style and are often produced in years that are not generally declared.

Vintages since 1945: '45 '47 '50 '52 '58 '60 '63 '66 '67 '70 '75 '77 '79 '80 '82 '83 '84 '85.

Niepoort   ★★★→
Rua Infante D Henriques 39–29, 4000 Porto, tel (2)
2001028; Rua Serpa Pinto 278, Vila Nova de Gaia, tel (2)

301640. Founded 1842. V'yds: 500 ha at Quinta de Napoles and Quinta do Carril. Stock 3,000 pipes. Additional brands: Dry White; Senior Tawny. Visits: no.

One of the few port firms that is still family run, Niepoort is now in the hands of the fifth generation. Its origins are Dutch; the founder, in 1842, was one Eduard Kebe, who took F M van der Niepoort as his partner in 1847. Today, Niepoort is one of the smaller houses. The firm specializes in vintage *colheitas*, some of which can be very fine; they hold up very well once bottled. The aged tawny ports have similar, though lesser, character (the 30-year-old is surprisingly fruity for a wine of this age). Unusually for a firm that is particularly good at vintage tawnies, the true vintage wines are equally fine, with excellent fruit flavours and a deceptive ability to age.

Vintages since 1945: '45 '55 '60 '63 '66 '70 '75 '77 '78 '80 '82 '83 '85 '87 '91.

Offley Forrester   ★★→

PO Box 61, Rua Guilherme Braga 38, 4401 Vila Nova de Gaia. Tel (2) 305111. Founded 1737. V'yds: 90 ha incl Quinta da Boa Vista. Stock: 28,000 pipes. Additional brands: Baron de Forrester; Boa Vista Vintage, LBV; Diez Port; Duke of Oporto; Offley.

Baron Joseph James Forrester was one of the great figures in the port trade in the 19th century. He entered the family firm (started by William Offley in 1737 and joined by James Forrester in 1803) in 1831. Joseph James Forrester, the nephew of James, was drowned at the rapids of Cachão in 1861, when travelling in the company of Dona António FERREIRA. During his lifetime he had been the first to map the Upper Douro and had saved the vineyards when oidium (a type of fungal disease) struck in the 1850s. For these and other services to port, he was created a baron by the King of Portugal. The Forrester family continued to run the company until 1929, when it was sold to a London firm of wine merchants. Later, in 1983, it was bought by Martini e Rossi.

Until its purchase by Martini, Offley Forrester had been going through a rather dull patch. Since then, the most successful improvements have been to the aged tawnies, such as the Baron Forrester 10-year-old, but the Duke of Oporto, a middle-range ruby, continues to be too soft and mellow to have much character. Softness and mellowness are also characteristics of the Boa Vista vintage ports, wines which come to maturity quite early, as is the style of Portuguese-owned port houses. The '77 was a middle quality wine, but the best of the firm's recent vintages was the '72, a year that was not generally declared. The '83 looks set to be one of the better vintages from this house. Some confusion exists over the fact that Boa Vista is the name for vintage and for LBV wines here.

Vintages since 1945: '45 '50 '54 '60 '62 '63 '66 '67 '70 '72 '75 '77 '80 '82 '83 '85.

Osborne ★→★★
Rua da Cabaça 37, 4400 Vila Nova de Gaia. Tel (2) 302648/394842. Founded 1967. V'yds: none. Visits: weekdays 9.30–12.30, 1.30–5.30.

Osborne is a part of the major sherry producer of that name. The Portuguese branch of the firm was started up in 1967 in association with QUINTA DO NOVAL, but since 1982 has operated from a separate lodge in Vila Nova de Gaia. It makes a full range of styles, from standard ruby, tawny and white ports to vintage wines, exporting a major part of its production.

Vintages since 1945: '60 '70 '82 '85.

A Pinto Santos ★
PO Box 39, 4401 Vila Nova de Gaia. Tel (2) 302320. Founded 1872. V'yds: none. Additional brand: Santos. Visits: weekdays 10–12, 2–5.

Founded in 1872 by A J Pinto dos Santos Junior and João António Luizelho, this was originally a trading company, but port gradually took over. It was sold after the Second World War to the BARROS, ALMEIDA company. While it makes all styles of port, the firm is most at home with its standard range and the wood-matured vintage *colheitas*. I have enjoyed the '77, a wine that has matured quickly and has been ready to drink since 1988. The LBV was simply commercial and dull.

Vintages since 1945: '55 '57 '58 '60 '63 '65 '66 '70 '74 '75 '77 '78 '80 '82 '83 '85.

Manoel D Poças Junior ★→★★
PO Box 56, Rua Visconde das Devesas 186, 4401 Vila
Nova de Gaia. Tel (2) 300212. Founded 1918. V'yds:
74 ha at Quinta das Quartas, Quinta de Sta Barbara,
Quinta de Vale de Cavalos. Stock: 10,200 pipes. Additional
brands: Almiro; Lopes; Pintão; Poças; Pousada; Seguro;
Terras. Visits: no.

A go-ahead firm, still family owned, making a wide range of wines
including the port sold in Portugal's *pousadas* (government-run
hotels). In fact, this is the only one of their wines I have had a
chance to taste. It is a light tawny style, and I found it pleasant but
unexciting. One of the peculiarities of the company is that it
exports its vintage wines already decanted. The firm's finest wines
are generally agreed to be the vintage *colheitas* and aged tawnies.
Vintage wines are relatively new to the firm, but they are certainly
of a good standard.

Vintages since 1945: '60 '63 '70 '75 '85 '91.

Quarles Harris ★★→
PO Box 26, Travessa do Barão de Forrester, 4401 Vila
Nova de Gaia. Tel (2) 3796063. Founded 1680. V'yds:
none. Stock: 2,800 pipes. Additional brands: Personal
Reserve; Royal Ruby, Tawny, White. Visits by appt.

The origins of this firm lie in Devon in England, from where
the Dawson family set up trading links with Portugal in the 16th
century. Among other items, the Dawsons shipped Douro wines
and were probably among the first to do so. In 1680, Thomas
Dawson set up in port shipping as Dawson & Harris (later to
become Quarles Harris). By the end of the 18th century, when the
firm was taken over by Warre, it had become one of the largest
shippers, although it is now one of the smaller houses. Since early
this century, the firm has been owned by the Symington family
(also the owner of DOW'S, W & J GRAHAM and WARRE).

Mellowness and balance are the hallmarks of Quarles Harris
ports. This is especially true of the vintage wines − the '85 for
example is much softer than some other vintages from the
Symington group (and will therefore mature more quickly). The
same applies to other recent Quarles Harris vintages, such as the
'83 (which will be a highly enjoyable wine in two or three years'

time) and the '77. An LBV, produced here in small quantities, is one of the better, more characterful examples of this style.

Vintages since 1945: '45 '47 '50 '55 '58 '60 '63 '66 '70 '75 '77 '80 '83 '85 '91.

Quinta do Cotto   ★→★★
Cidadelhe, Vila Real. V'yds: 52 ha near Régua. Additional brand: Quinta do Cotto. Visits by appt.

This was the first *quinta* to bottle its own port in the Douro region following the change in regulations concerning ageing in Vila Nova de Gaia. In fact, Miguel Champalimaud, the owner, was one of the most outspoken advocates of Douro bottling.

Although bearing a French name, the Champalimaud family is Portuguese in origin, and has certainly owned this land since the 17th century. Its vineyards are in the Baixo Corgo region, land usually considered only suitable for producing low quality ports. But the family champions this area, preferring it to the more popular Cima Corgo and Alto Douro, which lie up river.

The *quinta* made its name with table wines such as Grande Escolha, and the family believes that port should be made in much the same way as these wines (this includes preventing its oxidization), an attitude that has set it against the port establishment. So far only one port has been bottled by Champalimaud, the '82 vintage, although there has been talk of the '89 being bottled as well. In other years, the port is sold in bulk to shippers.

Vintages declared since 1945: '82.

Quinta do Crasto   ★★→
Gouvinhas Ferrao, 5060 Sabrosa. Tel (5) 492207. Founded 1615. V'yds: 42 ha. Additional brand: Quinta do Crasto. Visits by appt.

Quinta do Crasto is one of the new generation of ports, produced entirely in the Douro, on the estate where the grapes are grown: a true *château*-bottled wine. Jorge Roquette and four partners own the estate, based near Pinhão, which previously sold its crop to FERREIRA and, before that, to Constantino (a firm bought by Ferreira in 1961). The *quinta* has bottled only a few wines to date, but aims to make a premium range, such as vintage, LBV and aged tawny.

Vintages since 1945: '78 '85 '87.

Quinta do Noval ★★★→

Rua Cândido dos Reis 575, 4400 Vila Nova de Gaia. Tel (2) 302020. Founded 1803. V'yds: 106 ha incl Quinta da Barca, Quinta das Candas, Quinta do Silval. Stock: 6,600 pipes. Additional brands: da Silva; Nacional; Old Coronation Ruby; Quinta do Noval; van Zellers; Velloso & Tait. Visits by appt.

It was only in the 1970s that the family-owned company of Quinta do Noval changed its name from A J da Silva & Co to the name of its most famous vineyard. The firm was effectively established when António José da Silva bought the vineyard and farm of Quinta do Noval at Pinhão in 1894, although records of the *quinta* date back at least to 1715. The son-in-law of António da Silva, Luiz Vasconcellos Porto (an appropriate name indeed) transformed the *quinta*, creating the wide terracing which today makes it one of the show-places of the Douro vineyards. Noval was the pioneer of many aspects of port we now take for granted: the first to introduce the LBV style; the first to export port in bottle rather than pipe; the first to introduce aged tawnies, and the first to develop stencilled lettering on bottles.

Much of the firm's history – and its wine – went up in flames in 1981 when the lodges at Vila Nova de Gaia burnt down. This fire precipitated a family crisis and, after a period of management by the great-grandchildren of Luiz Vasconcellos Porto, Cristiano and Teresa van Zeller, ownership has now passed to the French insurance company and Bordeaux *château*-owner AXA Millesimes.

Today, much of the firm's port is shipped direct from the Douro rather than being stored in Vila Nova de Gaia. The most famous wine Noval produces is called Nacional. This is a vintage wine made from a small patch of 5,000 ungrafted vines, which, alone among the Douro vineyards, has so far proved able to withstand the phylloxera louse. Only 250 cases are made each year, and the fabled '31 still commands enormous prices at auction.

Back on a less rarefied plane, the tawnies are always of the highest quality, with the 20-year-old (pale, with fig, raisin and mature fruit flavours) being my favourite. Noval LB (no longer an LBV, having dropped the vintage designation) is full-bodied and has more character than many other late-bottled wines. The vintage wines have varied in quality, with those from the 1960s and 1970s (when the style was new to the company) being less impressive than more recent wines. Wood-aged vintage wines are also produced.

Vintages since 1945: '60 '63 '66 '67 '70 '75 '78 '82 '83 '85 '87 '91.

Quinta da Romaneira ★→★★
Rua do Campo Alegre 298, 4100 Porto. Tel (2) 667141. Founded 1850. V'yds: 47 ha. Additional brands: Quinta da Romaneira; Quinta da Pulga. Visits by appt.

Although the Vinagre family has been producing port at its *quinta* near Alijó in the Cima Corgo for many years, it has only been bottling since the change in regulations in 1986, which allowed shipments to be made direct from the Douro. The firm makes a single-*quinta* vintage, Quinta da Romaneira, and has a second label, Quinta da Pulga, for basic ruby and tawny. It is still feeling its way with the vintage wines, but the raw material is good.

Vintages since 1945: '85 '87.

Quinta de la Rosa ★★
5085 Pinhão. Tel (54) 72254. Founded 1906. V'yds: 40 ha. Additional brand: Quinta de la Rosa. Visits by appt.

The Bergqvist family, which owns this *quinta*, has long been associated with port. Related to the FEUERHEERDS, it was linked with that shipper until Feuerheerd was bought by BARROS, ALMEIDA. For many years the *quinta*'s wine was made and sold by ROBERTSON, now part of SANDEMAN, and it was only with the '88 vintage that the connection was finally severed, and the wine came to be sold by the Bergqvists. They have adopted an ingenious method of financing the operation by inviting investors to put up £1,000, in return for which they will receive five cases of port every year for five years. The winery and *quinta* are still very much in a traditional mould, superbly sited at the approaches to Pinhão, and the '88 shows that the *quinta* can produce fine wines.

Vintages since 1945: '88.

Quinta de Vale de Figueira ★★→
Covas do Douro, 5085 Pinhão. Tel (54) 72159. Founded 1759. V'yds: 19 ha. Additional brand: Quinta de Vale de Figueira. Visits: no.

This *quinta* is among those releasing some of their ports as single-*quinta* wines, bottled in the Douro. It is owned by Alfredo Cálem e Hoelzer, related to the CALEM port family, and much of the port from this *quinta*, which is close to Cálem's Quinta da Foz, is sold to that firm. However, some wine is kept back and both a '87 vintage and a 10-year-old tawny have been released here. These wines show the excellent style and quality you would expect of someone who has worked in the port trade all his life.

Vintages declared since 1945: '87 '91.

Quinta do Vesuvio ★★★
Travessa Barão de Forrester, 4400 Vila Nova de Gaia. Tel (2) 3796063. Founded 1820. V'yds: 67 ha. Additional brands: Quinta do Vesuvio. Visits by appt.

This was the showpiece *quinta* of Dona Antónia FERREIRA, the wine widow of the port industry, who did so much to open up the high Douro. It is still a magnificent estate, with by far the grandest house, its own private chapel and enormous open stone *lagares* (wine presses) for fermentation. Until its acquisition by the Symington family, in 1989, it was owned by Ferreira, but it was not included in the sale of that firm to Sogrape. The Symingtons are treating Vesuvio separately from their other port interests (DOW'S, W & J GRAHAM, WARRE) and currently make a single-*quinta* wine from the estate. They are restoring the estate house and undertaking extensive restructuring and replanting of the vineyards.

The first vintage port to be made under Symington control was the '89, but it is the '90 which fully justifies all the hype raised over this *quinta*. It is a huge wine, full of plum and fig flavours and built to last – seemingly for ever. With this exciting start, Vesuvio is obviously destined to regain its foremost place among Douro *quintas*.

Vintages declared since 1945: '89 '90 '91.

Adriano Ramos-Pinto ★★★
Avenida Ramos Pinto 380, 4400 Vila Nova de Gaia. Tel (2) 300716. Founded 1880. V'yds: 150 ha incl Quinta do Bom Retiro, Quinta dos Bons Ares, Quinta da Ervamoira, Quinta S Domingos, Quinta da Urtiga. Stock: 6,500 pipes. Additional brands: Dry White; Quinta do Bom Retiro; Quinta da Ervamoira; Quinta da Urtiga; Tawny Adriano.

Visits: June–Sept, weekdays 10–6, Sat 10–1; Oct–May, weekdays 9–5.

One of the most energetic companies in the port trade, founded by Adriano Ramos-Pinto when he was only 20. Adriano was soon joined by his brother António, and until 1990 the brothers' heirs continued to run the business. Family disagreements then led to a majority shareholding being taken by the champagne house of Roederer. In the early years of the century, Ramos-Pinto developed its spectacular art nouveau-style advertising, which is still used today.

The firm has earned a considerable reputation for its research into the matching of grape varieties with vineyards, and into the different methods of laying out vineyards in the steep valleys of the Douro (favouring the up-and-down system rather than the, officially-preferred, terracing method). The results of this painstaking research are apparent in the quality of the wines. The tawnies are the stars here – the single-*quinta* 10-year-old tawny of Quinta da Ervamoira and the 20-year-old Quinta do Bom Retiro are both very fine wines. They have quite a light, fruity character, and taste fresher than many aged tawnies. Some find the style too light, but it is very much in the tradition of Portuguese port. The ruby styles: the Quinta da Urtiga vintage character, the LBV and the vintage wines, are not as interesting, but the firm's two white ports (especially the dry style), which both have the Ramos-Pinto light touch, are highly successful.

Vintages since 1945: '50 '52 '55 '60 '63 '70 '75 '80 '82 '83 '85 '91.

Robertson Brothers ★★→

PO Box 7, Rua António Granjo 207, 4401 Vila Nova de Gaia. Tel (2) 304836. Founded 1847. V'yds: none. Stock: 3,100 pipes. Additional brands: Game Bird; Imperial 20-year-old Tawny; Privateer Vintage Character; Pyramid 10-year-old Tawny; Rebello Valente Vintage and LBV. Visits: no.

Although the Robertson connection with port dates back to the 18th century, the first formal partnership was in 1847, when James Nisbet Robertson went into business with Burdon & Gray, and the firm became John Gray & Robertson. Later, when James

Robertson's nephew joined the business, it was renamed Robertson Brothers. In 1881, it acquired the brand name Rebello Valente, which has been used on the firm's vintage ports ever since. For 53 years, until his retirement in 1946, the Robertson wines were made by Albert Kendall. In 1953, the firm was bought by SANDEMAN, which in turn was bought by Seagram, in 1980.

I have been impressed with the quality of Robertson's vintage wines and the aged tawnies. The '85 vintage was herby, with a hint of violets, and had a rounded, quite sweet finish, while the '83 was robust and full of fruit. The Rebello Valente LBV is an old-style wine which throws a crust and requires decanting. The 10-year-old Pyramid is mellow and amber-coloured, with quite intense fruitiness, while the 20-year-old Imperial is, inevitably, drier, but still has considerable warmth and vigour. The standard range is more memorable for the Game Bird labels, which stem from James Nisbet Robertson's interest in Douro wildlife.

Vintages since 1945: '45 '47 '55 '63 '66 '67 '70 '72 '75 '77 '80 '83 '85 '87.

Royal Oporto Wine Co (Real Companhia Velha) →★
PO Box 22, Rua Azevedo Magalhães 314, 4401 Vila Nova de Gaia. Tel (2) 303013. Founded 1756. V'yds: 177 ha incl Quinta dos Aciprestes, Quinta do Carvalhal, Quinta das Carvalhas, Quinta do Casal da Granja, Quinta do Sibio, Quinta do Sidrô. Additional brands: Dom José; Don Pavral; Navigators; Quinta dos Aciprestes; Quinta das Carvalhas; Quinta do Casal da Granja. Visits: weekdays 9–12, 2–6.

This is the second largest port shipper, after the Symington-owned houses. It was started up by the Portuguese government as the controlling body for the whole port trade – the Companhia Geral da Agricultura dos Vinhos do Alto Douro – at a time when the reputation of port was suffering because of sharp dealing practices and adulteration. As such, it certainly made some improvement by regulating how the wine was made and by controlling its sale to the shippers. But the organization, in turn, became venal and by 1848 was itself in need of reform. Ten years later it lost its monopoly and became simply one among many port shippers. Today, Royal Oporto is as much concerned with table wine as with port. The company is no longer government-owned.

The ports are not particularly fine wines, but they are produced in great quantity and are often to be found under the label of a wine merchant or supermarket. The best wines here are the *colheitas* and tawnies. The vintage ports (although no doubt deriving from one year) are really nothing of the kind, simply superior rubies that mature quickly; the firm also seems to declare nearly every year. Of the single-*quinta* wines, Quinta das Carvalhas is a full-bodied tawny with some character, Quinta dos Aciprestes is a ruby and Quinta do Casal da Granja is a white.

Vintages since 1945: '45 '53 '54 '55 '58 '60 '61 '62 '63 '67 '70 '77 '78 '79 '80 '82 '83 '84 '85 '87 '91.

Rozès ★
Rua Cândido dos Reis 526-532, 4400 Vila Nova de Gaia. Tel (2) 304580. V'yds: 4.5 ha. Stock: 5,600 pipes. Additional brands: Infanta Isabel; Prince Henry. Visits: June 1–Aug 31, weekdays 10–5.30.
Rozès was founded in Bordeaux as a merchant company for importing port to France, only later were lodges opened in Porto. It is appropriate therefore that the firm is now part of the Moët-Hennessy-Louis Vuitton-Veuve Clicquot empire, and that 70 percent of production goes to France. Inevitably, most of this is in the form of basic ruby, with lesser quantities of tawny. The vintage ports are of a reasonable rather than an exciting quality.

Vintages since 1945: '63 '67 '77 '78 '82 '83 '85 '87.

Sandeman →★★★
Largo Miguel Bombarda 3, 4400 Vila Nova de Gaia. Tel (2) 3706807. Founded 1790. V'yds: 88 ha at Quinta do Vau and Quinta das Laranjeiras. Stock: 53,000 pipes. Additional brands: Apitiv Dry White; Founders Reserve; Imperial 20-year-old Tawny; Original Rich Ruby, Tawny, White; Quinta do Vau; Royal 10-year-old Tawny. Visits: daily 9.30–12.30, 2–5 (Oct–March closed weekends).
Sandeman's lodge in Vila Nova de Gaia is the most prominent on the river front, with its huge figure of the Don – the cloaked figure, used as the firm's symbol for both its port and its sherry – looming large over the classical façade. The Don joined the company in 1928, when artist George Brown sold the copyright to

Walter Sandeman for 50 guineas.

Sandeman has been in existence since 1790, when George Sandeman left Perth in Scotland and founded a firm based in both Jerez and Porto, and the connections have remained ever since. The family was a pillar of the port trade: one of its members, George Albert, married into Portuguese nobility at the same time as becoming a governor of the Bank of England. The family continued to control the firm with an innovative spirit – it was the first firm to advertise port – until 1980, when Sandemans was encompassed by the massive Seagram organization.

The quality of wines from this firm has varied in the past decade. Some of the standard range has been very uninspired (but sells well in the, rather less discriminating, French market). Founders Reserve is a ruby style with a straightforward, rather sweet, commercial taste. But the aged tawnies are another proposition: the 10-year-old Royal is full of tawny character and good, nutty fruit. The 20-year-old can be of a high standard, but sometimes seems to suffer from too much young wine in the blend (perfectly legal provided the average age is 20 years). Sandeman's vintage ports are currently in a soft, comparatively quick-maturing, mainstream style, especially the '80 and '82, although the '85 showed much more class. It is to be hoped that the commitment to quality rather than quantity, announced in 1990 to coincide with the firm's bicentenary, and the arrival of a Sandeman as managing director will return the firm to some of the glories it enjoyed in the past.

Vintages since 1945: '45 '47 '50 '55 '60 '63 '66 '67 '70 '75 '77 '80 '82 '85 '88.

C da Silva ★→
Rua Felizardo de Lima 247, 4400 Vila Nova de Gaia. Tel (2) 3794128. Founded 1862. V'yds: 20 ha at Régua. Stock: 14,000 pipes. Additional brands: Dalva; House Reserve; Presidential. Visits by appt.

This house was founded in 1862 and, confusingly, is one of the three to have had the name Silva (the Portuguese equivalent of Smith). It is independent but under Dutch ownership, having at one point been part of the Spanish Rumasa group, and exports 95 percent of production round the world, mainly within Europe. The dry white port is very pleasant as an aperitif wine, and the tawny has some aged wines in it to give character. House Reserve is the biggest brand. The firm also produces the rare *colheita* ports, which here, as so often elsewhere, are the stars of the show compared with the vintage ports (sold at da Silva under the Presidential label), which are much too soft and sweet.

Vintages since 1945: '63 '70 '77 '78 '82 '85 '87.

Smith Woodhouse ★★★
PO Box 19, 4401 Vila Nova de Gaia. Tel (2) 3796065. Founded 1784. V'yds: 8 ha at Quinta de Sta Madalena. Stock: 6,400 pipes. Additional brands: Fine Ruby, Tawny, White; Old Lodge; Old Oporto. Visits by appt.
This is a firm with political origins. It was founded by Christopher Smith, a member of the British Parliament and later Lord Mayor of London. He was joined in business by his sons, and later by the Woodhouse brothers, at which time the firm took its present name. In 1970, it was acquired by the Symington family, but the lodges continue to be run independently.

The Smith Woodhouse style is fragrant and fruity, perhaps not quite as serious as some of the other Symington houses, but not without considerable quality especially in the old tawnies and vintage wines. The aged tawnies have plenty of ripe, mature fruitiness. The LBV is in a traditional style, unfined and unfiltered; it throws a crust, and is therefore matured in bottle. The vintage wines seem to reflect the quality of the year very accurately: the '77 is a huge wine with no sign yet of maturity; the '80 is soft and quick–maturing; the '83 is a concentrated wine, which will not be ready until the turn of the century; the '85 is closed, heavy, full of ripeness, weighed down with rich tannins and purple fruit, and the '91 shows signs of developing the same weight. Considering their high quality, the Smith Woodhouse ports are often under–valued.

Vintages since 1945: '45 '47 '50 '55 '60 '70 '75 '77 '80 '83 '85 '88 '91.

Taylor Fladgate & Yeatman ★★★→★★★★
Rua do Choupelo 250, 4400 Vila Nova de Gaia. Tel (2) 304505. Founded 1692. V'yds: 92 ha incl Quinta de Vargellas, Quinta da Terra Feita. Additional brands: Atlantic (tawny); Chip Dry; First Estate; Quinta da Terra

Feita; Quinta de Vargellas; Taylor; Taylor Fladgate. Visits: weekdays 10–6.

For many, this firm, founded in 1692 by Job Bearsley, is the most famous name in port. Peter Bearsley, Job's son, is believed to have been one of the first Englishmen to visit the Upper Douro, and Taylors was the first British-owned firm to acquire property in the Douro Valley, at Régua. The Casa dos Alambiques is now a winery; the 4XX symbol, which is always found on the firm's port bottles, hangs over its gates. In 1893, Taylors purchased the beautiful and spectacular Quinta de Vargellas in the high Douro – at the time one of the most easterly port vineyards. The single-*quinta* port, Quinta de Vargellas, and the Taylor vintage wines, come from here. More recently, the firm bought the large property of Quinta da Terra Feita, in the Pinhão Valley, which is also likely to produce single-*quinta* wine.

The name of the firm derives from a partnership between Joseph Taylor, who joined in 1816, John Fladgate, who joined in 1837, and Morgan Yeatman, who became a partner in 1844. There are still Yeatmans involved in the business, and it remains

Terraced port vineyards at Quinta de Vargellas

one of the three independent, family-owned British port houses (the others being the Symington group and CHURCHILL GRAHAM).

Taylor's ports are among the greatest – and the most expensive. Vintage Taylor's port is supremely elegant and long-lived, shot through with the smell of violets that pervades all the wines from Quinta de Vargellas. The '45 is legendary, while the '63 and '77 are among the finest of the last 30 years; the '80 is possibly the best of that lesser vintage, while the '83 is powerful and perfumed and the '85 is just beginning to hint at its potential. They all share the characteristic of being deceptively tough and tannic when young, only revealing their greatness over many years, and they all mature slowly: 20 years is often not long enough. The Quinta de Vargellas can be as fine as many other houses' vintage wines; Quinta da Terra Feita has richness and power. Of the aged tawnies, the 20-year-old is elegant and light, on the dry side and always fresh; the 10-year-old tawny sometimes lacks fruit, while the 30- and 40-year-olds are too woody for my taste, although many acclaim them as supreme examples. The recently introduced First Estate is a ruby reserve-style wine that is soft and sweet, designed to celebrate Quinta de Vargellas, the firm's premier estate and its main vinification centre. Taylor's LBV is the biggest-selling LBV on the market; it sometimes suffers from being too young, but at its best is a rich and heavy wine. Taylor, Fladgate & Yeatman's partnership arrangement with FONSECA, makes this firm the owner of two of the finest port houses.

Vintages since 1945: '45 '48 '55 '60 '63 '66 '70 '75 '77 '80 '83 '85.

Vieira de Souza   ★

PO Box 39, Rua Serpa Pinto 534, 4401 Vila Nova de Gaia. Tel (2) 302320. Founded 1925. V'yds: 95 ha (part of Barros group). Additional brand: Souza. Visits: weekdays 9–12.30, 2–4.30.

This firm was founded by the BARROS family in conjunction with Alcino Vieira de Souza. Today it mainly produces a range of very basic tawnies and rubies, which sell in Germany and the Netherlands. A small quantity of vintage wine is made.

Vintages declared since 1945: '65 '70 '74 '75 '77 '78 '80 '83 '85 '87 '89.

Warre ★★★→
PO Box 26, Travessa do Barão de Forrester, 4400 Vila Nova de Gaia. Tel (2) 3796063. Founded 1670. V'yds: 29 ha at Quinta da Cavadinha. Stock: 18,000 pipes. Additional brands: Fine Selected Ruby, White; Kings Tawny; Nimrod Very Fine Old Tawny; Quinta da Cavadinha; Sir William 10-year-old Tawny; Warrior Finest Vintage Character. Visits by appt.

This is the oldest existing British-owned shipper. It was founded by two young, opportunistic Englishmen seeking fame and fortune following the marriage of Charles II of England to Catherine of Bragança (Bragança being a city in northeast Portugal). But the first Warre to enter the business was William Warre, who became a partner in 1729, at which point the company acquired its present name. Until 1912, the Warres were in sole possession of the firm.

During the Peninsular War, one of the partners was Lieutenant General William Warre, who fought with distinction alongside Wellington and is believed to have sold the great man some of his port. Andrew Symington became a partner in 1892, and took charge of the Portuguese side of the business in 1912. The Warres finally sold their interest to the Symington family in the 1950s, although until very recently there was still a Warre representing the firm in Britain. The Warre lodge in Vila Nova de Gaia is distinguished by having the largest oak vat in the port trade: the Memel vat holds 178,091 bottles – roughly 2.4 m glasses of port.

Warre's wines are less voluptuous than some of the other ports in the Symington group – certainly less voluptuous than W & J GRAHAM's, and less powerful than DOW's. They tend towards elegance and balance, and although by any but the toughest standards they are great wines, they never quite hit the heights of Dow's or Graham's vintages. Warre vintages are on the dry side, and are often quite woody when young, but they do develop perfumed, fragrant fruit with maturity. That is true of the '66 and '63, while the '77 is richer and more intense. The '80 is a star of that year, but the '85 remains rather disappointing. The newly-introduced Quinta da Cavadinha is a single-*quinta* vintage wine from the Warre property in the Pinhão Valley. The LBV is quite the best of this style available: a crusted wine, bottled four years after the vintage. Other wines in the range are less exciting, although the

Nimrod tawny has a following and Warre's Warrior, a ruby, is a good example of a vintage character wine.

Vintages since 1945: '45 '47 '50 '55 '58 '60 '63 '66 '70 '75 '77 '80 '83 '85 '91.

Wiese & Krohn Sucrs ★★→
Rua Serpa Pinto 149, 4400 Vila Nova de Gaia. Tel (2) 301238. Founded 1865. V'yds: 9 ha at Quinta do Retiro Novo. Stock: 9,500 pipes. Additional brands: Arnsby; Carneiro; Coelva; Krohn; Roga. Visits: no.
A history covering many nationalities lies behind this firm. It was started by two Norwegians, Theodor Wiese and Dankert Krohn, but in 1906 two new partners (Portuguese J M Gomes Figueiredo and British Edmund Arnsby) took over. Later, the family of Edmundo A Falcão Carneiro became involved and the Falcão Carneiro family now runs it as an independent, family concern.

The firm specializes in wood-aged wines, aged tawnies and *colheitas*. It does however release frequent vintages – sweet, rounded wines – often in years that are not generally declared, and it also produces standard tawny and ruby ports. Strangely, while Wiese & Krohn exports most of its production, little goes to Scandinavia. From being relatively unknown, the firm's following has been increasing in recent years.

Vintages since 1945: '57 '58 '60 '61 '63 '65 '67 '70 '75 '78 '82 '84 '85.

Madeira

Madeira is a wine whose reputation ranges from a belief that it all disappears into cooking pots to a conviction – held by the relative few who have tasted great madeira – that it is a unique wine of great fascination. The fact that this wine nearly disappeared and that it is still produced in only tiny quantities makes its position as a great wine both precarious and even more mysterious.

The Island of Madeira

The island of Madeira and its companion, Porto Santo, are the inhabited portions of a small archipelago that rises from the floor of the Atlantic Ocean about 440 miles (700 km) due west of Casablanca. Some say they are the remains of the lost continent of Atlantis, others that they are no more than the tip of an extremely high mountain that happened to be left behind when the continents of Africa and South America moved apart aeons ago.

Madeira, the larger of the two, is an extremely lush, volcanic island, covered with vegetation but with virtually no flat land. It is an autonomous region belonging to Portugal and has been since it was discovered, in 1419. At first – and second – sight it seems impossible that vines could grow on this tiny, overcrowded piece of land. Small villages and the one large town, the capital Funchal, spread themselves over the lower slopes of the mountains, the buildings interspersed with banana and sugar cane plantations. It is not until you look closely and attentively that you discover straggling vines, trellised on narrow, irrigated terraces, growing above crops of sweet potatoes and other vegetables. Because the island is so mountainous, the land planted to vines can hardly be measured in hectares on Madeira – there are only 1,800 hectares of vines in total – it is better measured simply by the number of plants.

Vines can grow from sea level (although this is rarely put into practice since most of Madeira's cultivable land is on the top of cliffs), up to 600 or even 700 m altitude on the south side of the island, up to 400 m on the north side. The biggest concentration of vineyards is in the district of Câma de Lobos, around the village of Câmara de Lobos, made famous by the paintings of Sir Winston Churchill, who was a regular visitor to the island. From here, and from along the southern coast, come most of the finest wines. On the north side, the vineyards of Porto da Cruz and Santana make wines of lesser quality.

Grape Varieties

The official regulatory organization, the Instituto do Vinho da Madeira, permits the following varieties to be used in madeira.

Noble Varieties (*Castas Nobres*)

Bastardo Not necessarily, but probably, the same grape as that approved for use in port; very rarely seen now in Madeira.

Bual A medium-sweet grape; once the most widely-planted variety on the island although, until the tightening of regulations concerning grape varieties, in the late 1970s, it was in danger of extinction (*see* The History of Madeira).

Malmsey This variety is used for the sweetest style of madeira. Malmsey is an archaic British term for the Malvasia Candida grape, and a corruption of the even older term, Monemvasia.

Sercial This makes the driest style of madeira. It produces a perfumed wine that is astringent when young but ages well.

Terrantez A rare variety, much prized, that makes sweet, heavily-perfumed wines of great longevity.

Verdelho The medium-dry style of madeira comes from this variety. It is the one madeira grape that can, it seems, be successfully transplanted to other parts of the world (Australia in particular) and still produce madeira-style wines.

Good Varieties (*Castas Boas*)

Malvasia Roxa, **Verdelho Tinto**, **Tinta Negra Mole**, **Moscatel**. Of these, the most important variety – making up 70 percent of the total production of madeira – is Tinta Negra Mole, a hybrid vine, used widely to make cheap madeiras for use in the kitchen.

Approved Species (*Castas Autorizadas*)

Rio Grande, **Boal de Porto Santo**, **Tinta da Madeira**, **Complexa**, **Triunfo**. The grapes are grown at different levels on the island. Those destined to make the sweeter styles of madeira – Malmsey and Bual – are grown at lower levels than those intended for the drier styles – Verdelho and Sercial. The Tinta Negra Mole is grown throughout the island and has the strange quality of being able to take on a different character according to where it is planted. If grown near the sea, it takes on the character of Malmsey or Bual, but if planted higher up it adopts the character of Sercial or Verdelho. No wonder that, until recently, this grape was used heavily in blends.

How Madeira is Made

Madeira starts life as a table wine. The grapes are harvested at any time from mid-August onwards, depending on the variety and where it is grown, the Malmsey being picked first. They are then transported to the lodges in Funchal, where modern, mechanical presses are employed – few open *lagares* (wine presses) are still in use.

Fermentation takes place either in small oak casks or in huge oak *cubas* (vats), holding up to 25,000 litres. Fortification is carried out at different stages in the fermentation process according to the grape variety. The sweet Malmsey is fortified early, then the Bual, while there is still some residual sugar, and both Verdelho and Sercial are fermented until fully dry and then fortified.

The *vinho claro*, as the new wine is called, is then filtered, ready for the *estufagem* – the cooking process, that is the secret of madeira – which starts at the end of January. The wine is heated up slowly and then cooled over a period of months, a technique developed in the late 18th century and designed to imitate the passage of the wine by ship through the warm, equatorial waters of the Atlantic Ocean to America and the Caribbean. (The journey was found to improve the wine and to give it the sweetness and acidity that it is now characterized by and which, together with a slight oxidization, make it highly drinkable.) There are four different methods of heating and their use depends on the quality of the wine:

1   The traditional process is now reserved for only the very finest wines. The wine is put in casks (called lodge pipes) which hold 630 litres and placed in south-facing rooms high up in the lodges in Funchal, where it is left to soak in the hot Madeira sun for anything up to eight years. Some remain for 30 years or more.

2   The next best wines, from the noble grape varieties, are placed in lodge pipes and then put in *estufas* (rooms heated by hot water pipes). The casks are left for six months to a year while they are slowly heated to 40°C and then cooled down again.

3   Lesser wines are put into huge wooden vats with hot water pipes in their bases and are heated (up to 45°C) and then cooled over a period of six months.

4   Tinta Negra Mole wine is put into ceramic-lined tanks, heated up to 50°C and then cooled. The process takes four months.

After the *estufagem*, maturation starts. This – as is now apparent with all matters involving madeira wine – is a lengthy, leisurely process. The wine is put in casks, sealed in with a banana leaf, and left. The casks are not filled to the brim, but a space is left at the top to allow the process of oxidization – which is partly what gives madeira its character – to continue. The wine is left for at least three years – but finer wine is left for much, much longer (*see* Styles of Madeira). Vintage wine must remain in cask for 20 years at least, and may be left for up to 100 years before being bottled.

Styles of Madeira

Most madeira is a blended wine. An age indication on the label will be that of the youngest component of the blend. There are also vintage and *solera* madeiras.

Madeira is the world's longest-lived wine. I have tasted a 1795 Terrantez that was still fresh and deliciously drinkable. Vintage and *solera* madeiras dating from the early 20th century can still be found although, naturally, they are expensive. But most of the madeira that is readily available comes in a less rarefied form.

Three-year-old This is the basic style of madeira, much of which goes into cooking. At this level, the lesser grape varieties are used – especially the Tinta Negra Mole – rather than the noble varieties. No grape is indicated on the label, simply a description such as 'dry'. Other terms shown on the label may include 'finest', 'choice' or 'selected'.

Rainwater This is a soft, Verdelho (medium-dry) style. It originated during the 18th century, when casks left on the beach at Funchal for shipment (there was no dock at the time) absorbed rainwater during storms. The water lowered the alcohol level of the wine, but the eventual purchaser found he quite liked it. The name Rainwater stayed, and is now registered by the madeira firm of Barbeito. This is a three-year-old wine. No indication of grape is given on the label.

Five-year-old reserve At this level, noble grapes may be used. If one of them constitutes 85 percent of the blend, it will be indicated on the label. However, since 1 January 1993, most 5-year-old has simply carried a description of style – dry, medium, sweet – because the noble grapes are in such short supply that they are all destined for the next category. The youngest wine in the blend is five years old.

Ten-year-old reserva velha or special reserve Ten years is the age of the youngest wine in the blend. The noble grape variety used will be indicated on the label, provided that the variety makes up 85 percent of the wine.

15-year-old extra reserve The youngest wine in the blend must be 15 years old. The same grape variety regulation applies as for the 10-year-old.

Fresqueira 20-year-old vintage A vintage madeira stays in cask for 20 years before bottling. It must be made 100 percent from noble grapes and, of course, all be from one year.

Solera Bottles of *solera* madeira carry the date at which the *solera* was laid down. The *solera* system for madeira is very much the same as it is for sherry: casks are regularly topped up with newer wine, while a portion of the old wine is drawn off into casks containing yet older wine. Only ten percent of the contents of a cask may be transferred at any one time. This category of madeira is not permitted under European Commission regulations and the Portuguese government is currently appealing against this. While the resolution is awaited, no *solera* madeira is being made, although bottles dating back as far as 19th-century *soleras* are still available.

The History of Madeira

The first expedition to reach Madeira arrived from Portugal, in 1419, under orders from the Portuguese prince, Henry the Navigator, the man who later inspired Vasco da Gama. The island was initially colonized by convicts, and among the plants they brought with them were vines. These were the vine types that are now regarded as Madeira's major noble varieties: Monemvasia (Malmsey), which came from Crete; Sercial from Germany; Verdia (Verdelho) from Italy; Boal (Bual) from mainland Portugal.

The story of Madeira from that time on is comparatively peaceful, isolated as it was and far away from wars. The island lay on one of the major trade routes, and it was as a result of this that English merchants came to set up shop in Funchal, creating a small British colony with its own Factory House. As in the case of port, the English were the first to exploit fully the potential of the local wine. One of the treaties with England that helped the port trade –

giving England favoured nation treatment in Portugal, in 1654 – was also of benefit to Madeira. And a further action involving the English was soon to bring prosperity to Madeira and give a boost to the wine trade. In 1663, Charles II announced that anything exported from Europe to the English colonies in the Americas had to be transported in English ships. There was one loophole in this decree – the island of Madeira was exempt – and the colonists exploited it. So it was that madeira became the favourite drink of the southern states of America.

The wine was still unfortified of course. But it was while journeying that madeira developed the delightful character that gave it an extra dimension. The heat of the sun and the motion of the ship baked the wine in its casks, giving it an oxidized quality which, unlike in most other wines, where oxidization is a fault, turned out to be a virtue. The Americans liked this new taste so much that they exported the wine back to Europe – whereupon it was shown that two sea trips made the wine even better.

Fortification came later, in the 18th century, and, as so often with fortifieds, it was force of circumstances rather than design that led to the practice of adding brandy to the wine. France and England were at war in America and the transportation of wine was difficult and dangerous. Stocks built up in Madeira, and to save space the shippers began to distil part of the wine and then use this to strengthen the rest. When trade resumed, these fortified wines were found to be much better than their predecessors.

By the end of the 18th century, the producers had devised the process of *estufagem*, enabling them to avoid the expense of sending the wine on a long sea voyage to acquire its baked character.

It was now the heyday of madeira: the wine was more popular in England than port and was still very much in demand in America. English houses dominated the trade in Funchal, much as they did in Porto. Some families had been on the island since the 17th century – the Leacocks and the Boltons – while others, such as the Shortridges and the Gordons, arrived during next the century. More familiar names, such as Cossart, Rutherford & Miles and Blandy, arrived early in the 19th century. Portuguese firms were also established at this time, the first being Lomelino.

The twin evils of oidium and phylloxera hit Madeira in the mid-19th century – oidium in the 1850s, phylloxera in the 1870s.

The vineyards only survived through the efforts of one man, Thomas Slapp Leacock, who treated the vine roots with resin and tar and began the process of grafting onto American root stocks.

These root stocks were not only used for grafting. They themselves were planted and the fruit used to make table wines for the locals. At some point, however, wine from the American *vitis labrusca* began to be used in madeira and, at the same time, one of the island's European vine varieties, the highly prolific Tinta Negra Mole, began to replace the traditional, low-yielding varieties, Malmsey, Verdelho, Bual and Sercial.

As a result, the next 50 or 60 years saw a gradual decline in the fortunes of madeira. Traditional markets disappeared and were not replaced; exporters began to rely more and more on the use of madeira in cooking, rather than as a fine wine for drinking. Quality levels dropped as more and more cheap wine – labelled Bual, Sercial or whatever, but containing *vitis labrusca* or Tinta Negra Mole – was shipped to the kitchens of Europe. Of course there were still some fine wines being made – as madeiras from the last 100 years prove today – but standards fell and it seemed that the end of an era had been reached. In 1913 a decision was taken by most of the English producers to join forces and form the Madeira Wine Company, to protect themselves and to create a larger organization for more effective marketing.

It is largely only since the 1970s that controls on madeira have been tightened. With an eye to entry into the EC, the Portuguese government decided to set out new regulations which state that if a bottle is to be labelled with one of the noble grape varieties (*castas nobres*), 85 percent of its wine must be made from that variety. The rule was tightened in 1993 to ensure that even 5-year-old reserve wines, which previously carried noble variety labelling although not necessarily made up of the requisite 85 percent, may no longer do so. The use of noble variety labelling is now effectively restricted to 10-year-old wines. The use of *vitis labrusca* is banned in madeira (although it is still used in some rather noxious table wines) and Tinta Negra Mole must be kept for the final 15 percent of high quality madeira, and for use in the cheaper styles. The Instituto do Vinho da Madeira was set up to take overall control.

The major problem in improving the quality of madeira at the moment is that there are not enough of the noble grape varieties to go round. Of the island's vineyards, 40 percent is still planted with *vitis labrusca*, and a high proportion of the rest is Tinta Negra Mole. The island government has set a replanting programme in train, encouraging farmers to replace their vines with new, noble varieties and there is a grafting station on the eastern end of the island, selling grafted vines to farmers at a low price. But, at the moment, high quality madeira is still in short supply.

Storing and Serving Madeira

Madeira is unique in that the bottles should always be cellared standing upright. (There is, apparently, something in the cork that can taint the wine if the two come in contact.) The wine will keep almost indefinitely once bottled, although all madeira is ready to drink as soon as it leaves the shipper's lodge. It does not need decanting as the final filtering has been done by the shipper. Once opened, a bottle of madeira will stay fresh for many months – much longer than any other wine.

When considering how and when to drink madeira, sherry is a better comparison than port because the principal styles of madeira are quite similar to those of sherry. Thus a Sercial madeira, while not as dry as a *fino* sherry, can be treated in the same way and drunk chilled as an aperitif. Verdelho and Bual madeiras correspond to medium-dry sherry and can be drunk either as aperitifs or with a first course, such as soup. Bual and Malmsey madeiras can be used as equivalents to *oloroso* sherry; both are suitable after a meal or as accompaniments for cakes and puddings.

Producers

Barbeito ★★→★★★

Estrada Monumental 145, 9000 Funchal. Tel (91) 761829.
Founded 1946. V'yds: none. Stock: 490,000 litres.
Additional brands: Crown Barbeito; Island Dry; Island
Rich; Madeira Barbeito. Visits: Mon–Sat 9–12.30, 2–5.30.
Although this is a relatively new company, it operates in an old-fashioned way, from cramped premises perched precariously high above the sea, just west of Funchal. The present owner is the daughter of the founder.

The firm claims to have purchased the right to use the name 'Rainwater' in 1956, although other companies still seem to use it. It owns no vineyards but buys in grapes and makes its own wine. Stainless steel has yet to be seen here, and most of the *estufagem* takes place in huge wooden *cubas* (vats).

The house style is light, and tends towards sweetness. Of the standard brands, the Island Rich and Dry are basic 3-year-old wines. These are rather too soft and lack the kick of acidity that good madeira needs, but the range of 5-year-olds is better (Bual, Sercial and Verdelho), and shows some good varietal character, but still this lack of acidity. There is a new 10-year-old range from the same grapes that exhibits signs of good, aged material, and an impressive range of old vintage wines. Many of these vintage wines were of course purchased after the company was founded, and for this reason the Malmsey 1901, still fruity and with rich acidity, or the Terrantez 1832, perfumed, aromatic and amazingly fresh, have very little connection with Barbeito except for the skill shown in purchasing them and the storage space given them. However, younger vintages such as the Bual '60 (made by Barbeito) exhibit the distinct house style of lightness, consistent with the firm's more commercial ranges.

Blandy's Madeiras ★★★→

Madeira Wine Company, Rua dos Ferreiros 191, 9000
Funchal. Tel (91) 20121. Founded 1811. V'yds: none,
see **Madeira Wine Company. Stock:** *see* **Madeira Wine**
Company. Additional brands: Duke of Cambridge
Medium-Dry; Duke of Clarence Full Rich; Duke of

**Cumberland Medium-Rich; Duke of Sussex Special Dry.
Visits: weekdays 9–7, Sat 9–1.**
The firm was founded by Berkshire-born John Blandy, a member
of the garrison sent in 1807 to defend Madeira against the threat of
Napoleonic invasion. In 1811 he returned to establish himself as a
wine merchant. The Blandy home and lodges still exist in Funchal,
and the family remains involved in the business although the firm
is now part of the MADEIRA WINE COMPANY. The family is also
active on the island through its ownership of Reid's Hotel, the
island's most famous hotel and the favourite holiday resort of Sir
Winston Churchill.

Blandy is the most familiar name in madeira, and the brand is
the largest of those owned by the Madeira Wine Company. The
standard 5-year-old range is named after a series of English Dukes.
The Duke of Sussex is a fairly commercial wine without any astringency but with some nuttiness; the Duke of Cambridge is better –
light and full of flavour – while the good acidity of the Duke of
Cumberland brings out the fruit and stops it being too cloying.
The Duke of Clarence is one of the most widely-sold madeiras in
Britain. The range of 10-year-old special reserve is characterized
by considerable elegance and a clear-cut character that makes them
very appealing. The Verdelho and Bual are especially good, and
the Malmsey is almost on the same plane.

H M Borges Sucrs ★★→★★★
**PO Box 92, Rua 31 Janeiro 83, 9001 Funchal. Tel (91)
23247. Founded 1877.**
This family firm makes an attractive range of 5-year-old wines that
includes a quite firmly acid, dry example with good nutty fruit, a
medium-dry with similar acidity, which brings out the fruit and
considerable flavour, and a very burnt-tasting medium-sweet that
appears to contain a large amount of old wine. The firm's sweet
wine is also on the dry, acid side. Grapes are bought in from the
Câmara de Lobos area, and from a Sercial vineyard at Jardim de
Serra owned by one of the company's shareholders.

Cossart Gordon ★★★★
**Madeira Wine Company, Rua dos Ferreiros 191, 9000
Funchal. Tel (91) 20121. Founded 1745. V'yds: none,**

see **Madeira Wine Company. Stock:** *see* **Madeira Wine Company. Additional brands: Good Company Full Rich; Rainwater Medium Dry; Viva Dry Aperitif.**

Probably the most famous name in madeira, this firm was founded in 1745 by Francis Newton and William Gordon, who were fleeing the failed Jacobite uprising led by Bonnie Prince Charlie. Another Newton brother fled to Virginia and the two established a trade in madeira wines. William Cossart, descended from a Huguenot family, arrived in Madeira in 1808 after spending some time *en route* from Dublin in a French jail. During the 19th century, the firm sold quantities of madeira to the British Army in India, where it was laced with quinine to ward off malaria – not a practice seen today. The Cossarts are still actively involved in the madeira trade, although not in the firm that bears their name. David Cossart, a British Master of Wine, has written a splendid book on the subject. The firm is now part of the MADEIRA WINE COMPANY.

The Cossart Gordon madeiras tend to a lightness and elegance that makes them very stylish but also immediately recognizable. The Good Company Full Rich and Viva Dry Aperitif are in the basic range. The 5-year-old Rich is deliciously light, but hints at the typical, slightly medicinal flavour of Malmsey, coupled with richness and a very clean taste; the 5-year-old Dry is very dry. Cossart's Rainwater Medium Dry is rather too soft for my taste,

The 10-year-old Malmsey again has a light touch, which perhaps does not quite reflect this grape's character, but the range of 15-year-old wines is superb, and here richness takes over, as well as the harmony and elegance that comes with maturity.

Justinho Henriques Filhos ★★
Rua do Carmo 86, 9001 Funchal. Tel (91) 23301. Associated company: Companhia Vinicola da Madeira.

My contact with this company has been limited to a tasting of its Justinho Bual, which was smooth, with a pronounced burnt taste and plenty of attractive, rich fruit.

Henriques & Henriques ★★ → ★★★
PO Box 4290, Rua Dr Brito Câmara 32A, 9053 Funchal. Tel (91) 743541. Founded 1850. V'yds: in Câmara de Lobos. Additional brands: Century Malmsey; Monte Seco.

Associated companies: António Eduardo Henriques; Belem's Madeira Wines; Carmo Vinhos; Casa dos Vinhos da Madeira. Visits by appt.

Although there are no Henriques in the company (the last member of the family died in 1968), there is still a family feel here, with a small set of partners running what is the largest madeira firm outside the MADEIRA WINE COMPANY grouping. It was set up in 1850 by a vineyard owner in Câmara de Lobos, west of Funchal, and still owns vineyards in what is regarded as the best area for Malmsey and Bual grapes. Henriques is currently building a £4 million vinification plant at Câmara de Lobos, which will be the largest on the island.

The firm operates under its own name and under a confusing number of *sous-marques* from companies which it has taken over. It makes the madeira that is shipped under the Harveys of Bristol label and also the wines for Sandeman; both are ranges of basic 3-year-olds. The best wines go out under the Henriques & Henriques name. They come in a rich style, even at the level of the Sercial, and include a lovely, creamy Malmsey. The firm also has, like many other madeira companies, a limited range of old, vintage wines, and occasionally releases *reservas* up to 85 years old.

The style of the associated companies is less definitive, but I have enjoyed the Belem Light Rainwater, with its soft style and attractive fruit, and the mature, quite rich taste of the Casa dos Vinhos da Madeira 10-year-old Sercial, which evidently has a quantity of old wines in its blend.

Leacock ★★★ →

Madeira Wine Company, Rua dos Ferreiros 191, 9000 Funchal. Tel (91) 20121. Founded 1741. V'yds: none, *see* Madeira Wine Company. Stock: *see* Madeira Wine Company. Additional brand: St John range.

The Leacock family set up shop in 1741 and produced a remarkable range of characters over the next two centuries. One of the most interesting was Thomas Slapp Leacock, who is credited with having been the first to identify the phylloxera louse, and who almost single-handedly rescued the vineyards of Madeira from the pest, first by dipping the roots of the vines in tar and resin, and later by instituting the programme of grafting onto American root stocks. The company subsequently became part of the MADEIRA WINE COMPANY.

The current range of wines under the Leacock name consists of the basic St John range and the special reserve 10-year-old wines. They are all characterized by a considerable dryness, which makes them immediately attractive. I particularly like the special reserve Malmsey, with its flavours of burnt treacle balanced by good acidity, and the St John Dry, which is the nearest a dry madeira ever comes to a dry sherry.

Lomelino → ★★
Madeira Wine Company, Rua dos Ferreiros 191, 9000 Funchal. Tel (91) 20121. Founded 1820. V'yds: none, *see* Madeira Wine Company. Stock: *see* Madeira Wine Company. Additional brands: Dessert; Imperial.
The firm of T Tarquinio da Câmara Lomelino (usually known as Lomelino) is the oldest Portuguese-owned house. It was founded in 1820, at a time when the madeira trade was dominated by the British. In fact the firm began by taking over the business of an English firm, that of Robert Leal. Naturally enough, the Lomelino business developed away from the traditional British markets and concentrated on Europe, particularly Sweden and Italy, as well as mainland Portugal. The firm however went the way of most British madeira companies when it became part of the MADEIRA WINE COMPANY.

For some reason, the Lomelino wines have seemed much less interesting than other wines from the Madeira Wine Company stable. They are either light and a little dull (as are the Reserve Bual 5-year-old and the Dessert Malmsey 5-year-old) or are just plain dirty and unpleasant (the Imperial Special Reserve Sercial). They certainly seem to have too burnt a quality, without the fruitiness. The other Imperial 10-year-olds are certainly better – the Bual and Malmsey especially are full of rich, chocolate and toffee flavours and benefit from a slightly dry finish.

Madeira Wine Company
Lodges: Rua dos Ferreiros 191, 9000 Funchal. Tel (91) 20121. Founded 1913. V'yds: 5 ha. Stock: 4.5 million litres. Additional brands: *see* below. Visits: daily 9-5.30.

This firm was set up in 1913 to amalgamate all the British madeira firms. Subsequent mergers have meant that it now controls 26 companies, some of whose names are still seen on a range of wines, while other names seem to have disappeared. The lodges of the Madeira Wine Company in the centre of Funchal are a must for any visitor to the island, being full of history and character. The main winery, more prosaically, is in a converted army barracks on the outskirts of Funchal, where stainless steel and modern bottling lines are the order of the day. The quality of wine produced is generally high, and it has certainly managed to retain the distinctive house styles, building on its considerable holding of old wines. In 1988, the Madeira Wine Company went public and 46 percent of shares was bought by the port family, Symington, which now controls the company equally with the BLANDY family. Considerable investment both in winemaking and in marketing is likely to lead to a revitalization of the company.

The companies included under the Madeira Wine Company are: Aguiar Freitas; Barros, Almeida; Bianchi's Madeiras; Blandy's Madeiras; COSSART GORDON; F F Ferraz; Funchal Wine Company; Luiz Gomes; Krohn Bros; LEACOCK; LOMELINO; Madeira Meneres; Madeira Victoria; F Martins, Caldeira; Miles Madeiras; A Nobrega; Power Drury; Royal Madeira; RUTHERFORD & MILES; Socieda Agricola da Madeira; J B Spinola; C V Vasconcelos; Viuva Abudarham & Fos; Donaldson; SHORTRIDGE LAWTON; Welsh Bros.

Effectively, four names are used as the principal brands for the company: Blandy's, Cossart Gordon, Leacock and Miles.

Pereira d'Oliveira →★★★
Rua dos Ferreiros 107, 9000 Funchal. Tel (91) 20784. Founded 1820. V'yds: in San Martinho and Câmara de Lobos. Additional brands: Golden Malmsey 5-year-old; Old Bual, Sercial, Verdelho 5-year-olds. Visits: weekdays.
This is a small, family-owned company that over the years has built up an enviable stock of old vintage wines. Besides the rather touristy shop that acts as its sales-point in Funchal, it has a separate winery and owns small amounts of vineyard.

The house style is quite dry, with plenty of acidity in all the wines – even in one such as the Golden Malmsey 5-year-old, where the fruit is certainly not too sweet or heavy and there is good freshness and balance. The Old Sercial 5-year-old is less interesting being slightly too soft, and, while the Old Verdelho 5-year old is correct rather than exciting, I certainly enjoyed the Old Bual 5-year-old, fresh and round, with a distinctive nutty finish and plenty of burnt acidity. Older vintages, described as Reservas, continue the house style of lightness and dryness, but like all madeiras seem to survive indefinitely. Vintages are for sale by single bottles at the firm's shop.

Rutherford & Miles ★★★→

Madeira Wine Company, Rua dos Ferreiros 191, 9000 Funchal. Tel (91) 20121. Founded 1814. V'yds: none, *see* Madeira Wine Company. Stock: *see* Madeira Wine Company. Additional brands: Old Artillery House Malmsey; Old Customs House Sercial; Old Trinity House Bual; La Reina Verdelho.

The Rutherford in this firm came from Jedburgh in Scotland and, like many Scots, left that country after the failure of the 1745 rebellion, finally settling in Madeira in the early years of the 19th century. The first wine was shipped in 1814. Later, Henry Miles and Rutherford & Co ran a joint operation called Rutherford & Miles (the Rutherfords based in London, and the Miles family in Funchal). Today, both families are still involved in the wine trade, although the firm is now part of the MADEIRA WINE COMPANY.

The Rutherford & Miles (usually referred to simply as 'Miles') house style is full and quite rich – characteristics that are apparent right across the range. It means, to my mind, that the more successful wines are the sweeter ones, with the Bual-style wines being particularly interesting. Both the 5-year-old reserve Old Trinity House and the 10-year-old special reserve have considerable sweetness, with the 5-year-old having brighter fruit and a greater flavour of nuts and raisins. The 10-year-old special reserve is smooth, rich and elegant with a long, lingering aftertaste. The Sercial 10-year-old is really warming and ripe, with plenty of mature wines, even if it lacks some acidity.

Shortridge Lawton ★★★→★★★★

Madeira Wine Company, Rua dos Ferreiros 191, 9000 Funchal. Tel (91) 20121. Founded 1757. V'yds: none,

see **Madeira Wine Company. Stock:** *see* **Madeira Wine Company. Additional brand: Very Dry 5-year-old Reserve.**
Founded in 1757 by Murdoch Shortridge, who arrived at the same time as the Cossarts and Leacocks, this was one of the last firms to abandon the habit of sending wine round the world by ship. One member of the family, John Shortridge, was the first president of the Factory House in Funchal, in 1830. The firm is now part of the MADEIRA WINE COMPANY.

The wines have a very burnt character making them harder at first to appreciate than some madeiras. They seem old-fashioned in style and taste considerably of old wood. Together, these factors give the wine rather too much astringency, but combined with the intensity of fruit, they can be very fine indeed. The special reserve 10-year-old wines form the best range, although the 5-year-old Very Dry Reserve is just that – very dry – and is one of the best dry aperitif madeiras available.

Veiga França ★→
Avenida Arriaga 73, 9000 Funchal. Tel (91) 21057.
I have limited experience of this firm, apart from tasting a soft, sweet, very rich Bual, which appears under the label of a British supermarket. The firm is strongest in the French and other European markets, for which it supplies madeiras for cooking and for own-label wines.

Other Madeira Producers

Adegas do Torreão Vinhos, Rua dos Ferreiros 215, 9000 Funchal. Tel (91) 21937.

Sherry

Sherry is one of the world's great white wines. As such, of all the wines in this book, fortification is least important to its character. And because it is the only fortified wine which is fortified *after* fermentation, rather than during, it is the only one which in its natural state is absolutely dry.

It is also the most versatile of fortifieds. It can be bone dry or very sweet, light and fresh, or rich and luscious. It can be drunk at the beginning of a meal or at the end, by itself as an aperitif, or with a wide variety of dishes, ranging from seafood to desserts.

The Sherry Vineyards

The Jerez region of Andalucía is in the southwest corner of Spain, between Cádiz and Seville and between the rivers Guadalete and

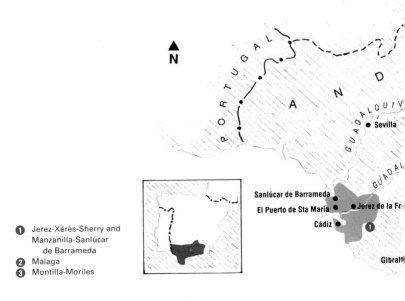

① Jerez-Xérès-Sherry and
   Manzanilla-Sanlúcar
   de Barrameda
② Málaga
③ Montilla-Moriles

Guadalquivir. It forms a rough triangle of land, bounded on one side by the Atlantic Ocean, with the towns of El Puerto de Santa María and Sanlúcar de Barrameda at two corners and the city of Jerez de la Frontera forming the apex, inland.

It is a white land. From the chalky soil of the vineyards through to the brilliant white of the houses, it coruscates in the bright, clean air from the ocean. The climate is regular – apart from recent drought years. It rains for about 70 days between September and April, while for the rest of the year the sun shines, often for days on end in cloudless, blue skies (giving an average of 3,000 sunshine hours – the highest count for any vineyard area in Europe).

The vineyard zone covers 13,000 hectares and lies inside the triangle formed by the towns and to the north of Jerez. There are three types of soil. By far the largest area, covering over 80 percent of the zone, also has the best soil type: the chalky *albariza*. This area spreads in a huge arc in the centre of the Jerez region, and covers a smaller area to the south of El Puerto de Santa María. It is known as Jerez Superior and is where all the most famous vineyards lie: Carrascal, Macharnudo, Añina, Balbaina. In its rolling hills and vast

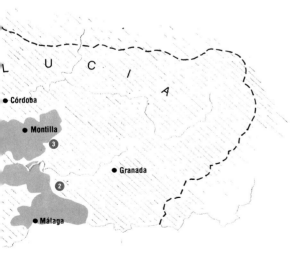

expanses it resembles Champagne in northern France – and it is perhaps no coincidence that both produce great white wines.

The two other vineyard areas are becoming less and less important. There is still some planting on the clay and sand soil of the *barros* near Chipiona and Rota, but that is being decreased, while the third area (of entirely sandy soil, known as *arenas*) has been almost completely abandoned.

Grape Varieties

Although there are a number of permitted grape varieties in the Jerez region, in effect almost all sherry is made from just one.

Palomino A local Andalucían variety, which may have been named after a knight in the army of Alfonso X, who recaptured Jerez from the Moors – the name is still recalled in the name of the *bodega* Palomino y Vergara. There are in fact two Palomino grapes, that are, as Julian Jeffs points out (*Sherry*, Faber & Faber, 1992), related but not the same. The original grape was called Palomino de Jerez or Palomino Basto, and although this grape is still found in older vineyards, in most places it has been replaced by the higher quality Palomino Fino.

The Palomino Fino produces the perfect base for sherry: a wine low in sugar and quite low in acid. It is not very good as a table wine (despite the efforts of some producers to persuade us otherwise), but is perfect for the maturing process of sherry.

Pedro Ximénez The other main grape for sherry, now planted less and less in the Jerez region. It is still used for sweetening wines, and occasionally can be found by itself in an intensely sweet sherry, but compared with the Palomino, which dominates 90 percent of the sherry vineyard, the PX (as it is usually known) is dwindling in influence.

Moscatel A small amount of this variety is still found. Again, it is used for blending with dry wines to make the sweeter wines popular in some export markets.

Other grapes that may legally be planted are the **Albillo Castellana**, **Beba**, **Cañocazo**, **Mantuo Castellano**, **Moscatel Gordo Blanco**, **Perruno**.

How Sherry is Made

Harvest time in the Jerez region starts at the beginning of September – officially on September 8, but it may be earlier or later, depending on the weather and the condition of the grapes. Once it has begun, harvesting will last for a month. Both hand picking and, increasingly, mechanical harvesting are practised.

Traditionally, the harvested grapes were left to dry on esparto grass mats. This reduced the moisture in the fruit and concentrated the sugars to produce wines higher in alcohol. Today, because of the expense, this practice is rarely seen unless sweet wines are being made from Pedro Ximénez grapes. The extra alcohol is obtained by the new vineyard procedure of training the vines on wires (rather than leaving them as low bushes), which gives them better exposure to the sun, and by timing the harvest more scientifically.

Another traditional practice that has almost disappeared is the treading of grapes in open stone *lagares* (wine presses). Workers wearing special hobnailed boots would tread the grapes into a pulp before the fruit was pressed using a huge screw fitted into the centre of the *lagar*. High labour costs have almost done away with this romantic way of pressing grapes and today they are more likely to be processed in huge *bodegas*, either in the sherry towns or at press houses in the vineyards, using the most modern pneumatic bag presses. (*Bodega* is the Spanish term for a winery, but it is also used to refer to a shipper's entire establishment.) The original method of carrying grapes from the vineyard to the press houses has also been transformed: gone are the wicker baskets, and in their place are hygienic, easy to clean plastic boxes, designed to hold between 14 and 16 kilos of grapes, a small enough quantity to avoid crushing the fruit at the bottom.

Initially, making sherry is like making any white wine. Fermentation takes place either in traditional oak butts (from the Spanish word for 'cask', *bota*) or, more frequently today in the modern *bodegas*, in stainless steel, temperature-controlled tanks. It is allowed to continue until a dry white wine is produced, with an alcohol level of between 13 and 14 percent. The wine is then transferred from its fermentation casks or tanks into 500-litre American oak butts .

It is at this point that the magic of sherry begins. Unlike other wine-growing areas, where every effort is made to prevent white wine having contact with the air and therefore oxidizing, in Jerez air contact is just what is wanted.

The butts are filled with wine, but a gap is left at the top for air. Instead of oxidizing, the wine develops a thick, yeasty layer on its surface that protects the wine from the air and allows it to develop slowly. This substance is known as *flor*. The theory is that the growth of *flor* is aided by the warm, moist wind, the Poñente, that blows in from the ocean. It would certainly help to explain why the *flor* in Sanlúcar de Barrameda – by the sea – is thicker than that in Jerez de la Frontera.

At one time, *flor* was considered to be a mysterious substance for which no rational or scientific explanation could be given. It was known to develop in the sherry region and, for some obscure reason, in the Jura Mountains of France, but in very few other areas of the wine world. Equally mysterious was the fact that one butt in Jerez would grow *flor*, while its neighbour remained defiantly yeast-free. Today, it is possible to predict the probability of *flor* appearing, and its development in barrel, by gas chromatography. But *flor* still has its peculiarities: it grows better in the late spring and autumn, and better in one corner of a *bodega* than in another.

After six months it is possible to see the *flor* development in a butt, and at this point the wines are classified according to their potential for future *flor* growth. The butts are marked with chalk into various categories. If they are going to develop a strong growth they are either marked '*palma*', as wines destined to become *finos* (*manzanillas*, in Sanlúcar), or '*palma cortada*', for those that will be *amontillados*. If they have little or no *flor* growth, they will be marked '*raya*' or '*dos rayas*', and these will become *olorosos*. A wine that falls in between the two categories is marked '*palo cortado*'. Such a wine has the delicacy of a *fino* but is not likely to develop *flor*, and may become either *amontillado* or *oloroso* sherry.

It is at this point that fortification, in the form of a blend of alcohol and mature sherry, takes place. In the case of the *palma* and *palma cortada* wines, fortification is slight, bringing the wine up to only 15 or 15.5 percent alcohol, because otherwise the *flor* would be killed. Wines in the other categories are fortified up to 18 percent alcohol, with the express purpose of killing the yeast.

The Solera System

After fortification, maturation begins, and the *solera* process commences. Much has been made of the complexities of this system, but in essence it is a maturing process, devised originally in Jerez to take advantage of the fact that when a young wine is introduced into a barrel of older wine, the young wine quickly takes on the older one's character.

A typical *solera* consists of tiers of butts, sometimes as many as four high, with each horizontal row containing wines of a different age. The *bodega* itself, in which the *solera* is housed, is usually high-ceilinged, dark and cool, like a cathedral, with sand-covered floors regularly watered to maintain the proper level of humidity and to keep evaporation of the wine to a minimum. It seems as though a breeze is perpetually blowing through the partly shuttered windows and dark doorways.

In this tranquil atmosphere, the wine may appear to be resting, but in fact it is frequently on the move. Wine for blending and bottling is drawn from the tier of casks containing the oldest wine. This is invariably at ground level and is the *solera* proper (the name is taken from the Spanish word for 'floor', *suelo*). Usually no more than a third of a barrel is removed at any one time, and the barrel is then replenished with younger wine from the row above. This process of replacement continues up through the rows of casks to the beginning of the system, which is topped up with the *bodega*'s newest wine. At each stage, the younger wine takes on the character of the older wine it has been added to.

The process of replenishment or 'refreshment' is usually repeated five times (passing through four tiers of butts) before the youngest wine has reached the *solera* proper – but it may be more. The butts through which the wine passes before it reaches the *solera* proper are known as *criaderas* (nurseries).

The *solera* process is used for all styles of sherry. *Oloroso* wines may be matured in the open to acquire a baked, burnt quality, while the more delicate *finos* mature in the cool of the *bodega*. The more stages in a *solera*, the finer the wine, but it is perfectly possible to draw wine off from one of the *criaderas* (from a stage of the *solera*) at any time after the minimum of three years' ageing required by law before bottling and sale has been completed: many less expensive sherries have been drawn off in this way.

Although sherry was once sold as a vintage wine, today it is invariably a blend, not only of wine from different years but also of wine from different *soleras*. Most sherries are put together to form an absolutely consistent product year in, year out. So, once the wine has been drawn off its *solera* it will go into another *solera* for blending, before moving on to the bottling line.

Styles of Sherry

Because *fino* and *manzanilla* sherries are living wines until they are bottled (since the *flor* yeast covering is slowly changing the nature of the wine), a sherry may fall into any one of a number of styles, whose characteristics blur into one another because these styles are so finely graded, before reaching the *amontillado* stage. Often the decision as to which stage a sherry should stop at in its development depends on the producer.

Manzanilla A style of *fino* that is aged only in Sanlúcar de Barrameda. It is the lightest and driest of all sherries, supposedly gaining its tangy, salty quality from being matured by the sea. Certainly the location helps to create the style – move a butt of *manzanilla* to Jerez and at once it changes character to a Jerez *fino*.

Manzanilla pasada A wine that changes from true *manzanilla* to take on some of the character of an *amontillado*. This usually happens after seven years' maturing. Again, this style can only be found in Sanlúcar.

Fino This is the dry style of wine that develops beneath the *flor* in the *bodegas* of Jerez de la Frontera and El Puerto de Santa María. It is fuller than *manzanilla* but still a delicate wine. It begins to deteriorate once removed from under its protective *flor* covering and needs therefore to be drunk as soon after bottling as possible (as does *manzanilla*). There should be a bottling or 'drink by' date on the label, but although some sherry shippers provide this, others seem reluctant to do so. A good shipper will only send small quantities for sale at a time, to ensure absolute freshness. *Fino* from Puerto *bodegas* tends to be in a softer, lighter style than that from Jerez. Both *fino* and *manzanilla* sherries are given additional fortification just prior to shipping – usually taking them up to 15.5 percent alcohol.

Fino amontillado This is a *fino* that is beginning to lose its *flor*, but has not quite reached the *amontillado* stage.

Amontillado A true *amontillado* is a *fino* that has been left in cask without refreshment from young wine until the *flor* yeast has been consumed and fallen to the bottom of the butt. The wine then begins to deepen in colour and to gain a dry, nutty flavour. Cheaper *amontillados* are made by giving a *fino* an extra shot of fortification to kill the *flor*. *Amontillado* proper is dry.

Medium This is a sweetened a*montillado*, intended in most cases for the export market. At one time, the sweetener was usually a little PX or Moscatel, but extra sweet Palomino grapes are now used.

Palo cortado This is a wine that started life as a *fino*, was left to develop as an a*montillado*, but started to deepen and become more like a rich *oloroso*. It is classified as Dos, Tres or Cuatro (two, three or four) Cortados according to its age. Inevitably it is a rare style of sherry and therefore expensive.

Oloroso This style did not develop much of a *flor*, and was fortified up to 18 percent alcohol at an early stage. It is often left in butts in the sun to take on a baked, burnt character, but even in the cool of a *bodega* it will naturally evaporate and reach a high level of alcohol – up to 24 percent. It is a rich, smooth, raisiny style, but a true *oloroso* is always dry.

Amoroso A sweetened *oloroso* made by adding PX or ripe Palomino and *vino de color* (colouring wine). The name comes from the Spanish word for 'loving', but actually refers to a vineyard. Most *amorosos* are now called 'cream sherry'.

Cream A dark, rich style of sherry; an *oloroso* sweetened with must from sweet grapes and darkened with colouring wines.

Pale cream A *fino* that has been sweetened with *dulce apagado*, a sweet wine made by arresting the fermentation with brandy.

Raya An *oloroso*-type sherry, usually used only for blending.

Brown A very sweet sherry that is a blend of *olorosos* and *rayas*. It is darker and richer than a cream.

Bristol Milk A traditional dessert sherry that was imported via Bristol. The earliest references to it date back to the 17th century. The familiar brand, Bristol Cream, owned by Harveys of Bristol, is a particular blend of Bristol Milk.

East India This is a brand name now, but the term originated when the maturation of sherry was speeded by sending it round the world – rather like madeira.

Tent A very concentrated wine made in Rota. It is rarely seen now as the town has become an American naval base and there are few vineyards left. Tent used to be made from black grapes called Tintilo de Rota, that were dried in the sun, left in tubs to begin fermenting and then pressed. The must was heavily fortified before fermentation finished, giving a very sweet, strong wine that was used for blending.

Controls on Sherry

The sherry region was one of the earliest wine regions in Spain to come under regulatory control. Following the Rumasa affair (*see* The History of Sherry), the region has become one of the most tightly regulated in the country as a result of a direct request by producers, not through an imposition by the government.

The region is covered by two denominations of origin (DOs). The Jerez–Xérès–Sherry DO covers the wines of Jerez de la Frontera and El Puerto de Santa María, while the Manzanilla-Sanlúcar de Barrameda DO covers those of Sanlúcar de Barrameda.

The governing body of the region is the Consejo Regulador, set up by government decree in 1935. This body has been responsible for implementing the Four Year Plan (*see* below), which has been bringing order to the chaos brought about by the Rumasa affair.

The DO regulations lay down the permitted vineyard areas, restricting planting to specific areas of soil (*see* The Sherry Vineyards). In practice, this now means that all planting takes place in the top quality, *albariza*, soil. In addition, they govern yields (80 hectolitres/hectare in Jerez Superior, 100 hectolitres/hectare elsewhere) and vine density, and determine when the harvest takes place. In order to maintain quality, every *bodega* must take a percentage of its grapes from the Jerez Superior region; the price of grapes is controlled by the Consejo.

The rules governing the maturing of sherry, also set out in the DO regulations, state that all the wine must be aged in *bodegas* in either Jerez de la Frontera, Sanlúcar de Barrameda or El Puerto de Santa María. Only *fino* aged in Sanlúcar may be called *manzanilla*. In addition, no wine may be released for sale before it has been aged for at least three years – in other words, it has gone through three stages of a *solera* system.

Only certain firms are allowed to export sherry, and a register of these is kept by the Consejo. There are 66 on the list at present. Other producers must sell the wines they wish to export to registered exporters, who are bound by a sales to stock ratio set by the Consejo. This body can also lay down a minimum selling price, which again ensures that the market is not flooded with cheap sherry, and encourages producers to mature their wines for longer.

There has been a move towards bottling sherry in Jerez rather than exporting it in bulk. Sherry bottled in Jerez has a seal of origin over the stopper, while any bottled outside Spain does not.

Almacenistas

These are wholesalers or stockholders of sherry who are not permitted to sell sherry direct to the wine trade, nor to export it. To register, they must have a minimum of 200 butts. In the days before the large firms made and matured their own sherry, there were many *almacenistas*, but now there are probably only about 50. They buy small quantities of wine, which they mature and then sell to exporting *bodegas*. While this wine can be blended (and much of it is), there has been a growing interest (led by the firm of Emilio Lustau) in selling *almacenistas'* wines as special selections. These are always top quality wines, usually from old *soleras*, and are only available in small quantities.

Jerez Brandy

Over half the profits of many a sherry producer will in fact come from brandy. Jerez is the main source of Spanish brandy, although it is not usually made from Jerez wine. The majority of the wine comes from the vast vineyard area of La Mancha in central Spain, where most Jerez brandy producers have distillation plants. The maturation however is carried out in Jerez de la Frontera, so many *bodegas* in the town will contain brandy rather than sherry.

The History of Sherry

The history of viticulture in the province of Cádiz dates back certainly as far as the Romans, possibly as far as the Phoenicians, Carthaginians and Greeks, who preceded them. Even during the Moorish occupation (from the 8th to the 13th centuries), wine was being produced in the fertile vineyards around the town of Jerez, or Seris, as it was then known. The name may be even older – some have suggested etymological links between Seris and Shiraz, the Persian town which certainly gave its name to the Shiraz grape of the Rhône Valley. A corruption of this Moorish name gave rise to the word 'sherry' in English (and only in English, since in France the wine is known as Xérès). By Chaucer's time, it was a recognized drink in England, and it was certainly fortified even then.

The Moors were driven out in the 1260s and the town of Seris became known as Jerez. For a long time it remained a border town between Catholic Spain and Moorish Granada, which is why, to this day, the phrase 'de la Frontera' is added to its name. (A number of other towns in Andalucía have a similar suffix.)

The Moors, of course, left behind their knowledge of the use of the alembic for distilling wine into spirits. Once the Catholic Kings of Spain were in control of the Jerez region, wine production expanded enormously, and it was not long before the English, already purchasers of the wines, came to Andalucía to trade in them as well. From the beginning of the 16th century, a flourishing English colony was in existence. Wine was exported from the region's main ports, El Puerto de Santa María and Sanlúcar de Barrameda (from where Columbus set sail), and from Jerez de la Frontera via a series of quays on the River Guadalete, two miles (1.25 km) from the town. According to Julian Jeffs (qv), 60,000 butts of sherry (one butt holds 500 litres) were exported in 1548 – 40,000 to England and Flanders, still the main markets for sherry – mainly from Puerto and Sanlúcar, which in the early days of the sherry trade were more important than Jerez de la Frontera itself.

The main English colony was in Sanlúcar. Rights were granted to it by the Dukes of Medina Sidonia, the region's main landowners, and were first set out in 1517. By the reign of Elizabeth I, despite the problems caused by the Reformation and the fact that England was at war with Spain, sherry sack was a firm favourite in English taverns. (The term originated in the fact that barrels were usually wrapped in sacking for transportation by sea.) 'Sack' could refer to wines from Madeira, Portugal or the Canaries as well as to those from the Jerez region. But sherry sack – the sack approved by Falstaff – was definitely from Jerez.

Considering the amount of time that England and Spain spent at war during the latter half of the 16th and much of the 17th and early 18th centuries, it is a wonder that any sherry left Jerez. Of course, England was not the only market – Flanders continued to take considerable quantities – but it was the British who developed the trade, and from the 16th century onwards some of the names that are still familiar, such as de Terry (an Irish family), were in place in the Jerez region. Unlike the port trade, however, which the English dominated for so long, the sherry trade was always shared between England and Spain.

Come the 18th century and the sherry trade was suffering from the effects of competition from port and madeira on the English market. Towards the end of the century, more Málaga was being exported from Spain than sherry. The situation was not helped by the restrictions placed on trade by the Gremio, the wine growers' association, which fixed prices at too high a level and refused to allow merchants to accumulate stocks.

But it was also a time when more familiar names arrived, such as the French émigrés Domecq, Lustau and Pemartín. From Ireland came William Garvey and Rafael O'Neale (who founded the first British *bodega* in 1724) and, from England, arrived James Duff and Thomas Osborne. At the same time, in England, two merchants, George Sandeman in London and William Perry in Bristol, were founding businesses based on sherry (and also on port, in the case of the Sandemans). The Sandeman name survives to this day, while the Perry business has become Harveys of Bristol.

The Peninsular War brought Jerez and the vineyard areas close to ruin. The French it seems drank most of the stocks and did not pay. Earlier, so the story goes, the Battle of Trafalgar could be heard resounding in the streets of the sherry towns. Many merchants packed up and escaped to the safety of Cádiz, and the vineyards were trampled and destroyed.

But success followed quickly upon disaster. And that success owes much to the energy and hard work of Pedro Domecq Lembeye – usually known simply as Pedro Domecq. Over a relatively short period he built up a prosperous business, and on his death, in 1839, he had an estate worth more than £1 million – an enormous sum for those days, of course. He also re-established the export trade and the integrity of sherry, which became a fashionable drink in the London of George IV. The town of Jerez thrived and yet more familiar names were attracted to the trade: John William Burdon, Luis Caballero and Manuel María González Angel.

The 1870s were the boom years for sherry. This was the time when the *bodegas* of Diez Hermanos and Williams & Humbert were founded. More sherry was being exported than ever before, demand outstripped supply, and then the inevitable happened: some merchants tried to cut corners, to send anything they could lay their hands on to keep customers happy. In 1873, there was an attack on sherry by a London doctor who accused the producers of selling grape juice that had been doctored with spirit and sulphate of lime (a process the Victorians called 'plastering'). It took some years before this scandal was proved to be groundless, but by that time (1894) phylloxera had arrived in Jerez, and the sherry trade entered another trough.

As always, of course, if a wine is of good enough quality it will regain favour. The sherry shippers were always luckier than some other wine producers because they had two products on which to rely – sherry itself and brandy. Brandy, for many companies then, as now, was a more profitable side of the business than sherry, certainly in Spain. It decidedly helped at the turn of the century.

In 1910, leading shippers formed the Sherry Shippers' Association, designed to promote the wine, particularly in the stagnant English market. Their efforts were rewarded after the First World War by the advent of the sherry party. Williams & Humbert can take credit for inventing this as an alternative to the cocktail party, but all sherry companies benefited from this clever idea.

The classic façade of Rancho Croft conceals ultra-modern equipment

Probably the same applies to the creation of the Don by Sandeman, which attracted attention to a major sherry brand and, by extension, to all sherry.

Since the inter-war years, while sherry's appeal may have fluctuated, the volume of trade has gone up and up. For example, 1979 saw greater shipments of sherry than ever before: 1.5 million hectolitres, compared with 0.7 million in 1970. Even in 1986, shipments were still above 1 million hectolitres, although more recently they have fallen below that level. The two familiar names of Harvey and Croft arrived in Jerez in the 1970s – Harvey to buy an existing *bodega*, Croft (until then only in the port trade) to set up a huge new one.

But these same years also saw the rise and subsequent fall of a remarkable empire that almost brought the entire trade in sherry crashing down with it. The Rumasa company was based at the small *bodega* of Zoilo Ruiz-Mateos, which in 1958 began to supply Harveys of Bristol – still without *bodegas* of its own in Jerez – with wine. In 1964, José-María Ruiz-Mateos signed a 100-year contract with Harveys to supply wine, and began to accumulate huge stocks. Within a few years he had begun to take over sherry. Williams & Humbert, Pemartín, Misa, Palomino y Vergara, Garvey, Varela, Bertola, de Terry and Bodegas Internacionales were just some of the firms controlled by Ruiz-Mateos. At one time he controlled 34 percent of sherry production, and that is aside from his banking and hotel interests, and his interests in Rioja wines and in Penedès Cava. His was the largest commercial grouping in Spain.

The story of how it all went wrong, and of how the Spanish government stepped in in 1983 to expropriate the group is still being unravelled, because Ruiz-Mateos has never been brought to court. But as far as sherry was concerned, it brought to light remarkable tales of the shipping of immature wines abroad to boost sales figures, and of the dumping of poor quality sherry on the Dutch, German and British markets. There was inevitably a great threat to the good name of sherry.

The threat has, however, proved to be of good effect. Sherry producers and shippers saw the need to achieve a balance between the vineyards (which had been increased dramatically in size in the 1970s to cope with the expected boom of the 1980s, which never came), the stocks of wine in the *bodegas* and the amount of wine shipped and sold. The Four Year Plan (which started in September 1983) fixed the minimum price of sherry to stop price wars, cut stock levels by fixing quotas for each house based upon how much the house shipped (as in the port trade), cut back the sherry vineyards by grubbing up vines in poorer quality areas, and set in train an intense campaign to promote sherry as a unique product.

A sales to stock ratio set up under the Four Year Plan meant that a *bodega* might only sell 29 percent of its stock in any one year. Previously, the figure was 35 percent. The drop was designed to ensure that wine did not flood the market, and that it was given time to mature.

The Rumasa-owned *bodegas* were all sold back to the private sector. Harveys of Bristol bought Palomino y Vergara and de Terry, and these, together with its existing *bodegas* (purchased in the 1970s), make it the biggest sherry firm in Jerez. The German supermarket group Coop bought Garvey; the Rioja businessman Marcos Eguizábal bought Bodegas Internacionales and Diez-Merito, and Williams & Humbert, the last to go, was bought by Barbadillo. The influx of new management into Jerez has transformed many *bodegas* and given stiff competition to those that remained independent.

At the end of the Four Year Plan's term, however, impressive as the results were in unifying a formerly disparate sherry trade, it was obvious that more work was needed. The price of grapes in Jerez continued to fall during the 1980s, badly affecting small-scale growers, while stocks continued to build up. And the price of sherry itself continued to drop, in real terms, in the wine's two principal export markets, Britain and the Netherlands. The provincial government then commissioned a report from management consultants Price Waterhouse, who, unsurprisingly, pointed out that supply continued to exceed demand.

As a result, it was finally decided by the provincial government, the shippers and the growers that it was essential to balance supply and demand. The vineyards are to be cut back by 4,000 hectares (although originally 5,200 hectares were to be removed), yields are to be reduced and quotas for the sale of wine are to be based on demand not production (to cut down on the dumping of young wine). The net result is that by 1998 there will be 11,000 hectares of vineyards, compared with 22,000 hectares in 1982.

When to Drink Sherry

Sherry is a highly versatile wine. With its plethora of different styles it seems appropriate for most occasions. The dry styles – *finos* and *manzanillas* – can double as aperitif wines (dry sherry is the best appetite stimulant I know), or equally can take the place of a white wine during a meal (a common practice in Jerez restaurants). With the current move to lower the alcohol level of *fino* from 15.5 to 15 percent, sherry will become even more attractive as a table wine. Always drink *fino* and *manzanilla* chilled.

An *amontillado*, in cold climates, is also a good aperitif, and a dry *amontillado* goes well with soups and starters including smoked salmon and other fish. Medium sherries can be drunk at any time. On warm days they are best chilled or at least cool.

The richer styles are almost meals in themselves. At the end of a dinner or last thing at night, a glass of *oloroso* tastes superb and is very relaxing. A favourite dish in the restaurants of Sanlúcar is ice cream doused in rich *oloroso*. Cream styles or wines made from PX lend themselves to use as dessert wines.

Visiting the Bodegas

As can be seen in the directory of producers that follows, only a few of the large *bodegas* are open to the passer-by. For the others, an appointment is usually necessary, but this can easily be made through a wine merchant or shipper in your home country. Once inside the *bodega*, you will discover that the sherry people are immensely generous, and the visit will be well organized. They will show you the sherry butts, stretching for what seems like miles in the cool of their lofty buildings, before offering you a glass of *fino* with some superb nuts.

Driving around the area presents no problems, and trips to Sanlúcar de Barrameda and El Puerto de Santa María are essential. A visit at the beginning of September will coincide with the harvest festival, when the whole town seems to be enjoying a continuous feast, and certainly never goes to bed. In mid-May there is the horse show – the passion of many a true Andalucían.

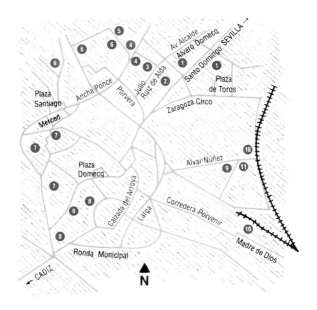

Jerez de la Frontera: The Sherry Bodegas

① Williams & Humbert
② Hijos de Agustin Blázquez
③ Garvey
④ A R Valdespino

⑤ Sandeman-Coprimar
⑥ Diez-Merito
⑦ Pedro Domecq
⑧ González Byass

⑨ La Riva
⑩ Diez Hermanos
⑪ John Harvey & Sons
  (Harveys of Bristol)

Producers

Tomás Abad ★★★
Playa del Cubo 4, Jerez de la Frontera. Tel (56) 341597.
Stock: 2,000 butts.
This bodega is a wholly-owned subsidiary of EMILIO LUSTAU, but does produce a top rate *fino* under its own name that is light, salty, austere and delicate.

Manuel de Argüeso ★★
**PO Box 6, 11480 Jerez de la Frontera. Tel (56) 331458.
Also based at Sanlúcar de Barrameda. Founded 1822.
V'yds: none. Stocks: 8,000 butts. Additional brands:
Señorita Manzanilla Oloroso; The Cream of Cream
Sherry. Visits: no.**

Founded by Don León de Argüeso, a wealthy farmer from the
north of Spain, Argüeso has expanded into a medium-sized company, with a separate *manzanilla bodega* in Sanlúcar. Owned by the
VALDESPINO family, it has recently stopped operating as an
almacenista and become an exporter, having in the process taken
over the *almacenista bodega* of Gutierrez Hermanos. The quality of
the wines is average rather than great, but I do like the dry *amontillado* and the *manzanilla*, which has just the right tangy freshness.

Antonio Barbadillo ★★★→★★★★
**Luis Eguilaz 11, 11540 Sanlúcar de Barrameda. Tel (56)
361242. Founded 1821. V'yds: 450 ha. Stocks: 60,000 butts.
Additional brands: Barbadillo; Fino de Sanlúcar; Fino de
Balbaina; Príncipe Amontillado; Sanlúcar Cream; Solear
Manzanilla Pasada. Visits by appt.**

One of the great names in *manzanilla*, Barbadillo is still run by
the founding family, although HARVEYS OF BRISTOL have a shareholding and the two firms jointly run a vinification centre in the
vineyards. The firm was started by Don Benigno Barbadillo
Ortigüela, a Castilian from Burgos, who moved to Sanlúcar,
bought some old *soleras* and began to sell sherry. The firm now has
extensive vineyard holdings in top quality *albariza* vineyards. The
huge Sanlúcar *bodegas*, which account for 70 percent of *bodega*
capacity in the town, are sited in what was formerly the bishop's
palace, a cool house surrounding a courtyard.

The wines are classics. The *manzanillas*, which often appear
under wine merchants' or retailers' own labels, are light, fresh,
tangy and bone dry. There is a rare Solear Manzanilla Pasada, an
old *manzanilla* with an average age of over 20 years and a great
intensity of flavour – very dry and salty at the finish. The Fino de
Balbaina (named after a vineyard area) is round and soft, but firm
and highly flavoured with *flor*. Both the Príncipe Amontillado and
the Barbadillo Oloroso are properly dry and nutty, while even the

sweet Sanlúcar Cream has a style and elegance that many of this type of sherry lack.

Bodegas Barón ★★→
Calzada de la Infanta 28, 11540 Sanlúcar de Barrameda. Tel (56) 360603. Founded 1895. V'yds: 140 ha. Additional brands: Atalaya; Pino Viejo; Solera Especial. Visits by appt.
A small group of *bodegas*, still family owned, including *bodegas* Carreteria, Malinillo, Regina, Tartaneros and Trabajadero. The Manuel Barón *bodega* itself is over 300 years old. The firm is particularly strong in *amontillados*, having a good reserve of old wines. The 100 percent Moscatel dessert wine comes from vineyards in Jara and Chipiona.

Bertola ★→
PO Box 33, Ca Madrid-Cádiz, 641-750, Jerez de la Frontera. Tel (56) 348946. Founded 1911. V'yds: 600 ha. Additional brands: Pale Dry; Gold. Visits by appt.
A relatively recent entrant to the sherry scene, Bertola was founded as the Jerez branch of the port firm of KOPKE. It was later sold to another sherry company, Diez Hermanos, which eventually became part of the Rumasa empire. After the break-up of Rumasa the firm was bought by Marcos Eguizábal and it is now run as a brand of BODEGAS INTERNACIONALES, in whose giant *bodega* its sherries are made.

If that sounds like a complex story of high finance, the sherries themselves are a much simpler proposition. The best-known is the Bertola Cream, popular in Scotland, but which I find too sweet and young-tasting. The full range of styles is made, however, and includes the rare *palo cortado*, and a lighter, *oloroso*, style that is strangely honeyed in taste. The *fino* is too heavy.

Hijos de Agustín Blázquez →★★★
Ca de Jerez a Algeciras km 2.3, 11406 Jerez de la Frontera. Tel (56) 348250. Founded 1795. V'yds: in Macharnudo and Balbaina. Stocks: 15,000 butts. Additional brands: Balfour; Carta Blanca Fino; Carta Oro Old Amontillado; Capuchino Palo Cortado; Carta Plata Old Amontillado; Carta Roja Oloroso; Medal Cream. Visits: no.

This is a small *bodega*, now wholly owned by DOMECQ but still selling its own range of sherries from its own *soleras*. The firm's most familiar brands are the Carta Blanca Fino and the Carta Roja Oloroso, both good examples of their kind. The Carta Oro Old Amontillado is a superb wine, ripely nutty with a mature, almost astringent, bitter character. A new range of sherries recently introduced to Spain by this company is called Balfour (showing the lure of a British brand name). Many of Blázquez' wines are sold under wine retailers' own labels.

B Bobadilla   ★★→★★★

PO Box 217, Ctra Circunvalación, 11407 Jerez de la Frontera. Tel (56) 348600. Founded 1882. V'yds: 150 ha. Stock: 15,000 butts. Additional brands: Alcazar Amontillado; Capitán Oloroso; La Merced Cream; Pedro Ximénez Romántico; Victoria Fino. Visits: no.

One of Spain's largest drinks companies, with a considerable interest in Jerez brandy as well as sherry (Bobadilla 103 brandy is one of Spain's best-known brands), this is still a family-controlled company. It started out in a *bodega* that formed part of a Jerez monastery, Los Padres Mercedarios (hence the cream sherry's name), but it has since moved to a large, modern *bodega* on the main Jerez ring-road.

Bobadilla is unusual among Jerezano companies in that its sherries are better known at home than on the export markets. Indeed, its wine has been described as 'sherry for the Spaniards' because the house style has a certain dryness that appeals less to some foreign markets. The best wine here is the bone-dry Victoria Fino (also known as Abanico). I have found the Alcazar Amontillado and the Capitán Oloroso to be on the dry side as well, which is definitely a point in their favour.

John William Burdon   ★★→

PO Box 6, El Puerto de Santa María. Tel (56) 851751. Additional brands: Don Luis Amontillado; Heavenly Cream; Pale Medium. Visits by appt.

In the middle and late years of the 19th century, this was one of the biggest of the English-owned *bodegas*. The firm was started by John William Burdon, who came out to work for DUFF GORDON and then set up in business on his own. When he died childless, the *bodega* became part of LA CUESTA, which in turn was sold to LUIS CABALLERO, in 1932. The Burdon *bodegas* are now used as stables for the Cartujano horses owned by DE TERRY.

Since the purchase of LUSTAU by Caballero, Burdon has been treated as a brand of Lustau, although stylistically the wines are kept separate. Until recently, the Burdon range was not particularly impressive, but of late the wines have definitely improved in quality, due to a very apparent upgrading in the range. The Burdon *fino* is in typical Puerto style, lighter and fresher than a Jerez *fino*.

Luis Caballero ★★★
PO Box 6, San Francisco 32, El Puerto de Santa María. Tel (56) 851751. Founded 1830. V'yds: 250 ha. Stock: 17,000 butts. Additional brands: John William Burdon; José la Cuesta; Emilio Lustau; Pavon. Visits: no.
The sixth largest firm in the Jerez region, Luis Caballero dominates El Puerto de Santa María in more ways than simply with its wine. Don Luis Caballero, of the sixth generation of his family, is a major figure in the sherry trade. He owns the splendid Moorish castle of San Marcos in the centre of the town, and as well as his sherries makes an orange brandy liqueur, Ponche, which is the brand leader in Spain. Caballero now owns EMILIO LUSTAU and this firm has been given responsibility for sherry production in the group.

Cabellero's origins date back to the 1830s, to the acquisition of a stock of wine from the Dukes of Medina, including a quantity of *oloroso* and *amontillado* that still forms the basis of the modern *bodega*'s *soleras*. Luis Caballero is rare among sherry firms in supplying all its grape needs from its own vineyards. The major brand names under which it sells sherry are BURDON, Troubador of LA CUESTA and Emilio Lustau.

Croft Jerez ★→★★
Ca Madrid-Cádiz km 636.3, 11407 Jerez de la Frontera. Tel (56) 306600. Founded 1970. V'yds: 660 ha. Stock: 70,000 butts. Additional brands: Croft Classic; Croft Delicado; Croft Original; Croft Particular. Visits by appt.
Croft is, of course, one of the oldest names in port, but it was not until it became part of International Distillers and Vintners (itself part of Grand Metropolitan, one of the largest wine, spirit and

brewing firms in the world) that it was decided that a Croft operation should be set up in Jerez. Once the decision was taken, no money was spared in two directions: one, in the creation of Rancho Croft, an enormous *bodega*, classical in style, if brand new in construction, backed by an equally large and impressive vinification plant, and, two, in the creation of brands. Of these, Croft Original was the first (and is still the biggest selling) pale cream sherry on the market.

It is perhaps symptomatic of Croft Jerez that Croft Original should not only be its biggest-selling sherry, but also its best. Of its type it is good, and it is certainly the best pale cream sherry on the market. The other wines, which are still seen as having small walk-on parts after the centre-stage success of Croft Original, are generally disappointing: Croft Delicado tends to flabbiness and sweetness, while Croft Particular is a very commercial (but no more) medium-style sherry.

José la Cuesta   *
PO Box 6, San Francisco 32, El Puerto de Santa María. Tel (56) 851751. Founded 1843. Additional brands: Troubador Cream; Troubador Medium Dry; Troubador Pale Dry. Visits: no.

This *bodega* is now part of the LUIS CABALLERO group. Its main brand name is Troubador: a range that tends towards dullness, sweetness and lightness.

Delgado Zuleta   ★★★
Carmen 32, Sanlúcar-Chipiona km 1.5. 11540 Sanlúcar de Barrameda. Tel (56) 360133. Founded 1719. V'yds: none. Stock: 8,500 butts. Additional brands: Amontillado Fino Zuleta; Amontillado Muy Viejo Quo Vadis; Manzanilla Barbiana; Manzanilla La Goya; Manzanilla Lola; B Rodriguez-La Cave. Visits: no.

One of the oldest Sanlúcar *bodegas*, Delgado Zuleta was started by Don Francisco Gil de Ledesma, and although it remained in the ownership of his family, it did not get its present name until the end of the 19th century. The firm is still independent. Early this century it became a supplier to the Spanish royal family, and there are butts in the *bodega* signed by King Alfonso XIII in 1930.

Its best-known wine is the Manzanilla La Goya, which is in fact an older style of *manzanilla*, a *pasada*. The wine is named after a famous flamenco dancer, and its age gives it an extra depth and character to add to this style's typical, salty tang. The *fino* is fuller and quite smooth but still dry, while the *amontillado* is fairly light and medium-dry; much more style, richness and dryness can be found in the Amontillado Muy Viejo.

Diez-Merito ★★★→

Ctra Nac IV km 641.750, Jerez de la Frontera. Tel (56) 341247. Founded 1884. V'yds: 176 ha. Stock: 72,000 butts. Additional brands: Don Zoilo; Fino Imperial; Merito; Oloroso Victoria Regina. Visits: no.

This firm, now controlled by Marcos Eguizábal (also owner of BERTOLA and BODEGAS INTERNACIONALES, is an amalgamation of a number of *bodegas*. It was started in 1884 as Diez Hermanos, but in 1974 merged with Marqués del Merito, and the current name was formed. After the break-up of Rumasa, Eguizábal bought the flagship *bodega*, Don Zoilo (which also makes the top-flight Gran Duque de Alba brandy), and the Celestino Diez de Morales *bodega*.

All the sherries from this *bodega* prove themselves to be of high quality. The various ranges are, it seems, kept separate, with Don Zoilo still regarded as one of the very best ranges of old sherry available, and the Merito name being reserved for an equally interesting spread of wines. Of the Don Zoilo set, the Very Old Fino is the best known: an extremely full wine and not quite as austere as some sherries, but with a good *flor* taste. The *amontillado* is full and rich, and definitely tastes of old wines. I have tasted the Diez Hermanos Palma Fino and found this a fascinating mix of old, nutty fruit and fresh fragrance.

Pedro Domecq ★★★→★★★★

San Ildefonso 3, 11403 Jerez de la Frontera. Tel (56) 331800. Founded 1730. V'yds: 1,600 ha. Stock: 92,000 butts. Additional brands: Amontillado 51-1a; Celebration Cream; Double Century; Fiesta Fino, Amontillado, Cream; La Ina; Primero; Rio Viejo; Sibarita; Venerable; Viña 25. Visits by appt.

One of the oldest and most famous firms in Jerez, Pedro Domecq was in fact founded by an Irishman, Patrick Murphy, who started trading in sherry in 1830. He brought a friend, Juan Haurie into the business, and on Murphy's death the Hauries took over the business. One of Juan Haurie's nephews, Juan Carlos, was in charge at the time of the French occupation of Spain during the Napoleonic wars and he made the mistake of siding with the French, selling them wine and acting as a local tax gatherer. When the French left, he inevitably became the most hated man in Jerez and the business was ruined. In stepped French-born Pedro de Domecq to rescue it, relinquishing the running of the Hauries' London office to take charge in Jerez. But Haurie was not only politically naive, he was also a hopeless businessman and not very pleasant to boot, and Domecq soon split with him and set up his own *bodega*.

Domecq died in bizarre circumstances: while being suspended over a cauldron of boiling water as a cure for rheumatism, the whole crazy contraption broke and plunged him into the water. The family carried on, and continues to be one of the greatest names in Jerez; José Ignacio Domecq is the current company chairman. Like many sherry firms, it probably makes more money from brandy (of which its most familiar brand is Fundador), but it undoubtedly takes its sherry-making very seriously. The firm's *bodegas* in Jerez are old but huge, and are complemented by a vast, modern bottling plant. It also owns a most beautiful palace in the centre of Jerez, which is used for entertaining.

The Domecq reputation luckily does not overshadow the wines. La Ina is one of the best *finos* on the market: very dry, very austere and truly elegant. A range is sold under the Fiesta label in the UK. The Double Century range is sound, with a slightly sweeter *fino* and a delicious, light *amontillado*. Rio Viejo is an old *amontillado*, dry, nutty and burnt. The newly-released old *solera* wines are superb: Sibarita is a cross between an old *amontillado* and an old *oloroso*, dating from a 1792 *solera*; Amontillado 51-1a (after the numbering of the *solera*) is an old, dry style of wine; Venerable is a rich, intense *oloroso*.

Duff Gordon   ★★→★★★

Fernán Caballero 3, 11500 El Puerto de Santa María. Tel (56) 855211. Founded 1768. Additional brands: No 28

Oloroso; Club Dry Amontillado; El Cid Amontillado; Fino
Feria; Nina Oloroso; Pinta Fino; Dry; Santa María Cream.
Visits by appt.

Although this firm is now part of OSBORNE, the Duff Gordon
name is still one of the most famous in Jerez and Puerto. Sir James
Duff was British Consul at Cádiz, and, together with his nephew
Sir William Gordon, he went into business in 1768 making sherry
and brandy in Puerto. During the next century or so, they supplied
a good number of the crowned heads of Europe. The Duff Gordon
interests were sold to its partner, Thomas Osborne, in 1872, and
the Osborne family has been shipping wines under the Duff
Gordon name since then, although they are not available in Spain.

The best wines are the Fino Feria – quite light and definitely dry
– and the two *olorosos*: the dry Nina, with its classic, burnt taste,
and the sweeter No 28, heavy, intense and rich. El Cid is the fuller
of the two *amontillados*.

José Estévez
**PO Box 167, Cristal 4, Jerez de la Frontera. Tel
(56) 349344.**

Linked with HEREDEROS DEL MARQUES DEL REAL TESORO.

Manuel Fernandez   →★★
**Ctra Circunvalación , Jerez de la Frontera. Tel (56)
348600. Founded 1880. V'yds: 150 ha. Stock: 14,500
butts. Visits: no.**

This firm represents half of the BOBADILLA group. It exports its
sherries mainly to Holland and Germany. Brandy also forms a large
part of production here.

Bodegas Jésus Ferris   ★★
**Avenida San Fernando 118, Rota. Tel (56) 363400. V'yds:
35 ha. Stock: 8,000 butts. Additional brands: Las 3
Candidas; Anfitrion; Don Jésus; J Ferris; La Liebre. Visits
by appt.**

This small firm is run from offices in Rota, with a *bodega* in Puerto.
A certain amount of its sherry is exported to Europe and the US. It
is only since 1976 that Don Jésus Ferris Marhuenda, the owner, has
been selling his wines direct rather than through a merchant.

Garvey ★★→★★★
PO Box 12, Bodegas de San Patricio, Divina Pastora 3, Jerez de la Frontera. Tel (56) 330500. Founded 1780. V'yds: 500 ha. Stock: 40,000 butts. Additional brands: Fino San Patricio; Flor de Jerez; International Range; Long Life Oloroso; Ochavico Dry Oloroso; San Angelo Amontillado; Tío Guillermo Amontillado.

The Irish connection is strong at Garveys. The firm was founded by William Garvey (the son of Patrick Garvey, who lived at Annagh Castle in County Wexford). He set up as a general trader, and among the goods he bought and sold was sherry, which soon dominated the business – so much so that he built what was then the largest *bodega* in Jerez, and one that is still among the most spectacular. (A new *bodega* for the firm has been built more recently on the outskirts of the town.) The Garvey family continued in ownership until 1978, when it sold out to Rumasa. Following the Spanish government takeover, Garvey was sold to the German Coop group, in 1985.

Garvey is unusual among sherry companies in that *fino* sherry is the company's dominant wine, accounting for 70 percent of production. The most famous is the Fino San Patricio (named, naturally enough, after Ireland's patron saint). It is always one of the finest *finos* available, an old wine in style, well balanced and with terrific *flor* character. Tío Guillermo is an old, dry *amontillado*, quite full-bodied, while the Ochavico Dry Oloroso is dry and full of old, burnt fruit: a very fine wine. I am less impressed by what the firm calls its International Range, which comes in four styles – extra dry, *amontillado* medium-dry, cream and pale cream. By comparison with the finer premium range these seem bland and commercial, with the extra dry particularly being too sweet, and the other wines also suffering from excess sweetness in some way.

Gil Luque ★★
PO Box 26, Jerez de la Frontera. Tel (56) 181386. Stock: 6,000 butts. V'yds: 15 ha. Additional brands: Deportivo; Luque. Visits by appt.

A small, private firm, based in attractive *bodegas* in Jerez.

Miguel M Gómez ★★→★★★

PO Box 73, Avenida de la Libertad 15, El Puerto de Santa María. Tel (56) 850150. Founded 1816. Additional brands: Amontillado 1855; Cream Leonor; Fino Alameda; Oloroso Dulce La Señora; Oloroso Seco Mentidero; Pedro Ximénez Triple Dulce. Visits: no.

This firm was founded in Cádiz in 1816 and it is still a family-owned business. It moved to Puerto in 1969 and has vineyards in Jerez Superior. The best wines here are the two *olorosos*, especially the dry Mentidero: rich and full-bodied but with a tangy, burnt taste. The Fino Alameda is very dry and quite light in character, typical of Puerto wines. A considerable amount of the firm's wine is exported under wine merchants' own labels.

González Byass ★★★→★★★★

Manuel María González 12, 11403 Jerez de la Frontera. Tel (56) 340000. Founded 1835. V'yds: 800 ha. Stock: 65,000 butts. Additional brands: Alfonso; Amontillado del Duque; Apóstoles; La Concha; Jerez Supremo; Matusalém; Noé; Tío Pepe; El Rocío; San Domingo; Solera 1847; Viña AB. Visits: weekdays 9.30–1.

It is almost 160 years since Manuel María González Angel founded the first of the González Byass *bodegas* in Jerez. His father, manager of the king's salt marshes in Jerez, had died suddenly, leaving a widow with five sons. Four sons went to study in Seville, but Manuel, constitutionally the weakest, was kept by the sea in Cádiz for his health, and put to work in a clerk's office. He soon tired of this and set up his own small *bodega* in Jerez. With the backing of a wealthy financier, he was able to build the La Sacristía *bodega* in 1835, on the site of a run-down vineyard of the same name. Success – and more *bodegas* – followed. Manuel González formed a partnership with his London agent, Robert Blake Byass, in 1863. In 1873, it was the first company to ship over 1,000 butts in a year, and by 1868 González Byass had become the largest sherry shipper.

The firm is still run by descendants of González and was, until 1988, run by descendants of Byass as well (they have now sold their shares to the González family). A minority shareholding is held by the multinational Grand Metropolitan, the owner of CROFT. The *bodegas* in Jerez remain some of the most interesting in the sherry country: Manuel González' laboratory has been preserved as a museum, while the semicircular La Concha *bodega*, built by Eiffel, is a splendid place for banquets. And then, of course, there are the white mice, who live in the *bodega* and can be seen sipping from saucers of sherry.

González Byass can boast that its range of sherries is the finest of them all. Much of the quality of these is built on the firm's huge stocks of old wines. Some *soleras* date back to 1847, and the range of blending material is enormous. Small quantities of a *manzanilla*, El Rocío, are made, but the firm's heart is in Jerez. The most famous of its brands is Tío Pepe (Uncle Pepe),a very fine, dry *fino*, always elegant and – an equally important factor – consistently reliable. The La Concha *amontillado* is comparatively light in style, but has a similar elegance. There is also a superb range of old sherries, of which the star to my mind is Amontillado del Duque, a dry, rich, fruity wine, concentrated and complex. Look out, too, for the Apóstoles dry *oloroso*, a wine of equal quality, and for the dessert sherries Noé and Matusalém.

Luis G Gordon ★★
PO Box 48, Colón 3, Jerez de la Frontera. Tel (56) 332195.
Founded 1734. Additional brands: La Giralda; Gordon &
Rivero; Manola Fino; Marqués de Irun; Royal Crescent.
One of the oldest firms, founded by a Scot, Arthur Gordon.

John Harvey & Sons (Harveys of Bristol) ★★→
Colón 1, 11401 Jerez de la Frontera. Tel (56) 151030.
Founded 1796. V'yds: 1,000 ha. Stock: 90,000 butts.
Additional brands: 1796 range; Bristol Cream; Bristol
Reserve; Club Amontillado; Finesse; Harveys 11/Tico;
Luncheon Dry. Visits: weekdays 9–1.30.
Although John Harvey has been a sherry-shipping company since 1796, until 1970 it bought all its wine from other *bodegas* rather than owning its own. In the 1960s, it purchased considerable quantities from José-María Ruiz-Mateos, which gave him the capital to move into the 'big time' Rumasa group. Since then, the firm has made up for lost time as *bodega* owners. In 1970, it purchased the small Mackenzie *bodega* in Jerez, and shortly afterwards acquired the adjoining Marqués de Misa *bodega* from the Rumasa

Mice at González Byass take fortifying sips of the *bodega*'s sherry!

group. The latter gave Harveys a fine site in central Jerez, and it is now adorned with a beautiful ornamental garden – and a pool of alligators! In 1985, following the Rumasa collapse, Harveys bought the two firms DE TERRY and PALOMINO Y VERGARA, which gave the company a huge, up-to-date complex in Puerto and the Palomino y Vergara *bodega* in Jerez. It has also invested heavily in vineyards (jointly with ANTONIO BARBADILLO and GARVEY) and has a modern winery complex at Gibalbin, altogether making it probably the biggest group in Jerez.

John Harvey's major brand, Bristol Cream, is the world's biggest-selling sherry. It is reliable and a tribute to the power of advertising. The *fino* Luncheon Dry, on the other hand, never seems to show well, being too heavy and sweet, and Club Amontillado suffers from the same faults. The range also includes Finesse, a pale cream sherry, and the John Harvey brand, which the firm describes as 'light and smooth'. There is a mixer sherry too, known either as Harveys 11 or as Tico, which is in fact a sweet-ened *fino*. Harveys does, however, redeem its reputation with the

fine, old-bottled Bristol Cream sherries (wines that show the year
in which they were bottled, and have taken on some bottle-age),
and with the high quality 1796 range, which includes a *palo cortado*
as well as a dry *oloroso* and a dry *amontillado*.

Emilio Hidalgo ★★→
Clavel 29, 11402 Jerez de la Frontera. Tel (56) 340424.
Founded 1874. V'yds: 100 ha. Stock: 8,000 butts.
Additional brands: Fino Panesa; Tresillo Amontillado;
Gobernador Oloroso; Magistral Cream. Visits: no.
A small, family-owned *bodega*, which acts as a *négociant* (merchant),
producing a range of wines from small, private vineyards, as well as
from its own land. It is perhaps typical of the way the sherry pro-
ducers are oriented towards exports, that even a modest-sized firm
such as this exports 85 percent of production.

Vinícola Hidalgo ★★★
Banda de la Playa 24, 11540 Sanlúcar de Barrameda. Tel
(56) 360516. Founded 1792. V'yds: 200 ha. Stock: 17,000
butts. Additional brands: Amontillado Napoleon; Fino
Especial, Oloroso Especial, Cream Especial; La Gitana
Manzanilla; Jerez Cortado Hidalgo; Pedro Ximénez
Viejo. Visits: no.
Although small, this family-owned *bodega* has begun to make quite
a name for itself through the quality of its wines. It supplies a number of wine merchants in England with own-label sherries blended
to a high quality. *Manzanilla* is obviously the firm's strong point
and the La Gitana is a very good example. A *fino* is also made, a
much heavier wine but still very dry. The *amontillados* and *olorosos*
have a definite Sanlúcar character – lighter, fresher and smoother-
tasting than the equivalent from Jerez de la Frontera. The firm's
Sanlúcar *bodega*, La Arboledilla, has the highest roof of any of the
sherry *bodegas*.

Bodegas de Los Infantes Orléans-Borbon ★★→
Baños 1, 11540 Sanlúcar de Barrameda. Tel (56) 360352.
Founded 1886. V'yds: 220 ha. Stock: 8,000 butts.
Additional brands: Amontillado Ataulfo; La Ballena; El
Botánico; Cream Orléans 1884; Fino Alvaro; Manzanilla

Torre-Breva; Oloroso Seco Fenicio; Pedro Ximénez
Carla. Visits: no.
Founded by members of the Spanish royal family, Don Antonio de
Orléans, the Duque de Montpensier, and the Infante de Orléans-
Borbon, this firm is now owned jointly by BARBADILLO (which
manages the *soleras*) and Compañía Agrícola Torre-Breva (which
grows the grapes). The *manzanillas*, Torre-Breva and La Ballena,
are the company's best wines.

Bodegas Internacionales ★★★
**Ctra Nac IV km 641.750, Jerez de la Frontera. Tel (56)
341889. Founded 1974. V'yds: 352 ha. Stock: 68,000 butts.
Additional brands: Duke of Wellington range. Visits: no.**
Bodegas Internacionales was the creation of Rumasa. Not content
with buying up every sherry company he could lay his hands on,
José-María Ruiz-Mateos decided to build himself the biggest
bodega in Jerez. He succeeded, and, as a result, created not only a
spectacular piece of modern architecture (covering 10,000 square
metres) but also a very good range of sherries. The firm is now part
of the Eguizábal group, which also includes DIEZ-MERITO. Apart
from the Duke of Wellington sherries, the Internacionales *bodega*
holds *soleras* for BERTOLA, J F Diestro, M Misa, Carlos de
Otaolaurruchi, J Pemartín, the Union de Exportadores de Jerez
and VARELA.

The Duke of Wellington Fino always shows well in tastings,
having a *fino-amontillado* style (a wine verging on *amontillado* in
richness while retaining a *fino* freshness). The others in the range
are of an equally high standard, especially the *amontillado* proper.

Lacave
**Avenida AA Domecq 5. Jerez de la Frontera. Tel (56)
346923. Founded 1810. V'yds: 370 ha. Visits: no.**
A *bodega* that started life in Cádiz and moved to Jerez when it
became part of the Rumasa group. I have not had a chance to taste
any of its wines.

Emilio Lustau ★★★→
**Plaza del Cubo 4, 11403 Jerez de la Frontera. Tel (56)
341597. Founded 1896. V'yds: 170 ha. Stock: 20,000 butts.**

Additional brands: Almacenista range; Dry Lustau Fino, Oloroso; East India Solera; Landed Age range; Solera Reserva range; Vendimia Cream. Visits: no.
This firm, now part of the LUIS CABALLERO group, has been highly instrumental in removing sherry's image as a cheap wine and in giving it a reputation for excellence, through its promotion of wines from *almacenistas*. More recently the firm has been innovative by returning to sherry-making traditions through its range of Landed Age sherries (wines bottled in the export country and then given bottle-age before being sold).

Lustau's *bodega* in Jerez is one of the most fascinating in the town, buried deep in the Moorish walls. In recent years, another *bodega* has been constructed, at the firm's Nuestra Señora de la Esperanza vineyard.

Lustau has always run a diverse sherry business, supplying wine merchants with own-label wines as well as promoting its own name through the Lustau range. In everything the company does, its quality shines out. From wines such as the Dry Lustau Fino, its standard *fino*, a delicate wine but absolutely properly bone dry, through the Dry Lustau Oloroso, a rounded wine, but with a very dry finish, to the rich East India Solera, sweet and concentrated, everything is of the finest standard. The *almacenista* wines vary in taste (but not in quality) because the firm buys small lots from different people and sells them separately. These wines make a fascinating exploration of the range of complex tastes to be found in old sherries. The Landed Age Sherries (available only in limited quantities) are another star turn. The range includes only *amontillados* and *olorosos*, since giving bottle-age to a *fino* sherry would ruin it. Out of these – and all are great wines – I particularly like the Rare Dry Oloroso, a rich and full wine even though it has a dry aftertaste, and the Amoroso, a very sweet wine, with toffee and rich caramel flavours.

Herederos del Marqués del Real Tesoro ★→★★★
PO Box 27, Calle Pajarete 3, Jerez de la Frontera. Founded 1879. V'yds: 200 ha. Stock: 16,000 butts. Additional brands: Almirante Oloroso Seco; Amontillado del Principe; Cream Réal Tesoro; Fino Ideal; Solera 1850. Visits: no.
The origins of the title of Marqués del Real Tesoro (Royal

Treasure) go back to 1760, when Señor Don Joaquin Manuel de Villena Guadalfajara Rodriguez de Manzano y Nieto, a lieutenant general in the Spanish Navy, was created a *marqués* for using his own silver as cannonballs in a naval battle when the ammunition was used up. Although the title died out, it was recreated in 1879 for the first *marqués'* grandson, and he it was who founded the *bodega*. Today it ranks as a small *bodega*, with two ranges of wines: a rather good set of older sherries (Fino Ideal, Almirante Oloroso Seco and the old *amontillado* Solera 1850), and a rather dull 'international' range that goes mainly to the Dutch market and is not particularly impressive.

José Medina
Banda Playa 46, Sanlúcar de Barrameda. Tel (56) 361456. Stocks: 30,000 butts.
This family firm has expanded in recent years to link up with several other *bodegas*: B M Lagos, Hijos de A P Megia, Luis Paez and Juan Vergara. It has vineyards at Carrasacal in Jerez Superior.

Antonio Núñez ★★
PO Box 349, Ronda del Caracol, Jerez de la Frontera. Tel (56) 345111. Founded 1927. Additional brand: Santacuna.
A family firm that originated in the wine business of Antonio Muñoz. Its sherries come in rather fancy, black bottles.

Rafael O'Neale ★★→
Jerez de la Frontera. Founded 1724. Additional brands: Casilda Cream; Spanish Arch; Wild Geese.
A modest-sized *bodega*, founded by an Irishman in 1724, and still run by an O'Neale. The Spanish side of the family has owned vineyards since 1264. The *bodega* itself has been designated a national monument because it includes a section of the Moorish walls of the old citadel and part of a tower. The firm's brands include a stylish *manzanilla*.

Osborne ★★★
Fernán Caballero 3, 11500 El Puerto de Santa María. Tel (56) 855211. Founded 1772. V'yds: 220 ha. Stock: 60,000 butts. Additional brands: 10RF; Bailen; Coquinero; Fino

Quinta; Pedro Ximénez Viejo; Solera AOS. Visits: week-days 10–3 by appt.

Another of the many firms that started out under an Englishman. Thomas Osborne Mann, from Exeter in Devon, arrived in Cádiz as a trader and – like many others – became involved in the sherry trade to the eventual exclusion of everything else. He bought a *bodega* in Puerto in 1772. His son, John Nicholas, became a diplomat and was created Conde de Osborne by Pope Pius IX. (There is still a Conde de Osborne in the family.) Gradually, the Osborne family (which owns the firm 100 percent) has became totally Spanish – so much so that English readers need to be reminded to pronounce the 'e' at the end of the name in a Spanish fashion.

Today the Osborne group is the biggest drinks company in Spain, with interests in brandy (30 percent of the market in Spain) and a whole range of wines and spirits. It also has an interest in port wine. Advertising hoardings showing the Osborne bull dominated strategically chosen hills throughout Spain until drinks advertising came under government control. The group has been linked with the DUFF GORDON name for many years.

Sherry, in fact, forms a relatively small part of the business, but it is in no way neglected because of that. The Fino Quinta is light, refreshing and soft, but still very dry, while the Coquinero *amontillado* is a nutty, fruity, dry style. The Osborne 10RF (or Reserva Familiale) is an *oloroso,* slightly sweetened – but not by too much; the Bailen is a dry *oloroso*. The Black Label Cream is very smooth and not too heavy.

Palomino y Vergara ★★★→
Colón 1–25, Jerez de la Frontera. Tel (56) 330950. Stock: 32,000 butts. Additional brands: Tío Mateo.

The firm could almost claim to be the oldest in Jerez because the Palomino family was certainly involved in wine in the 13th century – in fact it is quite possible that the Palomino grape take its name from this family. The Vergaras are more recent incomers, having set up as sherry shippers in 1765. The firm's home in Jerez, La Atalaya, has one of the most beautiful gardens in the town. Together with the *bodega*, it was taken over by Rumasa. After expropriation by the Spanish government, the *bodega* was sold to HARVEYS OF BRISTOL, but La Atalaya is now a national monument.

The offices at the *bodega* are splendidly elegant – all mahogany panelling and fine furniture.

Palomino y Vergara is a *fino* house, and quite rightly so, because Tío Mateo (Uncle Matthew), is a classic Jerez example, very dry but strong and firm with a marvellous *flor* taste.

Hijos de Rainera Pérez Marín ★★★
Misericordia 1, Sanlúcar de Barrameda. Tel (56) 182225. Founded 1825. V'yds: 152 ha. Stock: 8,000 butts. Additional brands: Bandera Fino; Hermosilla Manzanilla; Manzanilla La Guita. Visits by appt.

A small *bodega* whose chief reputation lies in its very fine Manzanilla La Guita, which is also the name of the *bodega* itself.

La Riva ★★★
Alvar Núñez 44, Jerez de la Frontera. Tel (56) 331877. Founded 1776. Additional brands: Guadalupe Amontillado; Oloroso Reserva; Royal Cream; Tres Palmas Fino. Visits by appt.

One of the older sherry houses, founded in 1776. During the 19th century, the De La Riva family made two major contributions to viticulture in the Jerez region. It began deep-planting its vines, a practice which is now universal, and it devised the method of *deserpia*, whereby each vine is enclosed in its own box in the soil to obtain the greatest benefit from low rainfall. The La Riva company has been controlled by DOMECQ since the two families became linked by marriage.

The wines are of a high quality, as would be expected from a firm controlled by Domecq. The Tres Palmas Fino is a classic of its kind – full and strong, with a tangy bitterness and excellent fruit and acidity. The Guadalupe Amontillado is dry and nutty, but still quite smooth. The fine Oloroso Reserva comes from a *solera* laid down in 1830 and is dry, but rich with intense, burnt – almost roasted – flavours.

Felix Ruiz y Ruiz ★★
Cristal 4,6 & 8, Jerez de la Frontera. Founded 1809. Stock: 10,000 butts. Additional brands: Don Felix; Ruiz. Visits by appt.

A small firm owning three *bodegas* and selling two ranges of sherry, in the usual three styles.

Sánchez Romate Hermanos ★★→★★★
Calle Lealas 26–30, 11404 Jerez de la Frontera. Tel (56) 182212. Founded 1781. V'yds: 80 ha. Stocks: 8,000 butts. Additional brands: Don José Oloroso; Iberia Cream; NPU Amontillado; Petenara Manzanilla; Romate; Marismeño Fino; Viva la Pepa Manzanilla. Visits: no.
Founded by Don Juan Sánchez de la Torre and later joined by the Romate family, this firm has long had a royal connection (it still supplies sherry to King Juan Carlos) and was owned by the Duque de Almodovar until he sold it to a group of businessmen 20 years ago, who have since expanded the vineyard holdings.

The firm is probably better known for its de luxe brandy – Cardinal Mendoza (or Cardinal, in the US) – but it does also make some good sherries, of which the NPU (Non Plus Ultra) Amontillado is perhaps the finest, a bone dry wine from a very old *solera*. The Marismeño Fino is light and very dry, while the Petenara Manzanilla is tangy and salty. Iberia Cream is definitely one of the better cream sherries available, with a good dry base to its richness.

Sandeman-Coprimar ★★★→★★★★★
Pizarro 10, 11402 Jerez de la Frontera. Tel (56) 301100. Founded 1790. V'yds: 369 ha. Stock: 61,000 butts. Additional brands: Armada Cream Oloroso; Character Amoroso; Character Medium Amontillado; Don Fino Superior Fino; Dry Fino; Imperial Corregidor; Royal Ambrosante, Corregidor, Esmeralda. Visits by appt.
Unusually, the House of Sandeman, founded in London in 1790, traded in both port and sherry from its beginning. However, for the first century of its existence it had no *bodega* in Jerez – that did not come about until 1879, when Sandeman took over the *bodega* of its supplier, Julian Pemartín. In 1894, the firm purchased a stock of 800 butts of *oloroso*, which today forms the basis of the Royal Corregidor and Imperial Corregidor. Disaster hit the company in 1912, when its Bodega Grande, full of old *olorosos*, caught fire and burnt down. Julian Jeffs (qv) tells of the whole town turning out

with pots and pans to scoop up the wine. The *bodega* has subsequently been rebuilt in the same style. After the First World War, Sandeman became the first firm to use advertising to sell its sherries and ports – using the silhouette of a Don as its symbol. The firm is now part of the Seagram group.

One of the greatest contributions Sandeman has made to Jerez in recent years is to release small quantities of very fine old *olorosos* and *amontillados* on to the market, thus enhancing not only its reputation but also the reputation of Jerez in general. Wines such as Imperial Corregidor are top class examples of wine based on old *oloroso soleras*. It is a pity, with this great stock of old wines, that the Character Amoroso, based we are told on a *solera* laid down in 1895, should not have more character and style. However, the situation is much better with the dry *finos*: Don Fino is the drier of the two (the other being Dry Fino) and is a light but very fresh wine, easy to drink and yet full of classic character. Royal Ambrosante is a based on an old *solera* of *palo cortado*, with a touch of Pedro Ximénez to give it a slight sweetness, while Royal Esmeralda is an old *amontillado* that, again, has some sweetness to balance its essential dryness.

José de Soto ★★
M Jésus Tirado 6, Jerez de la Frontera. Tel (56) 332162.
V'yds: 150 ha. Additional brands: Amontillado La Uvita;
Fino Campero; Fino Soto; Soto Amontillado, Cream,
Dry, Oloroso and Medium Oloroso. Visits by appt.
The firm was founded by José de Soto at the end of the 18th century. His son, also named José de Soto, expanded it considerably and also developed the Ponche Soto (a blend of brandy, sherry and herbs) for which, in Spain, the company is most famous. He also developed a new grafting system when replanting the Jerez vineyards after the ravages of phylloxera in the 1880s, for which he was awarded a Diploma of Honour by the Ministry of Agriculture. The firm is still independent and family-owned.

The sherries are good middle-of-the-road wines. I prefer the fuller styles – the *amontillado* and the *olorosos* – to the rather dull and, to my palate, slightly sweetened *finos*. The Dry Oloroso is especially good.

Carlos y Javier de Terry ★→★★

PO Box 355, Valdès 7–9, El Puerto de Santa María. Tel (56) 855511. Founded 1783. Additional brands: Sherry 501 range. Visits by appt.

A small *bodega*; its sherries are less well known than its brandies.

Fernando A de Terry ★★→

Sta Trinidad 2, El Puerto de Santa María. Tel (56) 862700. Founded 1883. Stock: 50,000 butts. Additional brands: Terry. Visits by appt.

The de Terry family, while originally from Ireland, was shipping wine from Spain as early as the 15th century. The family did not set up its *bodegas* until the end of the 19th century, when it built one of the most beautiful in the Jerez region, on the edge of Puerto, with a vast, arcaded courtyard. The de Terrys also established a herd of Cartujano horses, from which the horses for the Spanish Riding School in Vienna are taken, and set up a museum of carriages (the museum and stables are both still in existence and are well worth a visit). In the early 1970s, the de Terrys built the most extravagant modern *bodega*, on the Puerto-Jerez road, which bankrupted them and forced the sale of the firm to Rumasa. After the government takeover, it was sold to HARVEYS OF BRISTOL.

De Terry is much better known for its brandies than for its sherries. Indeed the only brand of sherry that is at all familiar is the Fino Terry, a light style of wine, soft, in the style of Puerto, and pleasantly fresh but quite unexciting.

A R Valdespino ★★★★

Pozo del Olivar 16, 11403 Jerez de la Frontera. Tel (56) 331450. V'yds: 190 ha. Additional brands: Amontillado Coliseo; Del Carrascal Palo Cortado; Don Gonzalo Rare; Don Tomás Amontillado; Inocente; Jerez Cream; Pedro Ximénez Superior; Tío Diego. Visits: no.

The Valdespino family has been connected with Jerez since the reconquest of the city in 1264, when Don Alonso Valdespino received some of the reclaimed land. It has long-established *bodegas* in part of an ancient monastery, with beautiful gardens and patios. Valdespino is still a family company, with important vineyard holdings in the top regions of Macharnudo and Carrascal.

The firm is traditional in the best sense, using wood for most of the fermentation, and preserving considerable stocks of old *soleras* for use in blending. It produces fine wines, perhaps its most familiar being the fresh, delicate and beautifully elegant Inocente *fino*, which is made, unusually, from a single vineyard in Macharnudo. Tío Diego is a good, dry *amontillado*. Older, very fine wines include the Don Tomás Amontillado, which is nutty and fruity but quite restrained, a *palo cortado*, Del Carrascal, very dry but delicately full, and the Don Gonzalo Rare, a bone-dry, rich old *oloroso*.

Varela ★→

Ca Madrid-Cádiz km 641.750, Jerez de la Frontera. Tel (56) 336062. Founded 1850. Visits: no.
This firm was founded by Ramón Jimenez Varela in the middle of the 19th century. It was taken over by Rumasa and subsequently its *bodega* was incorporated into the new BODEGAS INTERNACIONALES complex, owned by the Eguizábal group. Its best-known wines are Varela Cream and Varela Medium, neither of which are particularly distinguished.

Williams & Humbert ★★→

Nuño del Canas 1, Jerez de la Frontera. Tel (56) 331300. Founded 1876. V'yds: 218 ha. Stock: 48,000 butts. Additional brands: As You Like It Finest Sweet Sherry; A Winter's Tale Rare Old Amontillado; Canasta Cream Oloroso; Dos Cortados Oloroso; Dry Sack Medium-Dry; Pando Fino; Walnut Brown Sweet Sherry. Visits: weekdays 12–1.30.
The firm derives its name from those of Alexander Williams and his wife, Amy Humbert. He was a clerk working for WISDOM & WARTER in Jerez when he met Amy, who had come to visit friends in the town. The costs of married life were too much for his salary to bear and when his employers rejected the idea of a partnership, he decided to set up his own *bodega* with the help of his father-in-law. That was in 1876. In the following year he introduced Pando Fino to the British market, with considerable success (the name comes from a local farmer and not from the P&O shipping line as is sometimes suggested). Dry Sack, the most familiar name in the Williams & Humbert portfolio, dates back to 1906. The bottle is

famous for being packed with a sacking cover.

The Williams & Humbert *bodega* is also home to a fine stud of horses, which are used in the local races. It was also – until the post was abolished, in 1979 – the office used by British Vice-Consuls in Jerez: the room in which they worked is lovingly preserved.

The firm became a public company on the London Stock Market nicely in time for its shares to be bought by the Rumasa combine in the 1970s. It was expropriated by the government when this empire collapsed, but returned to private ownership when it was purchased by ANTONIO BARBADILLO.

The range of sherries from Williams & Humbert is considerable and a number rejoice in names from Shakespeare's plays. There is something curiously old-fashioned and homely about the sound of the As You Like It and A Winter's Tale. As a whole, the range tends towards sweetness and heaviness, with Dry Sack a typical example: a full *amontillado* that has been sweetened with Pedro Ximénez. The best wine is probably Dos Cortados, a *palo cortado* of some elegance.

Wisdom & Warter ★★
Pizarro 7, 11402 Jerez de la Frontera. Tel (56) 184306. Founded 1854. V'yds: 70 ha. Stock: 20,000 butts. Additional brands: Amontillado Royal Palace; Fino Olivar; La Guapa Manzanilla; Oloroso Mercedor; Tizon; Very Rare Solera; Viale; Wisdom's Choice; Wisdom's Manzanilla, Amontillado. Visits: weekdays at 11, 12.30 and 1.45.

The firm started with a tragedy: Henry Wisdom's elder brother, a wine merchant of Jerez, was drowned at sea, leaving behind considerable stocks of sherry. Henry then went into partnership with Joseph Warter and the business prospered quickly. It ranked tenth in the shipping list only six years after it was founded, and *Punch* magazine coined the slogan: 'Warter makes the wine and Wisdom sells it'. Although the death of Henry Wisdom ended the original families' connections with the firm, it was still an independent company until it became a subsidiary of GONZALEZ BYASS, although the *bodegas* (and the style of the wines) continue to be kept separate.

It is not a particularly exciting range, although certainly a wide one. The wines which go out under the Wisdom & Warter label (rather than simply Wisdom) are the better ones, especially La Guapa Manzanilla, Fino Olivar or the intensely sweet Pedro Ximénez. Wisdom's Amontillado is not too sweet and has a firm dryness that is attractive.

Other Sherry Producers

José Bustamente; Cuvillo y Cía; M Gil Galán; H de R Pérez Megia; Portalto; Bodegas Rayón; Rafael Reig y Cía; Pedro Romero; Bodegas San Cayetano; Bodegas Sánchez de Alva; Manuel Sánchez Ayala; Valderrama SA; Francisco García de Velasco.

Málaga

Málaga is a wine that saw fame and success snatched from it by a whim of nature, and has never found them again. The region itself (*see* map, pages 84-85) was the first area of Spain to be affected, and ruined, by phylloxera, in 1876, and since that time its wine has never recovered its position as one of the favoured fortified wines on the British and American markets, and it has completely lost its other market, Eastern Europe.

With today's growing interest in fortified wines, Málaga should be making a recovery, but economic pressures of a different kind are precluding that. The wine is produced in the hinterland behind the Costa del Sol, and, as any property developer will tell you, a vineyard does not offer much return on capital in comparison to a high-rise hotel or an apartment block.

There are now 16,000 hectares of vineyard in the Málaga denominated region, or DO (the equivalent of France's *appellation contrôlée*), but of those only 3,000 hectares are planted with vines for wine – the rest produce table grapes. It is a far cry from the time just before phylloxera, when 70,000 hectares were under vine and 175,000 hectolitres were produced annually (today's figure is only 82,000 hectolitres).

How Málaga is Made

The Málaga vineyards are concentrated in two small areas away from the coastal town of Málaga itself. The Moscatel (Muscat of Alexandria), one of the two major grape varieties used in the wine, is grown in the steep, coastal region of Axarquia, southeast of the town, where there is a moist but not too hot Mediterranean climate. This is now only a tiny vineyard region and many more vines for Málaga are to be found in new vineyards inland from Fuengirola and beyond the coastal hills on the plateau of Antequera. This plateau is searingly hot, an ideal growing area for Pedro Ximénez (PX), the other main grape variety used. However, up to ten percent of the wine can derive from outside the Málaga area (usually in the form of PX from the region of Montilla, to the west).

In most cases, the wine is made at the vineyard and then taken to wineries in Málaga for maturation. Fermentation takes place in large, earthenware jars, called *tinajas*, rather like Ali Baba jars. (The same type is used for Montilla-Moriles.) There is little of interest to see at the Málaga wineries today – many of the old premises have been taken over by tourists, and the wine companies have often moved out to industrial estates. But, by law, Málaga has to be matured in Málaga – and there is a good reason behind this, not simply bureaucratic mumbo-jumbo. The reason is that the moist air by the sea is better for slow maturation than the hot, dry air found inland – a factor also taken into account in the port-making.

Like sherry and port, Málaga is a blended and of course a fortified wine. But in one particular respect it is similar to Marsala. Both Málaga and Marsala have various concoctions of must and partially-fortified grape concentrates or syrups added to them to lend complexity and flavour.

The addition of these concentrates usually takes place before maturation starts, although it can take place after maturation if the producer prefers. There are five different additives:

Arrope A caramelized concentrate made from boiled grape juice that has been reduced to a third of its original volume.

Mistela Grape juice which has been fortified up to 13 percent to prevent fermentation.

Vino de color A further concentration of the *arrope*.

Vino maestro Grape juice fortified to 7 percent with wine alcohol before being fermented up to 16 percent.

Vino tierno A very sweet wine made from grapes that have been dried in the sun after the harvest and then partly fermented, before being fortified with alcohol up to 16 percent.

Maturation takes place in the cool of the *bodegas*, initially in large chestnut vats (*conos*) and then, after blending, in smaller, American oak casks (known as butts). Wine alcohol is added to bring the strength of the wine up to the level appropriate for the style being made. The quality of the wine depends on the length of maturation, although the rules of the *denominación de origen* (DO) of Málaga state that the minimum period in cask must be two years.

While less expensive Málaga will simply stay in cask for the required period of time, better wines go through a *solera* system (usually in six stages) (*see* Sherry, pages 89-90). In addition, some producers have butts containing very old wines, that are added to the *solera* or used as an ingredient in the final blend.

Styles of Málaga

There are a number of different styles of Málaga, which depend on the sweetness of the wine, its colour, the type of grape must used and the method of production.

Dulce Sweet Málaga.

Pajarete Medium-sweet Málaga.

Seco Málaga made from fully-fermented Pedro Ximénez grapes.

Dulce color This style contains a significant amount of *vino de color*, that gives the the wine richness, sweetness and a deep, almost black, colour.

Moscatel A style made 100 percent from Moscatel grapes.

Pedro Ximén Málaga made 100 percent from Pedro Ximénez. Other styles can be a mixture of this grape and the Moscatel.

Lágrima The top style of Málaga. The name, which means 'tears', refers to the fact that originally this wine was made only from the juice that oozed from grapes as they hung to dry. Since this method of obtaining juice is not only haphazard but also, today, impossibly expensive, *Lágrima* is now made from free-run juice collected before the first pressing in the *bodega*.

Solera This style is often the pride and joy of the Málaga house. If a date is shown on the label, it indicates not a vintage, but the year in which the *solera* was laid down. A few *solera* Málagas simply use a date as a brand name.

The colour of Málaga can vary from *blanco* (white), through *dorado* (pale gold) and *rojo-dorado* (deeper red-gold) to *oscuro* (quite dark) and *negro* (a deep, concentrated black).

The History of Málaga

Málaga is one of the richest fortified wines, and one of the oldest. The word 'Málaga' is a corruption of 'Malaka', the name of a Carthaginian colony of the 3rd and 4th centuries BC, and it is assumed that vines reached the area at about this time, through Greek traders. It is also probable that the Moscatel grape was planted as far back as this period. By Roman times, the sweet wines of Málaga were favourites in the Eternal City, and this popularity was taken up by the Arabs when they conquered Spain.

Through the Arabs' knowledge of distillation (and therefore of how to make brandy), Málaga, even at this time, was a fortified wine: the first, together with sherry, to undergo this process. Somehow, despite the Koran's strictures, the Arabs managed to encourage the production of Málaga's wine while discouraging the planting of vines in other areas. It is suggested, in fact, that the wine became known as 'Málaga syrup' and so avoided any association in people's minds with wine.

After the restoration of the Catholic kings, in the 15th century, Málaga came under royal patronage, with a Royal Charter being granted it in 1502. Málaga's heyday, however, was in the early 19th century, when it joined Marsala, madeira and port as one of the fashionable drinks at dinner tables in Britain and the US. It was sometimes known then as Mountain Wine, in reference to the precipitous hillsides behind Málaga, from where much of it came.

But why did its fortunes not revive after phylloxera? Certainly the development of the Costa del Sol as a tourist resort has been a contributory factor, but that is a relatively recent occurrence, and other reasons weigh more heavily. At the beginning of this century, Málaga's extreme, unctuous sweetness probably told against it. Add to this the high cost of growing the low-yielding Pedro Ximénez, and the emigration of many peasants after phylloxera, who were needed to work in the vineyards, and you probably have the answer.

A more recent development – apart from the tourist-centred building boom – is the worrying increase in plantings of Airén (a dull, white grape, known locally as Lairén). This is the most widely-planted vine in Spain and indeed in the world, and has the advantage over PX of being high-yielding and reliable. Although, by law, it is not permitted in Málaga production, there is some suspicion that it is used – and it certainly makes a cheap, cheerful and highly profitable white table wine.

Málaga's time could come again, however. There has been a small revival of interest among British wine-lovers, and anybody who tastes a fine Málaga goes on to rave about this wine. As so often with wines that are unfashionable, it simply needs a few people to taste and appreciate them for our attitude to be completely changed.

When to Drink Málaga

Málaga is less versatile than some of the other fortified wines. Even the dry styles, such as pajarete (which is rarely found outside the region) or seco, are simply too rich to be good aperitif wines unless they are diluted with soda water or mineral water. The wine certainly seems to be most suitable at the end of a meal, or as a dessert wine (chocolate is often cited as a good partner for a dulce Málaga). It needs to be served cool rather than at (centrally-heated) room temperature – a cellar temperature of about 10°C (50°F) would be about right, although in hot weather Málaga is delicious even cooler, especially when poured over ice cream.

Visiting the Bodegas

A few of the *bodegas* are open to visitors, but most are in industrial zones or on the outskirts of Málaga. It is surprisingly hard to drink good Málaga in the town itself – lager seems to be the beverage preferred by tourists, but some of the better hotels should be able to offer a range. I do not know of any tasting rooms in the town – but I would be delighted to learn of one.

Producers

Hijos de Antonio Barceló   ★★→★★★
Bodegueros, Polígno Industrial, 29006 Málaga. Tel (52) 313500. Founded 1876. Additional brands: Anibal; Lágrima Bacarles; Sanson; Solera Vieja. Visits by appt.
A family firm, that has expanded from its origins in Málaga to become a major Spanish exporter, taking in wines from Rioja and Rueda, as well as from Venezuela, Colombia and Chile. Its range of Málagas is found principally under the Bacarles label, and includes a 100-year-old *seco solera* wine, and an 1850 *solera* of *lágrima*. It also makes two very fine varietal wines – a luscious Moscatel and an intensely sweet, old Pedro Ximénez.

Flóres Hermanos   ★★→★★★
Avenida de los Guindos 20, 29004 Málaga. Tel (52) 321576. Stock: 300,000 litres. Additional brands: Flóres. Visits: weekdays 8–1.
A medium-sized, independent firm making the sweeter styles of Málaga. Curiously reluctant to tell the world about its wines.

Larios   ★★
Avenida de la Aurora 33, 29002 Málaga. Tel (52) 322350. Founded 1878. Additional brands: Seco Benefique; Colmenares Moscatel Viejo; Lacrimae Christi. Visits: no.
This is the largest gin producer in Spain, and Málaga is very much a sideline. The contrast between the high tech gin distillery and the quiet, secluded Málaga *bodega* is remarkable. Seco Benefique is a

dry, nutty wine, while the old Colmenares Moscatel is a classic of its kind.

López Hermanos ★★
PO Box 178, 29080 Málaga. Tel (52) 330300. Founded 1885. Additional brands: Flor de Málaga; Kina San Clemente; Málaga Virgen; Sol de Málaga; Trajinero. Visits by appt.

An old-established family firm that appears to produce the full range of Málagas (including one made, they say, with Airén grapes). But the company's finest wine is definitely the Málaga Virgen, made from 100 percent Pedro Ximénez. López uses a *solera* system for its finer wines.

José Sánchez Ajofrin ★★
Cno San Rafael, Polígno Industrial 29006 Málaga. Tel (52) 310996. Founded 1924. Additional brands: Embrujo. Visits: no.

Besides the Embrujo sweet Málaga and a 100 percent Moscatel wine, this firm also makes local table wines under the Costa del Sol and Viña Tachín labels. Quality is average rather than good.

Scholtz Hermanos ★★★→★★★★★
PO Box 1052, Málaga. Tel (52) 313602. Founded 1807. Additional brands: Lágrima Delicioso 10-year-old; Málaga Dulce Negro; Moscatel Pálido; Seco Añejo; Solera 1885. Visits by appt.

This is the *bodega* by whose standards all other Málagas are measured. In fact, it is the oldest *bodega*, founded by Germans but now Spanish-owned. It has a *bodega* building at Mollina in the hills north of Málaga, but maturation takes place in a modern building on the outskirts of the town. The firm's most famous brand is Solera 1885 (not, in this case, the year in which a *solera* was laid down, but simply a brand name). This is a bitter-sweet, tawny-coloured wine, but still with considerable richness, balanced by a satisfying, dry finish. The Moscatel Pálido is intensely sweet. Seco Añejo is a dry wine, *amontillado* in style but with greater acidity. Dulce Negro is deep, dark and very sweet, almost chocolatey. Nearly all the wines are made with a *solera* system.

Other Málaga Producers

Antiqua Casa de Guardia; Bodegas Montealagre; García Gomara; Salvador López García; José Garijo Ruiz; Antonio López Madrid; Pérez Texeira; Juan Sánchez y Sánchez; Hijos de José Suárez Villalba.

Montilla-Moriles

High up on the plateau that stretches across Andalucía is the small white-walled town of Montilla (*see* map, pages 84-85). Just to the south is the tiny village of Moriles. The area that surrounds them is one of the hottest in Spain in the summer – and is not particularly cool in winter. It is also the home of what could almost be one of Spain's forgotten wines. In fact, huge quantities are exported, although most people think of it simply as 'poor man's sherry'.

This description is, of course, dreadfully unfair to Montilla-Moriles (usually known simply as Montilla), and even calling it 'sherry' is not strictly accurate, because it differs from that wine in one essential respect: it is not always fortified. In truth, if it were not for the fact that we drink it like sherry, it would not be discussed in this book at all. The reason why Montilla-Moriles is cheaper in Britain than sherry is not because it compares unfavourably with the other wine, but because the wine for the British market is unfortified and therefore falls neatly into a lower duty band. In the American market, where similar duty considerations do not exist, it is sold as a fortified wine.

There are great claims for the antiquity of the wines of Montilla and Moriles. Relics of Moorish rule are to be found in the earthenware *tinajas* (like big Ali Baba pots) in which the wine is still fermented. In more recent times, the wine achieved success – but remained in anonymity – as part of a particular blend of sherry. Until controls on sherry production were introduced, in 1933, Montilla-Moriles was regularly shipped in large quantities to Jerez to be added to the blending vats, although there was no indication on the label that such a thing had happened. The practice continues (legally) on a much smaller scale, since sweet Pedro Ximénez wines from Montilla-Moriles are often added to sherry as a sweetener, but it is still economically important to the region, with some *bodegas* existing on nothing but the trade in PX wines to Jerez.

However, when sherry production was regulated, Montilla-Moriles suffered at the hands of the richer Jerez producers. Since then, Montilla-Moriles for export has not even been allowed to use the term *amontillado* to describe itself, although the word means 'made in the style of a Montilla'. Nor has it been allowed to use the

The pointed outcrop of La Lengue – the tongue

terms *fino* and *oloroso*, unless the wine is fortified. So, in Britain, the wines are described simply as 'dry', 'medium' or 'sweet'. Small wonder that most of those exported go under supermarkets' or wine merchants' own labels rather than the brand names of the *bodegas*.

The Montilla-Moriles Vineyards

There are two distinct areas where the best grapes for Montilla-Moriles grow, both with a soil known as *albero*, similar to the brilliant white chalk *albariza* found in the best areas of Jerez. One is the Sierra de Montilla, the other is nearer the village of Moriles, in an area called Moriles Alto (or Moriles Albero). About a fifth of the grapes for Montilla-Moriles comes from this chalk soil, generally for the dry wines. The rest comes from vines growing in sandy *ruedos* soil at the foot of the Sierra. Some 16,000 hectares are currently under vine, all in the province of Córdoba.

The predominant grape is the Pedro Ximénez. This grows

much better in Córdoba than in Jerez, hence the demand for Montilla-Moriles PX wine there (and also in Málaga). But unlike the wine destined for Jerez, that intended for Montilla-Moriles is fermented until dry. The resulting wine has a natural alcohol level of at least 13 percent, the hot summers having ensured that the grapes have a high sugar content. For this reason there is no need to fortify the wine. Other grape varieties are grown in small quantities. These include the Lairén (La Mancha's Airén grape), the Moscatel (Muscat of Alexandria), the Baladí (a grape that does not appear to occur elsewhere) and the Torrentes.

How Montilla-Moriles is Made

Production closely follows the pattern of sherry (*see* Sherry, pages 87-90). A major initial difference, however, is that Montilla-Moriles wines still go through their second fermentation in *tinajas*, the traditional, earthenware jars also found in Málaga. These are left open at the top during fermentation to prevent them from breaking. Walkways of planks are constructed at the level of the jars' necks so that the openings can be reached. The first fermentation, however, now takes place in either stainless steel or concrete tanks, both a recent innovation in the area.

Once fermentation is complete, the wines are classified according to their potential for growing *flor*. The classification system is similar to that used in Jerez (*see* Sherry, pages 88). *Flor* grows naturally on Montilla-Moriles wines, just as it does on sherry. Those intended for sweeter styles are prevented from developing this yeasty layer by being poured into butts until they are completely full so that there is no surface for the *flor* to develop on. A *solera* system is then used, similar to that of Jerez. The wine usually goes through four *criaderas* (or nursery stages) before reaching the final cask, the *solera* proper. For markets other than Britain, the wines will be fortified before shipping.

As in the case of sherry, there are two basic styles: *fino* (dry) and *oloroso* (sweet). The 'medium' style of Montilla-Moriles is usually a wine sweetened with Pedro Ximénez.

The Montilla-Moriles region does not produce the equivalent

of the great sherries, and it would be wrong to pretend that this is great wine country. But compared with some of the really cheap sherry that can easily be found, Montilla-Moriles is an acceptable and well-made wine, and with the introduction of modern *bodega* techniques it is getting better all the time.

Most of the wine is sold either as a Montilla or as a blend of Montilla and Moriles. Only rarely on the export markets is Moriles sold unblended, although it is available in Spain in distinctive, dark brown bottles (all the other Montilla-Moriles wines come in standard sherry-type bottles). The Moriles wines tend to be softer and lighter than those of Montilla.

Both wines should be treated in exactly the same way as sherry. Drink the dry style chilled as an aperitif or as an accompaniment to fish. In nearby towns such as Córdoba, and in Madrid, the dry style is sold in bars by the half bottle to drink with snacks. The sweeter styles are for more general consumption: at cocktail parties, on a cold evening or, again, as an aperitif.

Visiting the Bodegas

A number of *bodegas* are open to the public and they are definitely worth visiting, if only to see the rows of *tinajas*, full of *flor*-covered wine. Montilla-Moriles *bodegas* tend to be even more friendly than those of Jerez – after all they receive fewer visitors.

Producers

Alvear   →★★★
Avenida María Auxiliadora 1, E-14550 Montilla. Tel (57) 650100. Founded 1729. V'yds: 125 ha. Stock: 20 million litres. Additional brands: Fino CB; Fino Festival; Oloroso Asunción; Oloroso Pelayo. Visits: weekdays 9–12.
Almost certainly the oldest *bodega* in Montilla and one of the best, Alvear is also the biggest and most modern. All of this is good news for the wines, which are some of the cleanest and freshest coming

out of the region. I particularly like the Fino CB (the biggest-selling Montilla-Moriles in Spain), which has really pungent, tangy flavours, and the rich and not too sweet Oloroso Asunción.

Pérez Barquero ★★
Avenida de Andalucía 27, Montilla. Tel (57) 650500. V'yds: 100 ha. Stock: 8 million litres. Additional brands: Los Amigos; Barquero; Dos Reinos Superior Dry; Los Palcos; Solera 12. Visits by appt.

One of the two *bodegas* in Montilla that were part of the Rumasa group – and its collapse (*see* Sherry, pages 98). It has now been bought by local businessmen and things are looking up. I have sampled, and enjoyed, the Dos Reinos, with its bone-dry taste and dry, nutty finish.

Carbonell ★★→
Cira Aguilár-Puente Genil, Aguilár de la Frontera. Tel (57) 660643. Founded 1866. Additional brands: Flor de Montilla; Monte Corto; Moriles Serranío; Moriles Superior; Nectar. Visits: weekdays 8–1.

Almost as well known for olive oil as for wine, this *bodega* produces some very good *fino* styles. Moriles Serranío and Monte Corto are young, fresh wines; Moriles Superior is a *fino amontillado* (a *fino* that has almost become an *amontillado*). Flor de Montilla is a dry *amontillado* style. This is one of the few firms whose *bodegas* are not in Montilla itself but a few miles to the south of the town.

Compañía Vinícola del Sur ★→
Burguéo 5, Montilla. Tel (57) 650504. V'yds: 100 ha. Stock: 5 million litres. Additional brands: Don Enrico; Monte Cristo; Santa Amalia; Vinsur. Visits by appt.

The other formerly Rumasa-owned *bodega* (*see* Pérez Barquero). The brand name Monte Cristo was bought by Rumasa from the original producers of a Cyprus sherry and used for the leading export Montilla-Moriles. The wines have never been very exciting and it will be interesting to see how the new owners – local businessman – improve the quality.

Bodegas Crismona
Caelle Baena 25, 14860 Doña Mencia. Tel (57) 676000. Founded 1904. V'yds: 70 ha. Stock: 4 million litres. Additional brands: Los Cabales Fino; Dulce Crema. Visits by appt.

A small family-owned company that is still run on traditional lines (except that it produces bag-in-box wine for the export market).

Tomás García ★★→★★★
Llano de Palacio 7, Montilla. Tel (57) 650235. Founded 1921. Stock: 6.5 million litres. Additional brands: Flor Montilla; Solera Fina 1. Visits by appt.

This *bodega* is now owned by CARBONELL but the *soleras* are kept separate. The quality here is somewhat better than at Carbonell, particularly the Tomás García range and some of the own-label supermarket Moriles wines I have tasted in the UK.

Gracia Hermanos ★★★→
Avenida Marqués de la Vega de Armijo s/n, Montilla. Tel (57) 477052. V'yds: 75 ha. Stock: 10 million litres. Additional brands: Fino Corredera; Kiki; María del Valle; Montearruit. Visits: weekdays 8.30–2.

There is a surprisingly high quality to these wines that sets them apart from others. They have a depth and flavour, and taste much more of the richness of the *flor* (in the dry styles such as Kiki) than other dry Montilla-Moriles. The fact that they are also more expensive is a reflection of their quality. Apart from the good, dry style, the firm also makes some richly unctuous PX wines.

Bodegas Lama ★★→
Aguas 2, 14860 Doña Mencia. Tel (57) 676012. Founded 1885. Additional brands: Fino Angeles; Fino Camarena; Fino Lama; Oloroso Viejo Menciano. Visits: weekdays 11–4.

A small company producing an attractive range, especially the *finos*, which sell mainly on the domestic market. It is still family owned.

Bodegas Luque
Molinera 3, Doña Mencia. Tel (57) 676029. Founded 1925. Stock: 2.5 million litres. Additional brands: Fino Imperial;

Fino Los Luques; Fino El Pato; Oloroso El Abuelo. Visits: weekdays 8–1.

A small, independent firm that buys in grapes. I have not had a chance to taste its wines.

Bodegas Robles
Ca Córdoba-Málaga km 447, Montilla. Tel. (57) 650063. Founded 1927. Stock: 2 million litres. Additional brands: Abuelo Pepe; Cream Patachula; Fino Copeo; Fino Patachula; Sublime Robles. Visits: weekdays 10–3, 4–7.

A family-owned firm whose wines are only seen on the Spanish market, especially locally and in Madrid. The Fino Copeo is a young wine, while the Fino Patachula comes from older *soleras*. Abuelo Pepe is a particularly rich, old, *oloroso* style. A Pedro Ximénez wine, Dolce Robles, is made from sun-dried grapes.

Vins Doux Naturels

Muscat de Beaumes-de-Venise captured the after-dinner imagination of a whole generation of wine drinkers. With its sweet, honeyed taste, it proved immensely successful as a supposedly lighter alternative to port.

I say 'supposedly lighter', because I suspect that few people drinking their glass of Muscat de Beaumes-de-Venise realized that this was a fortified wine, nearly as strong as port and certainly as strong as sherry. What they probably also did not realize is that this wine is just one of a whole range of fortified dessert wines which come from the great arc of vineyards stretching around the coast of Provence and the Midi in southern France.

Their pedigree is ancient. They were invented by a medieval doctor, Arnaud (or Arnau) de Villanova, in 1285, presumably making use of what he had learned of spirit distillation from Arabs in Spain or North Africa. He found that if spirit was added to a wine during fermentation, the result was a sweet wine that was very acceptable to an age that had yet to discover sugar. This experiment was tried on the Muscat wines of Frontignan to good effect – in fact Arnaud wrote to the King of Aragon to say that drinking two glasses of his fortified Muscat de Frontignan made him feel years younger.

Frontignan was almost certainly the first Muscat wine to be made. In nearby Mireval, Muscats are not recorded until the 16th century, while in Beaumes-de-Venise, in the Rhône Valley, it is generally believed by growers that these wines were not produced until the 19th century.

Further south, the Muscat of Rivesaltes, a wine based on the discoveries of de Villanova, had achieved a reputation with the papal court by the 14th century, at which time Grenache-based wines were also being sweetened and fortified here. A fortified Grenache wine was also made in Banyuls in the 14th century, this time by the Knights Templar.

Sometimes it seems that *vins doux naturels* (VDNs) have changed little to this day. The Muscat-based and Grenache-based examples are certainly the most traditional styles of wine to come from a part of France brimming with new wines and modern techniques. And

The Vins Doux Naturels Appellations

it is curious – and certainly reassuring – to see old casks of *vins doux naturels* maturing slowly next to stainless steel tanks full of this year's fresh, young white wine ready for immediate consumption. As for any other fortified wine, wood ageing is essential to a fine VDN, in order to marry the spirit with the wine, to remove any harsh edges and to give it a soft, rich character.

1. Rasteau
2. Muscat de Beaumes-de-Venise
3. Muscat de Lunel
4. Muscat de Mireval
5. Muscat de Frontignan
   and Frontignan
6. Clairette du Languedoc

VAR

● Toulon

7. Muscat de St-Jean-de-Minervois
8. Maury
9. Rivesaltes and
   Muscat de Rivesaltes
10. Banyuls
11. Grand Roussillon

How Vins Doux Naturels are Made

One of the characteristics of all VDN production is that vine yields are low; the maximum permitted is 30 hectolitres/hectare. This is brought about by short pruning, which leaves only a few leaders (or main shoots) on the vines for growth during the coming season. The grapes need to be very ripe at the time of harvest so that the must contains the required 252 grams per litre of sugar.

There are white, rosé and red VDNs. The grape used for the red and rosé versions is Grenache. Most white VDNs are made from Muscat (either Muscat d'Alexandrie or, more often, Muscat Blanc à Petits Grains – known locally as Muscat de Frontignan), sometimes with a little Malvoisie, Spanish Maccabeu (in the Pyrénées-Orientales *département* only) and Clairette.

Fermentation is stopped by means of a *mutage*: the addition of a neutral spirit of 96 percent proof. The spirit must be added in the proportions of 1:10 – that is, for every 100 hectolitres of must, only 10 hectolitres of alcohol may be added. The process of *mutage* produces a wine of anything between 15 and 18 percent alcohol, with a potential alcohol level of 21.5 percent. As a rough guide, the sweeter the VDN, the lower the alcohol.

The wine must then be matured – either in small casks or in vats. The length of time varies according to the *appellation*, but anything from a year to 30 months is usual, although wines made from the Muscat are sold younger than this. A further method of maturing VDNs, traditionally used, is to place the wine in glass demijohns and leave a gap at the top so that the wine oxidizes, rather like sherry. A wine matured in this way is described as *rancio*.

The Appellations

VDNs are produced in a number of *départements* in the south of France. Starting in the east and moving west, the first two areas are Rasteau and Muscat de Beaumes–de–Venise, in the Côtes du Rhône. The next clutch occurs in the Hérault: Muscat de Lunel, Muscat de Mireval, Muscat de Frontignan, Frontignan, Clairette du Languedoc and Muscat de St-Jean-de-Minervois. The greatest concentration occurs in the Pyrénées-Orientales, with the fine wines of Maury, Muscat de Rivesaltes, Rivesaltes, Banyuls and Grand Roussillon.

Rasteau Made from the Grenache, this wine can be either red in colour (effectively, tawny) or white (effectively, a deep gold). It can be drunk young, or aged in cask for some years, after which it becomes *rancio*.

Muscat de Beaumes–de–Venise Made from the Muscat de Frontignan, this wine must have an alcohol content not exceeding 21.5 percent. It is certainly the most familiar of the Muscat VDNs, with its honeyed, grapey, mouth-filling taste.

Muscat de Lunel This is a Muscat de Frontignan wine, coming from the area of St-Christol near Montpellier.

Muscat de Mireval This wine, from the Muscat de Frontignan grape, comes from a small area just north of Frontignan itself.

Muscat de Frontignan The stony vineyards for this wine run right down to the sea, near Sête in the Hérault. It tends to be a richer style than Muscat de Beaumes-de-Venise, the result of using late-harvested grapes. Nearly all this wine is made in the local cooperative.

Frontignan A red, Grenache-based VDN from the same area as Muscat de Frontignan. Not very common.

Clairette du Languedoc A white VDN made from Clairette grapes. Very rarely found.

Muscat de St-Jean-de-Minervois Another small area of Muscat de Frontignan grapes, at the northern end of the Minervois vineyards, makes this wine.

Maury Red and rosé VDNs from the north bank of the Agly river, in the area of Rivesaltes just north of Perpignan. The wine is produced only from Grenache Noir, from very low yields (24 hectolitres/hectare). It must age for two years.

Rivesaltes A lesser version of the Maury, but the biggest of the VDN *appellations*. Red, white and rosé VDN can be made from Grenache Noir, Maccabeu, Malvoisie and Muscat.

Muscat de Rivesaltes 100 percent Muscat wine from Rivesaltes.

Banyuls Red and tawny-coloured wines, made from the Grenache Noir, with a blending of Grenache Blanc, Grenache Gris, Carignan, Maccabeu, Malvoisie and Muscat. The Grenache Noir must make up 50 percent of the wine, or 75 percent if it is a Banyuls Grand Cru. The wine must be aged for 30 months. A Banyuls *rancio* is one that has been matured over a period of years in small oak barrels left out under the summer sun. The effect created is similar to a rich, tawny-coloured port.

Grand Roussillon This wine and the *rancio* version may be produced anywhere in the Pyrénées-Orientales *département*.

Styles of Vin Doux Naturel

VDNs can be *doux* (the sweetest), *demi-doux* (medium-sweet), *demi-sec* (medium-dry) or *sec* (dry). Inevitably, all Muscat VDNs are *doux*. Red VDNs aged in cask for a long period are called *rancio* wines. Some producers are experimenting with blending *rancio* and un-oxidized wines to give a wine not unlike vintage port.

Producers

Rasteau

As in many other of the VDN areas, the local cooperative produces the bulk of the *appellation*'s wine. Most of what **Cave des Vignerons de Rasteau** makes is very good and typical of the *appellation*. The other producer is **Domaine de la Soumade (★)**, which makes a very sweet, light-coloured wine.

Cave des Vignerons de Rasteau, 84110 Rasteau

Domaine la Soumade, Vaison la Romaine, 84110 Rasteau

Muscat de Beaumes-de-Venise

Again, it is the coop, here the **Cave des Vignerons de Beaumes-de-Venise**, that makes the most familiar version (★★→), with its lusciously sweet, fruit and honey flavours, balanced with a hint of lemon acidity. **Domaine de Durban (★★★)** has a softer, orangey-flavoured wine. **Domaine de Coyeux** is a big, new estate of 130 hectares, owned by a Parisian, making good, tangy wine (★★→).

Cave des Vignerons de Beaumes-de-Venise, Quartier Ravel, 84190 Beaumes-de-Venise

Domaine de Coyeux, 84190 Beaumes-de-Venise
Domaine de Durban, 84190 Beaumes-de-Venise

Muscat de Lunel

Lunel produces one of the least interesting of the southern French Muscats, but one of the best comes from **Château du Grès St-Paul (→★★)**. It has a nice balance of acidity.

Château du Grès St-Paul, 34400 Lunel

Muscat de Mireval

The local cooperative (**Cave de Rabelais**) makes a pleasantly fruity and honeyed wine, quite light in style, which definitely needs to be drunk young (★→★★).

Cave de Rabelais, 34840 Mireval

Muscat de Frontignan

By far the largest proportion of Muscat comes from the local cooperative, the **Cave Coopérative Vinicole du Muscat de Frontignan**. It is the only wine it makes, and is very sweet and rather old-looking: raisiny rather than fruity (★→). The coop's best version is the Cuvée Hors d'Age, aged for 30–40 years in wood, which gives it a curious, almost *rancio* taste that, for a Muscat, works surprisingly well. The only other producer I know of is **Château de la Peyrade**, which makes a much better wine, all honey and oranges and with a very perfumed bouquet (★★→).

Cave Coopérative Vinicole du Muscat de Frontignan, 34110 Frontignan

Château de la Peyrade, 34110 Frontignan

Muscat de St-Jean-de-Minervois

By far the best producer in this small area is **Domaine Barroubio**, whose Muscat is fresh, floral and fragrant, with plenty of light fruit (★★→). Others firms are **Cave Camman** and **Domaine Simon**.

Domaine Barroubio, 34360 St-Jean - de-Minervois

Cave Camman, 34360 St-Jean-de- Minervois

Domaine Simon, 34360 St-Chinian

Maury

Mas Amiel is the best producer. It makes a *rancio* version in glass demijohns, which give it an oxidized, burnt-toffee taste – very spicy and nutty (★★→). Another important name is **Cave Lafage**, whose small estate produces a woody, long-lived wine (★★). The local coop, **Les Vignerons de Maury**, makes some very rich wines, heavier but fruitier than either of the other two (★→).

Cave Lafage, 29 avenue Jean Jaurès, 66460 Maury

SCV Les Vignerons de Maury, 66460 Maury

Domaine du Mas Amiel, 66460 Maury

Rivesaltes

A number of cooperatives are involved in the production of this wine. **Cave des Vignerons de Baixas**, **Cave Coopérative de Fitou**, **Cave Coopérative les Vignerons de Lapalme** and **Les Maîtres Vignerons de Tautevel** are the best known. None of them makes a particularly exciting example, but the **Vins Fins** cooperative at Riveslates has the best. The private estates do much better. Good names to watch include **Domaine Cazes**, whose vintage wines and Cuvée Aimé Cazes are both full of fruit, the vintage tasting more of richness and ripeness (★★★). **Château de Corneilla** makes a very sweet wine – rather too sweet for my taste (★→). **Alphonse Duffaut** has a version with more *rancio* taste(★). Further *rancio* tastes come from **Domaine Sarda-Malet** (★). **Château St-André** makes a really delicious *rancio*, not too heavy but packed with raisin and nut flavours (★★), while **Domaine St-Luc** has a younger wine with orangey tastes (★★→). **Raymond Laporte** also makes a well-matured wine, the Ambre Vieux (★★). Other producers worth looking out for are **Mas de la Garrigue**, **Charles Noetinger** and **Domaine Ste-Hélène**.

Muscat de Rivesaltes

The best Muscat comes from **Domaine Cazes**, floral and with really fresh, citrussy fruit (★★★). **Jean Radondy** makes a fuller wine, but again with citrus overtones (→★★★). **Domaine St-Luc** is less exciting, but has some pleasant enough fruit (★→). Aphrodis, from **SICA des Vins de Roussillon**, is an evocative name for a rather dull wine (★). Of the cooperatives, **Les Maîtres Vignerons de Tautevel** makes a beautifully gold-coloured, elegant wine (★★) and **La Roussillonaise** makes a well-balanced wine with just the right richness and freshness (★★→★★★). Other producers include **Domaine Bellavista**, **Serge Bourret-Danot** and the **Vins Fins** cooperative at Rivesaltes.

Cave des Vignerons de Baixas, 66390 Baixas
Domaine Bellavista, 66300 Thuir
Domaine Cazes, 66602 Rivesaltes
Château de Corneilla, Corneilla del Vercol, 66200 Elne
Alphonse Duffaut, Banyuls dels Aspres 66300 Thuir
Cave Coopérative de Fitou, 11510 Fitou
Cave Coopérative les Vignerons de Lapalme, 11480 Lapalme
Raymond Laporte, Château Roussillon, 66000 Perpignan

Les Maîtres Vignerons de Tautevel,
66720 Tautevel
Mas de la Garrigue, 17 avenue Général
de Gaulle, 66240 St-Estève
Charles Noetinger, 66000 Perpignan
Château St-André, 34120 Pézenas
Domaine St-Luc, 66300 Thuir

Domaine Ste-Hélène, 66690 Sorède
Domaine Sarda-Malet, Mas St-
Michel, 66000 Perpignan
Serge Bourret-Danot, 66300 Thuir
Société Coopérative Agricole des Vins
Fins, Salses le Château, 66600
Rivesaltes

Banyuls

There are a number of good producers of this wine. One of the
best is **L'Etoile**, whose Select Vieux and Grande Reserve vintage
wines always taste of long maturation in wood. They turn distinctly tawny with age, but still manage to retain tannin as well as
having sweetness and maturity (★★★). Another top producer is
Domaine du Mas Blanc, an estate that has been in the same family since 1635, and where both old-style wines and a younger,
fresher style, called Rimage (★★) are made. Only about 9,000 bottles a year are produced, some of which are bottle-aged rather than
wood-aged. **Banyuls Templers** makes an intensely-flavoured
Banyuls Grand Cru, full of burnt and roasted tastes and with quite
a strong suggestion of spirit (★★★). Other producers are **Robert
Doutres**, **Domaine de la Rectorie** and **Vial-Magnères**.

Banyuls Templers, 66650 Banyuls-
sur-Mer
Robert Doutres, 66000 Cases-de-
Pêne
Domaine du Mas Blanc, 9 avenue du
Général de Gaulle, 66650 Banyuls-
sur-Mer
Domaine Vial-Magnères, Clos St-

André, 14 rue Edouard Herriot,
66650 Banyuls-sur-Mer
Domaine de la Rectorie, 54 avenue
du Puig del Mas, 66650 Banyuls-
sur-Mer
SCV 'L'Etoile', 26 avenue du Puig del
Mas, 66650 Banyuls-sur-Mer

Pineau des Charentes

The Cognac region does not simply make cognac. Travellers, especially in the area away from the main Cognac towns will often see signs advertising Pineau des Charentes. This is a sweet aperitif wine, produced in red, white and rosé versions. It is made by stopping fermentation of the local wine with brandy (which must be cognac) to create a drink which I find unexceptionable but which is nonetheless popular in the Charentes and elsewhere in France. Because it is made with brandy, rather than a neutral spirit (as in the case of the *vins doux naturels* of southern France), it is described as a *vin de liqueur*.

There is a romantic – if not necessarily believable – tale about how Pineau des Charentes was developed. In 1589, it is said, a vintner in Burie put new must by mistake into a barrel already containing cognac. He realized his error, noticed that fermentation had not begun and pushed the barrel into a corner. Much later, wanting to use the barrel, he looked inside and found a delicious, sweet and fruity liquid. Thus Pineau des Charentes was born.

The grapes used for Pineau are: Ugni Blanc, Colombard, Montils or Sémillon (for white); Cabernet Sauvignon, Cabernet Franc, Merlot or Malbec (for red and rosé). The proportion of wine to cognac must be three-quarters to one-quarter. Pineau has to be aged for a minimum of one year; Vieux Pineau will have been aged for five years in small casks. The older Pineau acquires a slightly oxidized or '*rancio*' character and is less fruity in taste than the young wines.

Most Pineau des Charentes is made by small-scale farmers, although one or two big firms have become involved in production, notably **Camus** with its Plessis brand and the **Unicoop** cooperative with Reynac. Other Pineau is made by the **Unicognac** cooperative (Monalisa brand), by **Cognac Hardy** (Extra Vieux), and by **Marnier-Lapostolle** (of Grand Marnier fame). Of the small-scale producers, **Gérard Antoine**, **Dominique Chainier** and **Domaine des Gatinauds** (the brand is called François 1er) have good reputations. Pineau can be drunk chilled or with ice, or mixed with fruit juice. The requirement that it contains cognac means that it can never be inexpensive.

Gérard Antoine, Les Annereaux,
16370 St-Sulpice de Cognac
Camus Plessis de Luxe, BP 19, 16101
Cognac
Dominique Chainier, La Barde
Fagnouse, 17520 Arthenac
Cognac Hardy, 142 rue Basse de
Crouin – BP27, 16100 Cognac

Marnier-Lapostolle, 91 boulevard
Haussman, 75008 Paris
Unicognac, Route de Cognac, 17500
Jonzac
Unicoop, Union Coopérative de
Viticulteurs Charentais, 49 rue
Lohmeyer, 16102 Cognac

There are similar drinks in the Armagnac region (Floc de Gascogne) and in Champagne (*ratafia*). But, while consumption of Pineau des Charentes is nationwide in France – and a small amount is exported – these other two are very much for local consumption.

Marsala and Other Sicilian Fortified Wines

Can Marsala ever pull back from the brink of total decline into a wine that sees only the kitchen stove, is flavoured with any number of curious combinations of fruits, and is hardly ever encountered in the context for which it was created?

Until a few years ago, the answer might well have been 'No'. But with the arrival on the Marsala scene of a few dedicated individuals, and with one of its biggest producers maintaining standards, all is not lost, and Marsala may once again be spoken of in the same breath as fine sherry, the wine to which it is most closely akin.

The Marsala Vineyards

As the mountains of central Sicily soften and flatten towards the west of the island, in the provinces of Trápani, Palermo and Agrigento, so vineyards take over. Great swathes line the flat, coastal plain that runs south from the city of Trápani, past the port of Marsala to Mazara del Vallo.

More vines are found in this area than in any other part of Sicily. And while much of the production – certainly that of the higher altitude vineyards – is of table wines, the vines on the flatter, and hotter, plain are destined for Marsala.

Grape Varieties

The grapes used for the standard, unflavoured, white wine based Marsalas are: the Grillo, the original grape and still seen as giving the highest quality wines; two varieties of Catarratto, the Lucido and the Opaco; the Damaschino, and the Inzolia (or Anzonica), which is a table grape. Recent DOC rule changes have allowed ruby-coloured Marsala to be made from the red Perricone (or

Pignatello), the Calabrese (or Nero d'Avola) and the Nerello Mascalese. (DOC, or *denominazione di origine controllata*, is the category of Italian wine into which Marsala falls. The term applies to wines from specified grape varieties which are grown in fixed zones, and are made by set processes to meet certain criteria in terms of flavour, colour etc.)

How Marsala is Made

The Sicilian harvest begins in mid–August, but if the grapes are left on the vines into late August and early September, when picked they will be rich, heavy, small and sweet, and make the ideal material for Marsala. Unlike other fortified wines (except madeira), grapes for Marsala's base wine should be overripe. The aim is to achieve a naturally high level of alcohol in the wine: 12 percent is the minimum considered suitable.

While most of the grapes are converted into wine, some are held back to make the two sweetening agents that give Marsala its special character. One is *sifone* (or *mistella*): a blend of semi–dried, raisiny grapes and wine alcohol (known as *buon gusto* in the local Sicilian dialect). The other is called *cotto* (*calamich* in Sicilian): a strange concoction for which grapes are reduced in heated copper cauldrons until syrupy in consistency and somewhat burnt; it is this additive that gives Marsala its 'cooked' character. When mixed together, *sifone* and *cotto* are known as *concia*. They are usually added to the wine as a blend after fermentation and before maturation, the varying proportion of each giving the Marsala its particular character and degree of sweetness as well as its fortification.

Styles of Marsala

Marsala is aged in wood for different lengths of time according to the style being made. These styles are now closely controlled by the DOC rules, although they still follow pre-DOC commercial classifications.

Fine The basic Marsala. It has a strength of 17 percent alcohol, and is aged for at least 12 months, of which a minimum of eight should be in wood. More *cotto* than *sifone* is used in the blend. The same style used to be called Italy Particular (or IP), since Italy was its main market; the initials still appear on the label.

Marsala superiore This style must be stronger than the *fine*, with a strength of 18 percent alcohol, and be aged for two years. The degree of sweetness or dryness depends on the producer, but more *sifone* than *cotto* is used in the blend. Traditional descriptions of these wines are Superior Old Marsala (SOM), London Particular (LP) – because it was the category usually exported to Britain – and Garibaldi Dolce (GD). Again, those initials still appear on the label. For Marsala *superiore* to be called *riserva*, it must have been aged for four years.

Vergine and vergine stravecchio The top two categories of Marsala. They are sometimes made using a *solera* system (*see* Sherry, pages 89-90), but can also be produced by careful blending of old wines, known as *lieviti*. They are always dry wines. *Vergine* is matured in wood for five years, *vergine stravecchio* for ten. The wine is made from free-run juice, fermented off the grape skins using a method called *pesta-imbotta*. Both are often unfortified and achieve their 18 percent strength simply through evaporation and concentration in cask. They never contain *sifone* or *cotto*. *Vergine stravecchio* is the only Marsala that must be sold in bottle, although most Marsala is in fact now bottled in Sicily.

Speciale The flavoured Marsalas are now no longer permitted to be called DOC Marsala, but must nevertheless contain 80 percent Marsala wine in the blend. However, with a classic sleight of hand, producers bypass the first regulation by indicating on the label of their banana-flavoured wine that it is a blend made using DOC Marsala. One for political pressure?

In addition to the styles mentioned above, other terms appear on Marsala wine labels. The colour of white wine based Marsala, whose colour deepens with age, may be described as *oro* (gold) or *ambra* (amber). Red wine based Marsala may be labelled *rubino* (ruby-red). The sweetness of the wine, which corresponds to the amount of sugar it contains, may be described as *secco* (dry), *semi-secco* (medium-dry), or *dolce* (sweet).

The History of Marsala

If ever a wine benefited from British experience in fortified wines, it is Marsala. It was created by two Englishmen, John Woodhouse and Benjamin Ingham, in the middle years of the 18th century, using local wines from the Trápani area in western Sicily – the region from which the wine comes today. To create Marsala, they employed the existing knowledge of the advantages of fortification to Portuguese and Spanish wines.

Marsala ageing in locally-made oak barrels

As in the case of other fortifieds, it was the original wine that first attracted the creator of the new style. John Woodhouse was selling pharmaceuticals to the Sicilians when he discovered the white and red wines of Trápani, and decided that they would appeal to English tastes. Quite why he thought this, history does not relate, but it is surprising since apparently the wines were heavily oxidized and extremely flabby. But we can be grateful that he did think so, because he then decided that the only way they could be success-fully transported to England was as fortified wines. He added 2 gallons of brandy to every 100 gallons of wine (the capacity of his barrels), and then shipped the wine home. It became known as 'Marsala Wine' because that was the name of the small port from which it was shipped, but by the Sicilians it was always referred to as 'English Wine'.

The next name to appear on the scene was Benjamin Ingham, who arrived in 1806. He was the first to require his suppliers to follow a series of rules for making Marsala, which included taking account of the quality of the grapes, when they should be har-vested, how they should be fermented and in what way the fortifi-cation should be added. The same rules apply, in essence, today.

The names of Woodhouse and Ingham dominated Marsala dur-ing its early years. They supplied wine to Nelson's fleet when it went out to defeat Napoleon in Egypt, and built up a roaring trade in England. When they died, the value of the Marsala trade was reckoned to be some £5 million a year – a vast sum of money for that time.

The Sicilians themselves were quite slow to come in on this suc-cessful act. The oldest Sicilian firm is Florio, founded in 1833. Others followed during that century, but it was still the English who controlled the bulk of the trade. It is said that Garibaldi chose to land at Marsala with his 'Thousand' in 1860 because of the pres-ence of British ships in the harbour; he rightly concluded that the troops of the Bourbon kings of Naples would be reluctant to fire on him in case they hit British ships. The rest of that story, as they say, is history.

However, the inhabitants of Sicily were probably less enam-oured of their new rulers when, in 1864, the first tax on Marsala wine was introduced by the Italian state. While it affected local trade, it did not kill off the highly successful export trade, still mainly to England, although France was also now taking a share. By the turn of the century, about four million litres of Marsala were being exported annually.

It was at this time that Marsala became as popular as an ingredient in cooking as it was as a drink. But success in one field brought about downfall in the other, because although there was a continuous increase in Marsala production right up to 1960 – when 45 million litres of wine were produced – the quality of what was being made went in exactly the opposite direction. From being a wine that could be used both at the table and in the kitchen, the kitchen took over almost entirely.

Marsala formed the base of millions of *zabaglioni* produced throughout the world. So much so, in fact, that enterprising Marsala producers designed special blends with egg – *all'ouvo* – as the base for this delicious, frothy dessert. This was not the way to create serious friends for the drink, however, and when fairly ordinary Marsalas then had cream, banana, strawberry, chocolate and other flavourings added to them, the time of Marsala as anything other than a frivolity seemed past.

But, finally, the Italians came to their senses at a minute to midnight. In 1969, a DOC regime was introduced, and although the 'cheap and cheerfuls' continued to be produced and sold, there was now, alongside these, a system that firmly set out different levels of quality. Further regulations were laid down in 1984.

When to Drink Marsala

With its various degrees of dryness according to style, Marsala is a versatile drink. While the *fine* style is better suited to cooking, *superiore*, *vergine* and *vergine stravecchio* are definitely for drinking. The dryness of *vergine* and *stravecchio* makes them perhaps more suitable as aperitifs or as accompaniments to the first course of a meal, although they can also be enjoyed in place of a tawny port after a meal. *Vergine* also goes well with quite strong cheeses, even the blue varieties. *Superiore* tends to be taken as an after-dinner drink or as an accompaniment to puddings.

Other Sicilian Fortified Wines

The island of Pantelleria, the most distant of Italy's DOC zones, situated just off the coast of Tunisia, is home to two styles of fortified wine, both based on the Moscato grape (the Muscat Blanc à Petits Grains).

The island is volcanic, and its black earth is highly productive. Vines are grown low and against walls to avoid the worst effects of the constant winds whipping in from the Sahara, across the water.

Moscato di Pantelleria Made from very ripe Zibibbo grapes (the local term for the Moscato), this comes in four styles, some fortified, some unfortified. *Naturale* and *naturalmente dolce* are naturally sweet and high in alcohol (the *naturalmente dolce* containing as much as 17 percent alcohol). *Liquoroso* is a version of the other two styles that has been fortified with wine alcohol. Sparkling versions are also made.

Moscato Passito di Pantelleria Made from semi-dried, or *passito*, grapes, which have been laid out on grass mats in the sun. It·comes in three versions: *naturalmente dolce* (at least 14 percent alcohol); *liquoroso* (at least 21.5 percent, fortified from 15 percent); and *extra* (23.9 percent, fortified from 15.5 percent).

Both wines are superb examples: rich, sweet, concentrated dessert wines, made only in limited quantities (about one million litres a year). Recently, they have achieved a cult following in Britain.

Producers

Agricoltori Associati di Pantelleria ★★★
Via Arenella, 91017 Pantelleria. Tel (923) 911253.
Additional brands: Solimano; Tanit. Visits by appt.
The main cooperative on the island of Pantelleria makes a good example of Moscato Passito di Pantelleria *extra* under the brand name of Tanit. This is a fortified style, liquorous, full of honeyed, caramel fruit and with great richness and complexity of flavour.

The cooperative has around 1,000 grape-growers. It also makes table wines and musts for blending. A sparkling Moscato *spumante*, Solimano, is also made.

De Bartoli ★★★★
Azienda Agricola Vecchio Samperi del Dott, C'da Fornara Samperi 292, 91025 Marsala. V'yds: 20 ha. Additional brands: Bukkuram; Joséphine Doré; Marsala Superiore Tipo Miccia; Vecchio Samperi. Visits by appt.
Marco De Bartoli is one of those innovators that every wine area needs. He has flown against convention in Marsala by making a number of unfortified wines of *vergine* quality. Vecchio Samperi, a *vino da tavola*, because it does not obey the Marsala DOC rules, is the best of these: a nutty, dry, *amontillado* sherry-like style of wine that achieves great finesse from long wood-ageing. It comes in 10-, 20- and 30-year-old versions. Joséphine Doré, also a *vino da tavola*, is a drier Marsala-style wine, with attractive acidity. The Marsala Superiore Tipo Miccia is superbly sweet and raisiny, made from very old *solera* wines, deep in colour and richness.

He also makes wines from grapes grown on Pantelleria. Both the Moscato di Pantelleria and the Moscato Passito di Pantelleria Bukkuram are unfortified wines with a naturally high sugar content, high in alcohol and intensely sweet – the nearest thing in Europe to Australian liqueur Muscats.

Curatolo Arini ★
Via Sappusi 15, Marsala. Tel (923) 989400. Founded 1875. Additional brands: Superiore Secco; Superiore SOM Dry; Superiore GD Sweet.
Table wines and Marsalas are produced in this modern plant, still family owned.

Tenuta di Donnafugata ★★★
Terre di Donnafugata, Via Mazara 73, Marsala. Tel (923) 999555. Additional brand: Opera Unica.
Rallo is one of the most famous names in Marsala, and although the family sold its name to Alvis in 1989 (*see* Rallo Alvis), it is good to see that it continues to make one Marsala under the brand name used for its table wines: Donnafugata. Opera Unica, is a *superiore*

riserva, rich and medium-sweet, aged in wood for ten years, and a splendid after-dinner drink. The Rallos also make wines from Pantelleria – the star is a sweet, rich and very concentrated *passito*.

Fratelli Fici ★★
Via Sebastiano Lipari 5, 91025 Marsala. Tel (923) 999053. Founded 1945. Stock: 25,000 hl. Additional brand: Marsala Martinez.
The firm sells wine under its company name and under the brand name Marsala Martinez. It also makes a full range of average quality wines. The dry Marsala Vergine, aged for five years, is certainly the best product here.

Florio ★★★→
Via Vincenzo Florio 1, 91025 Marsala. Tel (923) 951122. Founded 1833. Additional brands: Baglio Florio Marsala Vergine; Ingham; Morsi di Luce; Targa Riserva 1840; Terre Arse Marsala Vergine; Vecchio Florio; Woodhouse. Visits: weekdays 8.30–12.30, 2.30–6.
The oldest of the Sicilian Marsala houses, and owner of the two oldest firms: Ingham and Woodhouse (which it bought in 1929). In turn, Florio has been owned by Cinzano, since 1924, and jointly with Saronno (the producer of Amaretto di Saronno) since 1987. In 1932, it was the first to create a Marsala *all'ouvo*, not necessarily a recommendation, but certainly a shrewd marketing exercise at the time. Florio is still one of the largest Marsala producers, despite selling part of its cellars to the new RALLO ALVIS company.

The Florio range is one of the best in Marsala, and the firm is at the forefront of efforts to improve the wine's image. Its dry Terre Arse Marsala Vergine (literally 'land drenched by sunshine') is a classic, nutty wine; the newly introduced Baglio Florio Marsala Vergine, matured in small casks, is somewhat sweeter but with good, dry, wood flavours. Vecchio Florio, the biggest selling brand, a *superiore*, is certainly commercial, but good of its type. Targa Riserva 1840 (the year the wine was first made) is a sweet after-dinner wine. The firm also makes a fortified dessert wine, Morsi di Luce, from Zibibbo grapes grown on Pantelleria.

It continues to sell wines under the Ingham and Woodhouse labels, but these are of a lower quality.

Ingham
See Florio

Lombardo Marchetti ★★→★★★
Via Sirtori, 91025 Marsala. Tel (923) 951256.
A firm making some good, dry wines. The Superiore SOM Secco has a definite, cooked, burnt taste from *cotto*, and a nice touch of acidity. The Vergine is made from a *solera* system, it is light in colour, but has plenty of older wines in the blend – again, it is dry.

Mirabella ★
Corso Gramsci, 91025 Marsala. Tel (923) 951886.
A firm that seems to produce rather coarse Marsalas. The Superiore GD has a burnt, cooked character, but with a rather unpleasant, appley acidity to it. The Superiore SOM has a strange, chocolatey taste clashing with acidity, and rather too high a level of oxidization. Mirabella also continues to produce some rather sickly, flavoured wines, of which the almond is, marginally, the best.

Carlo Pellegrino ★★
Via del Fante 39, 91025 Marsala. Tel (923) 951177.
Founded 1880. V'yds: 500 ha. Stock: 10,000 hl. Visits by appt.
One of the most important Marsala producers. The Pellegrinos, already wine producers in the area, decided to become involved in Marsala production in the 1880s, and have subsequently developed exports as the main side of their business. Their range encompasses the extremes: from the high quality, classic, dry Marsala *vergine soleras*, to the frankly peculiar ruby Marsala, a recently-launched product that tastes like a failed ruby port. The Marsala Superiore Oro, golden-coloured and with hints of honey, is more attractive.

Rallo Alvis ★★→
Via Sebastiano Lipari 18, 91025 Marsala. Tel (923) 951037.
Founded 1860.
This is the successor firm to Diego Rallo. Alvis, a Genovese company, bought the brand name Rallo from the Rallo family in 1989, and took up residence in part of the Florio *cantina*. It has refurbished and renovated the former Florio premises in great style,

installed new equipment, and housed itself in a fine villa in the gardens. The firm makes both table wines and a full range of Marsalas, from a *cremovo* (egg-flavoured) up to some excellent 12-year-old Marsala *vergine soleras*. Standards are still good at the top end of the range, and the appearance of a firm such as this is an encouraging sign of revival in the fortunes of Marsala.

Solunto ★
Cantine Solunto, Via Sirtori 53, Marsala. Tel (923) 981511.
A cooperative making wines from large areas of the island, but also Marsalas, which are of average, rather than exciting quality.

Woodhouse
See Florio

Other Marsala Producers

Francesco Intorcia e Figli, 91025 Marsala; Sala Spano, 91025 Marsala; Fratelli de Vita, 91025 Marsala.

California and other US Fortified Wines

Table wines may be the modern success story in California and the other American wine-producing states, but certainly in California – and to a lesser extent in New York State – today's wine industry was founded on fortifieds.

This is less surprising when you realize that vineyards first arrived in California with the Spanish missionaries. Their vinous requirement was for sweet altar wines, and they planted vines accordingly. Grapes reached San Diego in southern California in 1796, and the red grape they employed then, the appropriately-named Mission, is still planted in the hotter parts of the California vineyard today. It made then – and still does make – a sweet, dessert-style wine, one with not very much character initially but which improves with a little ageing (something I suspect the Franciscan fathers were not very interested in).

Winemaking therefore started in southern California and moved north. It was the gold rush to San Francisco in 1849 that brought grapes to the Napa Valley to satisfy the suddenly increased local thirst. But the growth in vine-planting, and the greatly improved viticultural techniques, were followed by the scourge of the vineyard, phylloxera, a louse that destroys vines not grafted onto resistant root stocks. This is endemic in the eastern states, but did not reach California until the early 1860s. It effectively concluded the first stage in the development of California wines.

The second stage was short and ended abruptly with Prohibition. This destroyed the commercial wine industry and, when Prohibition was repealed, left it with no skilled winemakers and no knowledgeable customers. Repeal did however create a market for cheap sherry-style and port-style wines. And while these did the industry's image no good, they did at least keep it in existence until the table wine boom began in the early 1960s.

The variety that formed the basis of these cheap fortifieds was the Thompson Seedless. This table grape, upon which California's table grape and raisin business is built, was planted in the huge expanses of the central San Joaquin Valley, and its natural, raisiny

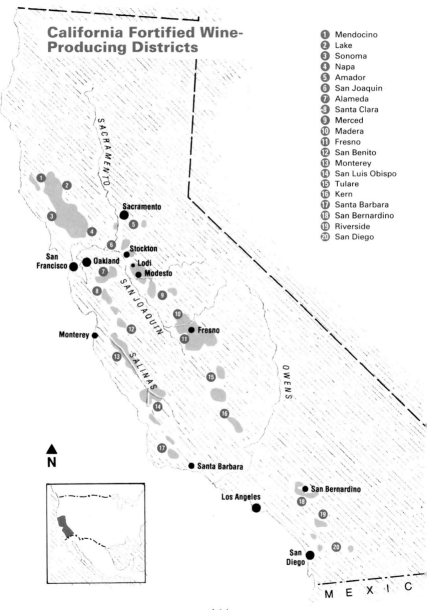

California Fortified Wine-Producing Districts

1 Mendocino
2 Lake
3 Sonoma
4 Napa
5 Amador
6 San Joaquin
7 Alameda
8 Santa Clara
9 Merced
10 Madera
11 Fresno
12 San Benito
13 Monterey
14 San Luis Obispo
15 Tulare
16 Kern
17 Santa Barbara
18 San Bernardino
19 Riverside
20 San Diego

qualities helped to give some of these early wines more than simply a sweet character.

But it is, in a sense, only since the table wine boom – which left sherry-style and port-style wines accounting for less than a fifth of wine production in California – that an increase has been seen in the quality of fortifieds and the development of premium wines. This has been particularly true in the case of vintage port styles, whose improvement has obviously been stimulated by a greater awareness in America of port from the Douro Valley. Sherry styles have fared less well, but even here there has been a growth of interest in the use of proper *solera* systems (*see* Sherry, pages 89–90) to make blends which can include older wines.

However, there is now another area of fortified wines, which may prove to be of equal interest. Perhaps in emulation of Australia, there are now a few producers making fortified liqueur Muscats, and to quite considerable effect. Muscat-based wines have already been employed in sparkling dessert wines as well as in some still California wines.

Where California Fortified Wines are Made

California does not exist in the perpetual heatwave that everybody watching Hollywood movies imagines. The wine-producing areas particularly are often affected by the cool Humboldt current, which travels up the Pacific Coast. The most dramatic effect of this current is in the San Francisco Bay area, where hot air from the land meets cool air from the ocean and creates fogs that roll inland up the nearest valleys, such as Napa and Sonoma. As a result, these valleys are quite cool at their southern ends, but become progressively warmer towards the north. The current has a similar effect on other coastal wine-producing regions north of Los Angeles – Monterey, Salinas Valley, Santa Barbara and San Luis Obispo.

The University of California at Davis (UC Davis), California's foremost institute of oenology and viticulture, has divided the vine-growing areas of the State into regions by 'degree days' (a 'degree day' is one with an average daily temperatures above 10°C

(50°F)). The regions range from the coolest, Region I, to the warmest, Region V. Coastal areas are placed in Region I, and are regarded as only suitable for producing table wines. It is not until Region III status has been reached that conditions are considered suitable for producing fortifieds.

Since coastal regions are the most affected by the cool, ocean waters (and produce the majority of the top quality table wines), it follows that inland areas will, conversely, be more suitable for making fortified wines. The bulk of the fortified wine-producing areas lies in the central San Joaquin Valley, a hot, baking but fertile trough that runs for 300 miles (480 km) from Lodi in the north to Bakersfield in the south. This is the source of California's basic wines (the 'jug' wines), of its huge crops of Thompson Seedless table grapes, and of its fortifieds. While some producers of fortifieds may have their wineries elsewhere, they will usually buy their grapes – or their wine – from the San Joaquin Valley.

Even here, however, the effects of the ocean can be felt in certain places. At the north end of the San Joaquin Valley, in Lodi, the mountains that line both sides of the valley drop away to reveal a flat plain that stretches towards the San Francisco Bay. Cool air can creep in here and distinctly alleviate the heat. So the northern end of the San Joaquin Valley (and the eastern vineyards of the Sierra Nevada Foothills) are in Region IV, while the hot southern end, beyond Madera, is in Region V. It is worth noting however that, while Madera produces some of the State's best fortifieds, there is an increasing interest in the potential of the cooler Sierra Foothills as a fortified wine-producing region.

Styles of California Fortified Wine

Although California's sherry-style, port-style and madeira-style wines may be labelled 'sherry', 'port' and 'madeira' in the US, in Europe the terms are protected and may only be applied to those wines from Spain, Portugal and Madeira. For export purposes, such California wines would have to omit the words 'sherry', 'port' or 'madeira' – but since none is exported, the problem of what to label them instead does not arise.

Sherry-style wine There are two basic types of sherry-style wine. The first is a barely dry style, usually called 'dry'; the second is a much sweeter style, called 'cream'. Essentially they are made the same way, with the degree of sweetness being governed by the timing of fortification. Typically, a wine will be fortified to between 17 and 20 percent alcohol, and then allowed to oxidize so that it attracts some of the character of Spanish sherries. There is no *flor* growth (*see* Sherry, page 88), but some producers of superior products use a *solera* system, which produces a constant blend including a proportion of older wines. Occasionally, sherry styles are vintage wines – a strange aberration and something that seem to contradict the whole idea of sherry and sherry-style wines.

The classic sherry grape, the Palomino, produces the bulk of sherry-style wines in California. Pedro Ximénez, the other sherry grape from Spain (where it is used for sweeter styles), is employed in blends to create California's cream sherry styles.

Madeira-style wine There are a few examples of madeira-style wines to be found. These tend to be dry in taste and red in colour, and to bear little resemblance to madeira proper. The grape used is the Zinfandel, California's most famous indigenous grape. There have been suggestions that it derives from the Primitivo of southern Italy, but this is not entirely proven. It makes big, sturdy, deep-coloured table wines, which can be elegant, but are often simply 'bruisers'. Its qualities make it highly suitable for fortified wines with higher alcohol requirements (*see* port styles). It grows anywhere in the State, but is probably better in warmer areas than in cooler ones.

Port-style wine There are about 50 wineries in the US making port-style wines. Well over half are in California, while New York State is the other major source.

California is the source of the most interesting port styles because, while the most widely-publicized changes in California winemaking have been in the area of table wines, there has also been something of a revolution here in port-style wines. The bulk of California's fortifieds have been made for a traditional, if declining, market, but the growth of interest in 'quality' wine has spread to fortifieds as well. A small – but increasing – number of producers is now making vintage port styles employing the traditional California grapes, Zinfandel and Ruby Cabernet (a variety developed at UC Davis to bring out Cabernet Sauvignon flavours in the heat of the San Joaquin Valley) and, to a lesser extent, Petite Sirah (the Durif of Australia). But a number of the more serious producers are now also using Portuguese varieties – Tinta Cão, Souzão and Tinta Madeira – as well as Cabernet Sauvignon, Shiraz and Pinot Noir.

Liqueur Muscats Orange and Black Muscat grapes are used for these wines, which are mainly produced in the area around Madera in the southern San Joaquin Valley.

Visiting California Wineries

Most producers welcome visitors to their tasting rooms. Since the fortified wine producers are widely scattered, you will probably need to plan a number of excursions, but the best areas in which to visit a number of wineries together are Madera, in the Central Valley, and Lodi, south of Sacramento. Take Highway 99.

California Producers

Chateau Julien   ★★→
8940 Carmel Valley Road, Carmel, 93923. Tel (408) 624 2600. Founded 1982. V'yds: 3 ha. Additional brands: Carmel Cream Sherry. Visits: weekdays 8.30–5; weekends 1–4.
The bulk of production at this boutique winery is of table wines, but when the winery opened, in 1982, it purchased an old *solera* of cream sherry-style wine, which was laid down in 1954. This forms the basis of the Carmel Cream Sherry, an old gold-coloured wine, soft with some nuttiness and acidity, even if tending towards too much toffee-sweetness.

The Christian Brothers ★→
**PO Box 394, St Helena, Napa, 94574. Tel (707) 9634480.
Founded 1882. V'yds: 486 ha. Additional brands: Golden
Sherry; Meloso Cream Sherry; Zinfandel Port. Visits by
appt (also to Greystone Winery, 2555 Main Street,
St Helena, daily 10–5).**
This is one of the largest firms in the California fortified wine business, and I do find its fortifieds of better quality than some of its
table wines, which can be rather dull. It is still run by a Catholic
teaching order – the cellar-master is Brother Timothy – and makes
quite a range of fortifieds, using grapes bought from independent
growers in the the San Joaquin Valley. By far the best fortified is a
vintage port style from Tinta Madeira, which is not nearly as sweet
as their basic ruby and tawny nor as heavy as the Zinfandel port
style. The dry sherry is not really dry, but is certainly more attractive than the heavy, sugar-water character of the cream sherry styles.

East Side Winery ★★
**6100 East Highway 12, Lodi, 95240. Tel (209) 3694768.
Founded 1934. Additional Brands: Handel & Mettler;
Oakridge Vineyards. Visits: daily 9–5.**
The best wines that I have tasted from this large growers' cooper-
ative in the northern San Joaquin Valley come under the Handel &
Mettler label. These include a light, tawny vintage port style from
Tinta Madeira grapes, and a successful Victoria Cream Sherry from
Muscadelle grapes (although, strangely, for a sherry style, it is a vin-
tage wine), which is in a convincing, dry *oloroso* style, with acidity
and nutty fruit.

Ficklin Vineyard ★★★→
**30246 Avenue 7½ Madera, 93637. Tel (209) 6744598.
Founded 1947. V'yds: 16 ha. Additional brand: Tinta Port.
Visits by appt.**
One of the pioneers of the new wave of high-quality port style
wines in California. Ficklin Vineyard started out with a bang with
its superb 1948 port style, and continues to make a vintage wine,
releasing it when it is considered ready for drinking. The firm uses
Portuguese varieties – Tinta Madeira, Tinta Cão, Touriga
Nacional and Souzão – to produce a wine lighter in style than a

Portuguese vintage port, but one that certainly ages over a long period like such a wine. Plans for the future include the introduction of a 10-year-old tawny port style, which is due for release in 1995. Ficklin is probably the closest that you can come to Portugal in California.

E & J Gallo ★→★★
600 Yosemite Boulevard, Modesto, 95323. Tel (209) 5213111. Founded 1933. Visits: no.
The largest winery in California – and probably in the world. It makes about 50 million cases a year, and in terms of fortifieds produces more port style wine than the whole of Portugal's Douro Valley. Colossal figures are always bandied about when Gallo is discussed, but the firm refuses to tell the world anything about what it does or how it does it. It produces some good, reliable fortifieds (as it does other wines and brandies), and has developed several new techniques, including a submerged *flor* process for a dry cocktail sherry style. Reliable, safe and well-made, Gallo fortifieds continue to dominate the market.

Greenstone Winery ★★
PO Box 1164, 3151 Highway 88, Ione, 95640. Tel (209) 2742238. Founded 1980. V'yds: 2 ha. Visits: Wed–Sun 10–4.
Founded by two teaching couples in 1980, this small winery, based in an attractive greenstone building, makes two fortifieds: a nutty, rich sherry style based on Palomino and Mission grapes, and a port style, made with high sugar content Zinfandel. The aim, especially with the port style, is for richness and weight.

Hecker Pass Winery ★→
4605 Hecker Pass Highway, Gilroy, 95020. Tel (408) 8428755. Founded 1972. Visits: weekdays 10–5, weekends 10–6.
Hecker Pass is a long-established area of wineries west of Gilroy in Santa Clara County. The Hecker Pass Winery itself, run by the Fortino family, makes a concentrated, stalky, quite tannic, fairly dry, ruby port style, and a rather vegetal, not very pleasant cream sherry style (which carries a vintage date).

Llords & Elwood →★★★
PO Box 2500, Yountville, Napa, 94599. Tel (707) 9448863. Founded 1955. Additional brands: Ancient Proverb; Dry Wit; Great Day D-r-r-y (*sic*); The Judge's Secret Cream. Visits: no.

Owned by Jay Corley of Monticello, this firm produces a range of sherry styles and port styles in a winery at Fremont in Santa Clara Valley, while its table wine business is conducted separately in the Napa Valley. Despite the somewhat twee names, the wines are very good: the Tinta Madeira-based Ancient Proverb port style has a good, tawny character; and if the Dry Wit medium-dry sherry style, made using an oak-ageing *solera*, is somewhat bland and a little too sweet, the Judge's Secret Cream has a good, mature taste, with a pleasant brown colour and some satisfying, raisiny fruit.

Louis M Martini Winery ★★
PO Box 112, 254 South St Helena Highway, St Helena, 94574. Tel (707) 9632736. Founded 1922. V'yds: 4 ha. Additional brands: California Cream Sherry; Golden Anniversary Dry Sherry. Visits: daily 10–4.30.

This family-owned winery buys grapes from Fresno County in the San Joaquin Valley for its fortifieds, while reserving its huge acreage in Napa for table wines. Palomino grapes are used for the small production of two sherry styles. I found the Golden Anniversary Dry, while being more medium-dry than dry, had some good, raisiny fruit and a nice bite from the spirit, while the California Cream, with its pale gold colour, was rather light, too sweet and a little bland.

Paul Masson →★★
700 Cannery Row, Monterey (museum and tasting room). Tel (408) 6465446. Founded 1852. Additional brands: Rare Cream Sherry; Rare Souzão Port. Visits: daily 10–6.

Paul Masson's winery facility is at Gonzales, but the new museum is the place to taste the wines and cover some wine history. The fortifieds continue to be packed in absurd, heart-shaped bottles that contain – in the case of the port styles at least – some surprisingly acceptable wine. The port style, made from Souzão grapes grown in the San Joaquin Valley, is firm, elegant and quite dry, with some tannin, but is perhaps spoilt by a little too much spirit. The cream sherry style is vegetal, sweet and, again, too spirity.

J W Morris Winery/Black Mountain Vineyard ★★★
PO Box 988, 101 Grant Avenue, Healdsburg 95448. Tel (707) 4317015. Founded 1975. V'yds: 150 ha. Additional brands: Black Mountain Vineyard Vintage and LBV. Visits: Thurs–Sun 10–4.

This firm was originally founded, with vineyards in Alameda County, as the J W Morris Port Works, and concentrated totally on port style wines. Now, while the move to Sonoma and the change of ownership have meant an increase in table wine production, the firm still makes some excellent port styles, now using grapes from its Alexander Valley vineyard. Zinfandel, Petite Sirah and Cabernet Sauvignon are used in the wines, as well as Ruby Cabernet. The general house style creates wines with a certain amount of dryness. Although some claim to discover Portuguese tastes in these wines, I find them quite green and stalky, and definitely at quite a distance from the Douro – although none the worse for that. The best wines are the vintage port styles, but the LBV port style, which spends four years in wood and is produced from 70-year-old vines in the Black Mountain Vineyard, is an elegant wine and ready to drink when released.

Mount Palomar Winery ★★
33820 Rancho California Road, Temecula, 92390. Tel (714) 6765047. Founded 1975. V'yds: 40 ha. Additional brand: Limited Reserve Port. Visits: daily 9–5.

This South Riverside County winery, 1,400 feet up in the coastal mountains, makes small amounts of a Palomino-based cream sherry style, and a Limited Reserve port style from Petite Sirah and Zinfandel. The sherry style is matured in an outdoor *solera*, while the port style is a ruby wine with some ability to mature.

Novitiate Cellars ★→
Los Gatos, Santa Clara. Founded 1888. No visits.

Although this winery, run by Jesuits, is primarily concerned with making altar wines, they do also make a reasonable *flor*-based dry sherry style as well as dessert wines.

Papagni Vineyards ★★★
31754 Avenue 9, Madera, 93638-8404. Tel (209) 4852760. Founded 1920. Additional brands: Finest Hour Dry and Cream Sherry. Visits: weekdays 8.30–4.

Angelo Papagni was a San Joaquin Valley grape-grower until he turned winemaker in 1975. While he is certainly producing some decent Central Valley table wines, he has shown what good quality sherry styles can be produced in this hot region if somebody tries. About seven years ago, he made two sherry styles, which I tasted then but have not seen since. The Finest Hour Dry was a very superior *amontillado* style, nutty, with some dryness and a good amount of acidity; the Finest Hour Cream was another classy wine, based on some old wines and again with a certain amount of acidity to balance its soft fruit and sweetness. They were two of the best sherry styles in California.

Prager Winery & Port Works ★★→★★★
1281 Lewelling Lane, St Helena, Napa, 94574. Tel (707) 963 3720. Founded 1980. Brands: Noble Companion Port; Petite Sirah Port; Pinot Noir Port. Visits: Mon–Sat 10.30–5.

Jim Prager is probably the only winemaker in California who has considered the Napa Valley as a source of good grapes for port style wines, and proves his point with some quite dry examples that have a definite ruby quality about them. I particularly enjoyed the Cabernet Sauvignon-based Noble Companion.

Quady Winery ★★★→
PO Box 728, 13181 Road 24, Madera, 93639. Tel (209) 6738068. Founded 1975. V'yds: 2 ha. Additional brands: Elysium; Essensia; Frank's Vineyard Port/Starboard. Visits: weekdays 9–5, weekends by appt.

One of the great originals in fortified winemaking, and with a very stylish, modern winery, Andrew Quady has not only made some very fine port style wines, but also virtually single-handedly inspired the production of fortified Muscat wines in California. He started off by making port styles, in 1975, and now produces vintage wines from two vineyards in Amador County. One is planted with Zinfandel and produces a deep, classic port style, with

Zinfandel's typical, slightly vegetal smell. The other vintage wine is Frank's Vineyard, (now also called Frank's Vineyard Starboard, since Quady reasons that if he cannot call his wine 'port' in Europe, he can at least call it 'starboard'). It is made with a mixture of Portuguese grape varieties, and is the more elegant wine. Both are aged in wood for two years before bottling (in the correct Portuguese vintage wine manner) and need some bottle-age before being drunk.

The fortified Muscats came a little later in the development of the Quady Winery. Essensia is an Orange Muscat wine, vintage-dated and sold two years after harvest. Elysium is made from Black Muscat and has a delicate, rose-like perfume and a magenta colour. Both are fermented to about two percent of natural alcohol and then taken up to 14.5 percent by the addition of brandy.

Rancho de Philo ★★→★★★
10050 Wilson Avenue, Alta Loma, 91727. Tel (909) 9874208. Founded 1832. V'yds: 2.5 ha. Additional brand: Triple Cream Sherry. Visits by appt.
Working in the oldest continuously-operating winery in California, Philo Baine makes small quantities of a cream sherry style in the Cucamonga district southeast of Los Angeles, in San Bernardino County. This is a well-balanced wine, not too sweet, with some *oloroso* character.

Santino Wines ★★→★★★
12225 Steiner Road, Plymouth, 95669. Tel (209) 2456979. Founded 1979. V'yds: 17 ha. Visits: daily 11.30–4.30.
This enterprising Amador County winery makes a vintage port style from a mix of Barbera, Zinfandel and a clutch of Portuguese varieties, of which the most important is Souzão. Vinified in open *lagares*, it spends 22 months in a number of large and small barrels before bottling. There is also a late-bottled vintage port style, vinified in the same way but then aged longer in wood. Both show considerable style, with a good balance of sweetness and tannin. The firm's Orange Muscat, fortified to 16 percent alcohol, is rich without being too heavy or cloying.

V Sattui Winery ★★★
1111 White Lane, St Helena, Napa, 94574. Tel (707) 9637774. Founded 1885 (re-founded 1975). Visits: daily 9–5 (winter), 9–6 (summer).

The only California madeira style that I have experience of, and one which shows very well. Made from the Zinfandel, it has a definite, burnt, intense character, considerable acidity and ripe, sweet fruit. The only negative point to this otherwise very convincing wine is a slightly raisiny touch. Sattui buys in grapes from the San Joaquin Valley.

V Sattui Winery, producer of one of the State's few madeira styles

Sebastiani ★★→
389 Fourth Street East, Sonoma, 95476. Tel (707) 9385532. Founded 1904. V'yds: 122 ha. Additional brand: Amore Cream Sherry. Visits: daily 10–5.
In this old–established, family–owned winery, they make a range of cream sherry styles, of which the best is the Amore Cream, a dry-ish *oloroso*-style wine, with good fruitiness and some nuttiness.

Shenandoah Vineyards →★★
12300 Steiner Road, Plymouth 95669. Tel (209) 2454455. Founded 1977. V'yds: 2 ha. Additional brand: Zinfandel Port. Visits: daily 10–5.
A rather mixed bag of wines from this Amador County producer. The firm makes heavy, porty table wines, and seems to repeat the heaviness – and certainly the tannin – in the port styles. The vintage port style is better than the crusting port style, having some Cabernet Sauvignon and Portuguese varieties in the blend, although it is spoilt by a vegetal edge from Zinfandel. The Zinfandel port style is rather musty, with too much bitterness from being in contact too long with the skins and stalks during fermentation. The Black and Orange Muscat wines, however, have good character and a rich, liquorous taste.

Valley of the Moon Winery ★→
777 Madrone Road, Glen Ellen, 95442. Tel (707) 9966941. Founded 1939. Visits: daily 10–5.
The Parducci family (which owns the winery of that name in Ukiah, Mendocino) makes a range of fairly standard fortifieds – port styles and sherry styles – at this Sonoma winery, as well as its table wines. Few excitements here.

Woodbury Winery ★★★
32 Woodland Avenue, San Rafael, 94901. Tel (415) 4594040. Founded 1977. Additional brands: Old Vines Vintage Port; Reserve Varietal ports. Visits by appt.
One of the new generation of winemakers aiming to produce quality fortifieds. Russ Woodbury's winery in Marin County, north of San Francisco, makes a vintage port style using Petite Sirah, Zinfandel, Pinot Noir and Cabernet Sauvignon, with grapes

coming from the Alexander Valley. Fortification is carried out using brandy made at the winery's own pot-still. The wine is rich, quite heady, but not too sweet and has just the right amount of firmness and tannin to give it some ability to mature. The quality of winemaking here has already excited admiration amongst port experts in Europe.

Other US Fortified Wine Producers

In New York State, two firms make fairly standard fortifieds. The Taylor Winery makes sherry styles and port styles from the foxy-tasting *vitis labrusca* (native American vines) rather than European *vitis vinifera*, and the wines' quality reveals the poor nature of the vines. Widmers Wine Cellars use a mixture of *vitis labrusca* and hybrids of European and American vines: the quality is no better.

Australian Fortified Wines

Outside Europe, Australia produces the most interesting and individual fortified wines in the world. Not only has it emulated European styles – notably port and sherry – but it has created two styles of its very own: liqueur Tokay and liqueur Muscat.

Where Australian Fortified Wines are Made

Fortified wines are made in virtually every wine-producing region of Australia. But some areas, of course, lend themselves more satisfactorily to the fortifieds than others. Some, like Coonawarra in South Australia, are simply too cold, but only a 100 or so miles north (close, by Australian standards) there is the fortified wine area

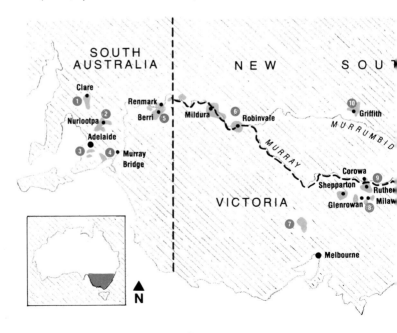

of Langhorne Creek and its neighbour McLaren Vale. Barossa Valley, also in South Australia, is the source of some fine vintage and tawny port styles, while Riverland, on the border between South Australia and Victoria, has been a reliable source of the cheaper fortifieds.

In New South Wales, the Hunter Valley and Mudgee both produce a few fortifieds, almost all port styles but with a few sherry styles, and there is considerable production of less expensive fortified wines in the Murrumbidgee Irrigation Area. In Western Australia, the Swan Valley north of Perth, the warmest growing area in the state, is most suitable for fortifieds, both port styles and liqueur Muscats and Tokays.

But it is in Victoria that the greatest fortifieds are produced, a fact generally recognized even among producers in other states. The stars of this show are the liqueur Muscats and Tokays of Rutherglen in the northeast of the state and in the neighbouring area of Milawa/Glenrowan. This area is covered in greater detail on pages 196-209.

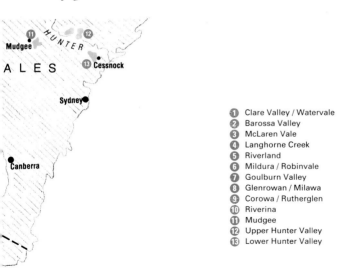

1. Clare Valley / Watervale
2. Barossa Valley
3. McLaren Vale
4. Langhorne Creek
5. Riverland
6. Mildura / Robinvale
7. Goulburn Valley
8. Glenrowan / Milawa
9. Corowa / Rutherglen
10. Riverina
11. Mudgee
12. Upper Hunter Valley
13. Lower Hunter Valley

The Australian Fortified Wine-Producing Districts

Styles of Australian Fortified Wine

There are three distinct styles of Australian fortified wine: sherry-style wines; port-style wines (both tawny and vintage), and fortified dessert wines.

Neither Australia's ports nor its sherries may be exported to Europe under those names. A tawny port intended for sale abroad will be described as a 'tawny'. (I do not know of any vintage ports that are exported.) The name 'liqueur Muscat' is permitted in Europe, but 'liqueur Tokay' must go by the name 'liqueur Muscadelle' to avoid confusion with the Hungarian dessert wine. Sherries tend not to be exported, but would go under terms such as 'dry' or '*fino*', 'medium', and 'sweet' or 'cream'.

Port-style wine There are two distinct types of port-style wine made in Australia. One is a tawny style, made, as in Portugal, by leaving the wine in cask for a considerable time where, while it loses colour, it gains the complexity of oxidation and wood flavour, and becomes a dry style. In Australia, it is also the practice to ferment the wines intended for tawnies for a shorter time on their skins than vintage wines, thereby also diminishing the colour of the wine. On the whole, as a style, these are more successful in Australia than vintage port styles.

Vintage wines, colloquially called VPs, are made in a ruby style. (Wines known as 'liqueur ports' are in a vintage style but do not usually have a vintage date.) VPs are younger wines than tawnies, made to age in cask, not in bottle. Many, especially those made with Shiraz, have a sweetness and a vegetal character that you tend either to love or to hate. Certainly, to my mind, vintage port-style wines are very much an acquired taste, and the public appears to agree, since the vintage port styles are losing out in popularity to the tawnies.

One of the major differences between making port in Portugal and making port-style wines in Australia is that Australian winemakers will decide what style of port they are going to make right at the beginning, when they see the grapes. In Portugal, the tendency is to wait and see how the wine begins its maturation before deciding what to do with it.

In the early days, port styles were made from very ripe

Shiraz and Grenache and tended to be soft and rather too sweet, lacking tannin. There have been three changes in approach since the Second World War. First, grapes are picked when less ripe and the wines are fermented until drier, which gives them a greater ability to age in barrel or bottle.

The second change has been a widening of the range of grape varieties used in port-making. Cabernet Sauvignon is now used, as is Durif (the grape known as Petite Sirah in California, and which in Australia is only found in Rutherglen). Similarly, the Touriga Nacional and other varieties from Portugal's Douro Valley are being planted more widely to make port-style wines.

The third change has been to the way the wine is fortified. The spirit used traditionally to fortify was a neutral grain spirit that lent no character to the wine, but took none away either. Now the practice – as in Portugal – is to use grape spirit, which produces a drier wine.

Madeira-style wine To my knowledge, this style of Australian fortified is made by only one producer. The madeira-style uses Verdelho grapes, and a considerable quantity of old stock is needed to achieve a blended wine with the right raisiny, luscious, quite volatile style.

Sherry-style wine This is the style on which Australia's wine trade with Britain was founded. It is also the style that has suffered most from the recent change in drinking habits. While the sweeter styles of sherry-type wines were popular, Australia could cope with ease. But its winemakers have found it more difficult to make really good dry sherry styles using *flor* yeast. Only by a few producers in Rutherglen, and a few in South Australia, has the dryness and the yeasty character of a true *flor* sherry style been captured.

Palomino and Pedro Ximénez, the grapes used in Jerez, have been used almost exclusively for Australia's better sherry-style wines, while Muscat of Alexandria (known as Gordo Blanco or Lexia, in Australia) has been used in the cheaper, sweeter styles. What winemakers lack here, of course, is the natural *flor* that grows on the wine in Spain (*see* Sherry, page 88). Although *flor* can be induced to grow, it never creates quite the same character as it does in true sherry. Moreover, the popular sherry style in Australia has been vaguely sweet and rather alcoholic, without any of the finesse or delicacy of the Spanish product. Only a few producers seem able to create the right conditions and taste, and those few are hardly encouraged to continue making their wines by a complete lack of interest on the part of the wine-drinking public. A pity, because those few good sherry-style wines exhibit a coherent style in their own right.

Liqueur Muscat With this style and with the liqueur Tokay or Muscadelle, we come to the heart of Australian fortified winemaking. Although fortified Muscats are made in the south of France, the Australian style, with its liquorous character and blend of old and young wines, is much more intense, while at the same time being less 'Muscaty'. The grape used is the Muscat à Petit Grains Rouges, or Brown Muscat, a small, red-skinned grape that imparts a reddish tinge to the wine when young and gives it a honey and caramel flavour, and a raisiny style. When these wines age in cask – which they seem able to do for ever because of their intense sweetness – they turn almost black in colour and develop some acidity, but remain remarkably fresh. Like the Tokays, the finest Muscats come from the Rutherglen and Milawa/Glenrowan areas of Victoria.

All liqueur Muscats are blended wines made in a *solera* system (*see* Sherry, pages xx–xx). While the less expensive, commercial wines consist mainly of young fruit, more costly versions will include wines of considerable age – even if only in minute proportions. Every producer makes a range of styles; the bottles may or may not have an age indication.

Liqueur Frontignac Simply another name for the liqueur Muscat.

Liqueur Tokay Although not quite as well known as the liqueur Muscat, the Tokay (or muscadelle as it must be referred to in Europe to avoid confusion with Hungary's dessert Tokay wines) is an even finer style, with greater complexity. The

Muscadelle grape produces big, luscious wines which smell of orange marmalade and are ripe, honeyed and smooth.

As with the Muscats, it is the age of the wines used in the blend that makes a significant difference to the quality of the final product. Some producers have wines of great age which they can add to induce considerable intensity and depth. To my mind, this is Australia's most interesting fortified.

How the Fortified Wines are Made

The use of wood for maturation is the secret of success in fortified winemaking the world over, and Australia is no exception. But one added advantage that Australia can give its wines is a high level of sugar in the grapes used, which frequently leads to wines with a natural alcoholic content of 15 or 16 percent. Interestingly, the introduction of Portuguese varieties for port styles has shown that they do not ripen as well here as the Shiraz. Those port styles that include Portuguese grapes in their blend achieve a greater dryness, and the high level of ripeness in Shiraz may explain why some Australian port styles have, in the past, been too sweet.

After the harvest, a fortified wine begins life like any other wine (although the stalks are often left on, to impart some tannin, which promotes ageing ability in the wines). The wines are fortified with grape spirit. In the case of liqueur wines and port styles, fortification is carried out to stop fermentation, while with *fino* sherry styles, fortification is often held back until fermentation has finished and the wine is dry. (In the traditional, sweet sherry-style wines, fortification was, again, carried out to stop fermentation and to add sweetness to the finished product.)

Then follows maturation, the longer the better for all styles, from the dry sherry styles, through the tawny port styles, to the luscious aged liqueur Muscats. All fortified wine producers have a vast array of old casks – old because it is not the taste of wood that is needed, but a measure of oxidization and concentration.

Blended fortified wines – the sherry styles and liqueur wines – are matured in a *solera*-type system, while vintage port-styles are matured in casks holding wines from only one year.

The History of Australian Fortified Wines

Fortified wines are not exactly new to Australia. Some of the earliest wines to be made, soon after the First Fleet arrived in 1788, were what the Australians like to call 'stickies'. And, during the years of Imperial Preference, Australian sherry and port were sent in great quantities by the Emu Wine Company back to the mother country, where they were consumed as one of the least expensive alcoholic beverages available.

Probably the first memory of alcohol that comes to mind for many Britons of a certain age is of consuming sweet Australian sherry at Christmas time, when anything considered truly alcoholic (as this, of course, was thought not to be) would never pass the lips of Great Aunt Mabel.

With the ending of Imperial (and later Commonwealth) Preference, when the United Kingdom joined the EEC in 1973, and with the Australian government's decision in 1953 to put a high excise duty on fortified wines, Australian fortifieds lost not only a captive market but also their low prices. Whether by luck or by judgement, this came at a time when the table wine boom was just beginning. And Australian producers, with a flexibility denied to their European counterparts, were able to switch to table wine production. The results of this change of tack are now coming to fruition, with a huge boom in the export of top class table wines, and a high per capita consumption of table wines in Australia (over 18–20 litres per head every year, according to recent counts).

So, the bulk fortified wine business has slumped in a relatively short time. In 1960, fortified wines accounted for 70 percent of Australian wine consumption: today the figure must be less than 10 percent. Although older Australians may still buy their flagons of cheap sherry- and port style-wines, the younger generation has turned away from such sweet, hangover-inducing substances.

But while that may have been bad news for the producers of such wines in bulk, the makers of top quality fortifieds have seen a resurgence of interest in their unique products. There has been renewed curiosity worldwide in the liqueur Muscats and Tokays – albeit, with production on such a small scale, this attention has been on a limited basis only. And a large spectrum of producers – from some of the smallest to some of the largest – makes a premium port style of which each is just as proud as he is of a Chardonnay or a Cabernet Sauvignon.

Visiting the Wineries

Virtually every winery in Australia, even the smallest, is delighted to welcome visitors. It may not have a formal tasting room, but the people will be happy to show you round, give you a sample to taste and entice you to buy: most wineries have a licence to sell by the bottle. Weekends are highly popular and the wineries can become rather crowded, especially those that are close to big cities, such as the Barossa Valley and McLaren Vale vineyards in South Australia, and the Swan Valley vineyards near Perth.

How the Directory of Producers is Organized

The directory that follows includes fortified wine producers from across Australia, except for those from northeast Victoria, who are discussed and listed separately on pages 196-209. Given the vast array of fortified wines produced in Australia, I have limited my comments to covering those producers whose wines are widely distributed and to those who have achieved a high reputation in their field. (The details of vineyards included only refer to land planted to vine for fortified wines.)

Producers

Angove's   ★★
Bookmark Avenue, Renmark, South Australia 5341. Tel (85) 851311. Founded 1886. V'yds: 104 ha. Additional brands: Bookmark; Paddle Wheel. Visits: weekdays 9–5.
Still family owned, this firm produces a full range of fortifieds, from

all the sherry styles, to tawny and vintage port styles, and even flavoured fortifieds. Bookmark is the brand for the 75 cl bottles, Paddle Wheel the one for the casks.

D'Arenberg ★★→
PO Box 195, McLaren Vale, South Australia 5171. Tel (8) 3238206. Founded 1928. V'yds: 4 ha. Additional brand: Nostalgia. Visits: weekdays 9–5, Sat 10–5, Sun 12–4.
Fine stone buildings, and the largest barrel – 40,000 litres – in the southern hemisphere, make this a popular tourist spot, only an hour from central Adelaide. Traditional winemaking methods and equipment, such as open fermenters, are still used for the fortifieds, which include a white Muscat, a vintage port style and Nostalgia – a liqueur port style that is very luscious and toffee-like.

Jim Barry →★★★
Main North Road, Clare 5453, South Australia. Tel (88) 422261. Founded 1959. Additional brands: Old Walnut Tawny; Sentimental Bloke Vintage. Visits: weekdays 9–5, weekends 9–4.
Together with some recent fine red table wine releases, such as the Shiraz-based Armagh, Jim Barry makes two excellent port-style wines, of which I prefer the nutty, not too sweet Old Walnut Tawny (although Sentimental Bloke is one of the best names for a fortified I could imagine).

Basedows ★★→
161–165 Murray Street, Tanunda, South Australia 5352. Tel (85) 632060. Additional brand: Old Tawny. Visits: yes.
The smaller of a pair of wineries (PETER LEHMANN is the other). Basedows operates from the more historical, stone-built premises, on main street Tanunda. The firm produces a sweet tawny port style, called Old Tawny.

Bleasdale ★★★→
Langhorne Creek, South Australia 5255, Tel (85) 373001. Founded 1850. V'yds: 11 ha. Additional brand: Pioneer Port. Visits: Mon–Sat 9–5, Sun 11–5.
This small family-owned winery is the only one I know of in

Australia to specialize in madeira-style wines. Verdelho grapes and some ancient blending material are used to make wines such as the 6-year-old, which has the characteristic acidity of madeira, but plenty of fruit and nuttiness as well. A full range of sherry styles, made with Palomino and Doradillo grapes, and both vintage and tawny port styles, complete this fascinating range.

De Bortoli ★
De Bortoli Road, Bilbul, New South Wales 2680. Tel (69) 635253. Founded 1928. Visits: Mon–Sat 9–5.30.
While the firm's table and dessert wine production has moved into the late 20th century, De Bortoli's fortifieds are firmly stuck in the age of the flagon. Large quantities of tawnies, vintage port styles and liqueur Muscats are sold in cellar-door sales to loyal locals who have drunk these wines all their lives.

Botobolar ★→★★
Botobolar Lane, Mudgee 2850. Tel (63) 733840. Founded 1970. Additional brand: Cooyal.
The Wahlquists are pioneers in organic viticulture in Australia and their methods certainly seem to help in producing concentrated red wines. This trait is also evident in the rich, full Cooyal port-style vintage.

BRL Hardy and Chateau Reynella ★★★
Reynell Road, Reynella, South Australia 5161. Tel (8) 3812266. Founded 1853 (Hardy), 1916 (Berri). Additional brands: Alicante Flor; Berri Estates Fine Old Port, Liqueur Muscat and Gold Crown range; Browns Bin 60 Port; Chateau Reynella Old Cave and Vintage Port; Hardy's Tall Ships Port; Lauriston Show Port and Show Muscat; Renmano Rumpole and Cromwell Port; Show and Vintage Port. Visits: Mon–Sat 9–5.
A combine formed by the merger in 1992 of Thomas Hardy & Sons and Berri Renmano. Both parties have made large quantities of fortifieds: those from Berri Estates are generally of the jug or cask variety, while those from Hardy are some of Australia's finest. Vintage styles go under the Hardy and Chateau Reynella labels – the Chateau Reynella wines being lighter and more elegant,

although the '75 Hardy vintage was a very great wine indeed. Hardy's Show Port is a top quality tawny port style, coming from old stocks, while Tall Ships is a good, mature tawny. Rumpole and Cromwell are simple, drinkable young tawny port styles from Riverland fruit. Sherry styles are still made, but, sadly, in decreasing quantities, although Alicante Flor, a dry wine, has plenty of yeasty *flor*, flavours.

Cape Clairault ★★
Henry Road, Willyabrup, Western Australia 6284. Tel (97) 555229. Founded 1976.
Small quantities of a vintage port-style wine are made in this Margaret River winery.

Chateau Tahbilk ★★★
Off Goulburn Valley Highway, Tahbilk, Victoria 3607. Tel (57) 942555. Founded 1860. Visits: yes.
One of the show-places of Victoria's viticulture, this ancient winery is just the right place to find a good fortified wine. Its Shiraz-based late-bottled vintage, matured for 3–4 years in casks that formerly held whisky, and then aged further in large barrels, is full of nettly, brambly fruit with quite a bit of spirit, but also a chocolatey intensity.

Craigmoor ★★→
Craigmoor Road, Mudgee, New South Wales 2850. Tel (63) 722208. Founded 1858. Visits: yes.
Housed in what is believed to be the oldest winery building in Australia still in use, Craigmoor – now owned by Wyndham, and therefore part of the Orlando group – produces a firm, quite tannic vintage style, as well as a liqueur Muscat which has some good, concentration.

Pieter van Gent ★
PO Box 222, Black Springs Road, Mudgee, New South Wales 2850. Tel (63) 733807. Founded 1979. V'yds: 10 ha. Additional brands: Mudgee Liqueur Frontignac; Mudgee White Port; Pipeclay Port and Muscat. Visits: Mon–Sat 9–5, Sun 11–4.

This winery is unusual in that 70 percent of the production is of fortifieds. I have tasted a selection over the years and, while I have liked the Pipeclay port-style wines, I do find that on the whole these wines are strictly commercial and not exciting.

Grant Burge ★→★★★
Barossa Way, Jacobs Creek, Tanunda, South Australia 5352. Tel (85) 633700. Founded 1988. V'yds: 10 ha. Additional brands: Very Old Liqueur Frontignac; Very Old Tawny Port. Visits: daily 10–5.
Grant Burge, owner of huge vineyard tracts in the Barossa Valley, the grapes from which are sold mostly to other producers, still manages to make some wines under his own name. There are a few fortifieds: the Very Old Tawny port style, made from Shiraz, Grenache and some Mataro, which is light and on the sweet side but still with some good, mature flavours, and a Very Old Liqueur Frontignac, based on red Frontignac and Muscat. This has a good *rancio* character, although it is lighter than Rutherglen Muscats. Sherry-style wines are also made.

Happs ★★→★★★
Commonage Road, Dunsborough, Western Australia 6281. Tel (97) 553300. Founded 1978. V'yds: 1 ha. Additional brands: Garnet; Pale Gold; Nine Year Solera. Visits: daily 10–5.
An interesting range of port-style wines, which includes a *solera* wine made from Portuguese grape varieties and employing blending material laid down since 1981, the year the first fortified wine was made at this winery. Pale Gold is a white port style, made from Sémillon, Verdelho and Chardonnay. The use of neutral spirit for fortification is the only failing in these wines.

James Haselgrove ★★
Foggo Road, McLaren Vale, South Australia 5171. Tel (8) 3238706.
I have tasted a pleasant, minty vintage port style from Haselgrove, made from Shiraz and Grenache, with good spirit and tannin.

Houghton →★★
Dale Road, Middle Swan, Western Australia 6055.
Tel (9) 2745100. Founded 1836. Additional brand:
Centenary Port.

From a company with a long pedigree, and many traditions, comes an attractive tawny port style, Centenary Port, which exhibits the virtues of consistency in such wines.

Lamont ★★→
Bisdee Road, Millendon, Western Australia 6056. Tel
(9) 2964485. Founded 1978. Additional brand: Navera.

Run by the daughter of Jack Mann, the legendary winemaker of HOUGHTON, this small winery makes a good vintage port style, and Navera, a liqueur fortified which is produced in small quantities.

Peter Lehmann ★★
Samuel Road (off Para Road), Tanunda, South Australia
5352. Tel (85) 632500. Founded 1979. Visits: yes.

A vintage port style from Shiraz grapes is made here, a good even if slightly too vegetal wine – solid and rich, as befits a production from the 'King' of the Barossa, Peter Lehmann.

McWilliam's ★★→★★★
68 Anzac Street, Chullora, New South Wales 2190. Tel
(2) 7071266. Founded 1877. Additional brands: Alberta;
Gallery Port; Hanwood Port; Hillside Oak Cask Tawny
Port; Royal Reserve Port; Show range. Visits: Hanwood,
Griffith, Mon–Sat 9–5.30, Sun 10–4; Mount Pleasant
Winery, Hunter Valley, weekdays 9–4.30, weekends 10–4.

This large family firm, whose main winery for fortifieds is at Hanwood, in the Murrumbidgee Irrigation Area in New South Wales, makes a wide range of fortifieds, from the basic cask ranges, such as Alberta and Hillside, to some classic examples of Australian styles. Sherry-style wines such as the Show range tend towards too much sweetness, especially the *oloroso*, although the *amontillado* has some nuttiness. The firm has good material for *flor* sherry styles, but the tawnies are its best port styles, particularly the Hanwood.

Mildara Blass ★★→
170 Bridport Street, Albert Park, Victoria 3206. Tel (3) 6909966. Founded 1888. Additional brands: Benjamin; Cavendish Port; Chestnut Teal Supreme Dry Sherry; Statford Port. Visits: yes.

The high production vineyards of the Murray River region provide the base wines for a range of sherry styles here. Mildara was in fact an entirely sherry style based company until the 1960s. Its dry sherry style is a good *flor* type. This wine was known originally as 'George' because it was developed for the company's chairman at the time, George Cato, who had a sugar free diet. The port styles are less fine, although Cavendish and Benjamin are good examples of their kind.

Montrose →★★★
Henry Lawson Drive, Mudgee, New South Wales 2850. Tel (63) 733853.

Montrose is now part of the Orlando/Wyndham group. I have tasted attractively perfumed vintage port styles from this firm.

Penfolds ★★★→★★★★
Tanunda Road, Nuriootpa, South Australia 5355. Tel (85) 620389. Founded 1844. Additional brands: Club Port Old Vintage; Grandfather; Royal Reserve; Samuel Port. Visits: yes.

As befits its position as Australia's premier — and largest — red winemaker, Penfolds produces some of the best port styles in the country. The firm can draw on huge stocks of old material — up to 30 million litres at any one time — and on the right mix of old and new technology to make a full range of wines. I have always found the tawnies here to be better than the vintage versions. The star is Grandfather, a blend of Shiraz and Mataro, light, clean, elegant and liquorous in style, with a strong underlay of old wines. The 10-year-old is bigger, with rich, mature fruit, and I never fail to enjoy the Samuel Port, made from grapes grown in the Murrumbidgee and again light and elegant. Vintage and ruby wines include Royal Reserve and Club Port Old Vintage. The sherry styles are left to SEPPELT (also in the same group).

Pirramimma ★★→★★★

A C Johnston, McLaren Vale, South Australia 5171. Tel (8) 3238205. Founded 1892. V'yds: 12 ha. Visits: weekdays 9–5, Sat 10–5, Sun 12–4.

One of the old-style wineries, as is fitting for a firm that produces some old-fashioned port styles, which can be very good. The wines here are in a drier, more Portuguese vein, even though Grenache and Shiraz are used. Three styles of tawny are made: a 5-year-old, an 8-year-old and a 13-year-old, the last of which has plenty of *rancio* character. The vintage port style is dry, rich and pleasantly perfumed.

Plantagenet ★★→

PO Box 122, Mount Barker, Western Australia 6324. Tel (98) 512150. Founded 1968. V'yds: 1 ha. Additional brand: Vin du Sud. Visits: weekdays 9–5, weekends 10–4.

One of the longest established wineries in the Mount Barker region, Plantagenet produces a good range of port-style wines, especially a vintage, made from Cabernet Sauvignon and Shiraz. Vin du Sud is made from fortified grape juice, a sweet curiosity, perhaps modelled on the *vins doux naturels* of southern France.

Rockford ★★★

Krondorf Road, Tanunda, South Australia 5352. Tel (85) 632720. Founded 1984. Visits: yes.

If Robert O'Callaghan (Rocky) is one of the characters of the Barossa, it is quite right and proper that he should make a fine port style, in his case it is a 20-year-old tawny, mature and dry, and including many wines of considerable age.

Romavilla Winery ★★

Northern Road, Roma, Queensland 4455. Tel (76) 221822. Founded 1863. Additional brands: Dry, Sweet, Semi Sweet Sherry; Maranoa Madeira; Reserve Bin Amontillado Sherry; Taurus Imperial Port; Timbury Hills Liqueur Muscat; Very Old Liqueur Muscat; Very Old, Old and Liqueur Port. Visits: weekdays 8–5, Sat 9–12, 2–4.

Half the production at this vineyard, in Queensland's Granite Belt region, is of fortifieds. A full range of styles is made, of which the older port styles and Muscats are the best. Taurus is a 20-year-plus tawny, made from Shiraz and and a grape the firm refers to as 'Syrian', which must be a relative of Shiraz. Romavilla has enormous stocks of old Muscats, which, while some may have suffered with time, do show a deep, dense and concentrated character.

Rosemount Estates ★★→★★★
Rosemount Road, Denman, New South Wales 2328. Tel (65) 472467. Founded 1975. Visits: Mon–Sat 10–4, Sun 12–4.
I have tasted a vintage liqueur Tokay from this ever-expanding Upper Hunter vineyard, which was ripe, with caramel flavours and some acidity, almost like a madeira in its burnt character.

Saltram Wine Estates ★★★→
Salters Gully, Angaston, South Australia 5353. Tel (85) 638260. Founded 1844. V'yds: 6 ha. Additional brands: Ludlows; Mr Pickwick. Visits: weekdays 9–5, weekends 10–5.
Saltram, now part of the Seagram empire, is the producer of one of Australia's premium tawnies, Mr Pickwick, which is made in a light, fruity style. The firm clings to a fine tradition of winemaking, with quantities of old wines held in stock.

Sandalford ★★
West Swan Road, Caversham, Western Australia 6055. Tel (9) 2745922. Additional brand: St Nicholas.
A liqueur port style and St Nicholas tawny port style are the two main fortifieds here, together with a liqueur wine called Sandalera.

Scarpantoni Estates
PO Box 84, McLaren Vale, South Australia 5171. Tel (8) 3830186. Founded 1979. V'yds: 3 ha. Visits: daily 10–5.
A liqueur Riesling – an unusual combination of an aromatic wine and fortification – is a speciality here. There is also a really rich, dark, chewy vintage port style.

Seppelt (incl Queen Adelaide) ★★★★
Seppeltsfield via Tanunda, South Australia 5352. Tel (85) 632626. Additional brands: Amontillado DP 116; Flor Fino

DP 117; Mount Rufus; Old Trafford; Oloroso DP 38; Para Liqueur Port; Queen Adelaide; Solero. Visits: daily.

Still Australia's most important fortified winemaker – and owner of the historic Seppeltsfield winery, with its atmospheric, wood-floored storage halls and beautiful stone buildings – Seppelt continues to make the country's best sherry styles by building upon huge *soleras*. The Flor Fino DP 117 has a true *flor* taste and aroma; the Amontillado DP 116, made from old *finos*, is dry and nutty, and the Oloroso DP 38, although sweet, still has an underlying streak of dryness and elegance that sets it apart from other sweet Australian sherry styles. There is also a basic sherry style range, called Solero, and a further range produced under the Queen Adelaide label. Para Liqueur Port is one of Australia's most famous port styles, but the firm's vintage wines are still somewhat vegetal in style. Mount Rufus is a sweet tawny. The excellent liqueur Muscats hark back to the days when Seppelt was a major player on the Rutherglen scene.

Sevenhill Cellars ★★→

PO Box 13, Sevenhill via Clare, South Australia 5453. Tel (88) 434222. Founded 1851. V'yds: 18 ha. Additional brands: Touriga Port. Visits: weekdays 8.30–4.30, Sat 9–4.

Founded by the Jesuits, and still run by that Order, it is inevitable that sacramental wines should still form an important part of production here. But in recent years table and fortified wines have also been made. About a third of production is of fortifieds, which include a range of vintage and tawny wines, made using both Shiraz and Touriga grapes. Liqueur wines from Frontignac and Muscadelle grapes are also made, the liqueur Tokay (Muscadelle) being a good example of its kind. There is also a good *flor* sherry style, made with Pedro Ximénez grapes.

Thistle Hill Vineyard →★★★

McDonalds Road, Mudgee, New South Wales 2850. Tel (63) 733546. Founded 1977. V'yds: 1 ha. Visits: daily 9–5.

The Robertsons make wine, as they put it, 'in a tin shed on top a hill with a magnificent outlook', but that belies the reputation their wines have achieved. The liqueur Muscat and vintage port style are classically – traditionally – made, fortified with brandy, and matured in brandy barrels. The port style is made from Shiraz and Cabernet Sauvignon.

Tolley ★★
30 Barracks Road, Hope Valley, South Australia 5090. Tel (8) 2642255. Founded 1892. V'yds: 14 ha. Brands: Cellar Reserve; Pedare. Visits: Mon–Sat 9–5.
Barossa Valley and Murray Valley vineyards are the source of grapes for a wood-matured tawny made by this family-owned company.

Veritas Winery ★★→
94 Langmill Road, Tanunda, South Australia 5352. Tel (85) 632330. Founded 1955. Visits: weekdays 9–5, weekends 11–5.
In earlier days, the Binder family seems to have made a full range of sherry styles and port styles (including Oom Pah Pah Port), but rationalization has left only a good liqueur tawny, made from a huge mixture of grapes, in which Shiraz, Grenache and Mataro feature largely, and a liqueur Tokay. Fermentation is carried out traditionally, in open fermenters.

Wendouree Cellars ★★
Wendouree Road, Clare, South Australia 5453. Tel (88) 422896. Founded 1892. Visits: Mon–Sat 10–4.30.
While at present it seems that only a fortified Muscat is made here, in the past I have certainly tasted a dry, raisiny vintage port style, that echoed the full-blooded red table wines made by the Bradys at Wendouree.

Woodstock Winery ★★→
Douglas Gully Road, McLaren Flat, South Australia 5171. Tel (8) 3830156. Founded 1974. V'yds 3 ha. Visits: weekdays 9–5, weekends 12–5.
A good tawny port style from Shiraz and Grenache is the major fortified wine here, based on well-aged material and with distinct fruit and nut flavours. Good handling of the old wines and careful blending produce a complex wine.

Yalumba Winery ★★★→
**Eden Valley Road, Angaston, South Australia 5353. Tel
(85) 642423. Founded 1849, V'yds 10 ha. Additional
brands: Clocktower; Director's Special; Galway Pipe;
Museum Release; Old Show Sweet White. Visits: weekdays 9–5, weekends 12–5.**

One of the largest Australian wineries still in family ownership,
Yalumba (owned by the Hill-Smiths) makes one of the widest
ranges of fortified wines in the country. Of the tawnies,
Clocktower, aged for four years, is a good, commercial brand.
Director's Special is quite sweet, while the 10-year-old is drier,
with some Portuguese Touriga Nacional in the blend. The
premium tawny is Galway Pipe, named after a former governor of
South Australia and aged, on average, for 15 years. To my mind,
this is one of the best Australian tawny port styles: smooth, nutty
and almondy. There is also a wood-aged Tokay, called Old Show
Sweet White, and an excellent liqueur Muscat.

The Fortified Wines of
Northeast Victoria

The fortified wines from two areas of Victoria hold a special place
in the hearts of Australian wine producers and drinkers.
Rutherglen and Glenrowan/Milawa, both in the northeast corner
of the state, almost in New South Wales, are generally considered
to make the finest examples of two styles of wine that Australia has
made peculiarly its own: fortified Muscats and fortified Tokays.

The Rutherglen region also has one of the most characterful
and colourful histories in Australian viticulture. And the tradition
continues today, with many descendants of the families who first
settled here in the 1850s still in place at their vineyards and wineries. Firms such as Campbells of Rutherglen, Chambers Rosewood,
Gehrig and Morris are still run by the families who set up the
wineries over 100 years ago.

Vines were planted as soon as the area was opened up and by
1870, when gold was discovered in what became main street,
Rutherglen, there were 2,400 hectares of vineyard in the shire,

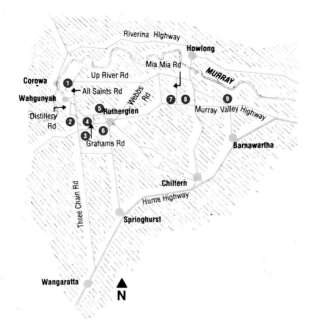

The Rutherglen Wineries

1. All Saints Estate
2. Pfeiffer
3. R L Buller & Son (Bullers Calliope)
4. Stanton & Killeen
5. Chambers Rosewood

6. Campbells of Rutherglen
7. Fairfield
8. Morris
9. Gehrig

All the wineries of Rutherglen are within 5–10 minutes' drive of each other. All those marked on this map have tasting and sales rooms. Details of the Rutherglen trail are in the local 'Tourist News', available from the Rutherglen tourist office, from Corowa, or in any motel in the area. Rutherglen is just off the Hume Highway about four hours' drive northeast of Melbourne.

making it the largest wine-producing area in Victoria. It gained a great reputation in the 1880s, the vineyard expanded and one producer, Morris, built the largest wine cellars in the southern hemisphere.

Phylloxera struck Rutherglen and the surrounding areas in 1899, and today this scourge remains endemic in the region, requiring grafting with American root stocks, as in many other vineyards worldwide, and the maintenance of a quarantine zone to prevent the louse spreading to ungrafted areas in the state. Inevitably, vineyard planting diminished and today the region has just 800 hectares in cultivation, compared with nearly 5,000 hectares before phylloxera struck.

From the early days, it was apparent that Rutherglen's fortified wines were something special. The climate is right – much hotter than the vineyard areas in southern Victoria or in South Australia – and the soil, especially the red loam which runs in a band around the town, gives a richness to the wines which makes them just the right base for fortifying.

The Rutherglen area has one of the most continental climates among Australian vineyards. The summers are hot and dry, the winters cold (with frosts) and comparatively wet. Because the spring is normally later than in regions closer to the oceans, the harvest can also run on well into the autumn, giving a long ripening period.

Of course, table wines are produced here as well – the reds from the same grape varieties as those used to make port-style wines, for which the area is also famous. Since 1953, with a drop in demand for inexpensive fortified wines, the proportion of table wines produced has increased. But what remain in the realm of fortified wines are the great wines which this area is uniquely equipped to make. So much so, in fact, that the base wines for many fortifieds made by producers elsewhere in Australia come from Rutherglen, or at least have a significant proportion of Rutherglen wines contained in them.

Methods of making Rutherglen fortifieds have remained very traditional. In an industry where irrigation is widespread, many vignerons in Rutherglen eschew the use of extra water, relying entirely on natural rainfall and believing that the resultant strain on the vines from low moisture levels is positively beneficial to the quality of the grapes. The wineries themselves, in many cases, are more like large sheds, and while tanks are used for fermentation, storage is always in wood, with casks of varying sizes filling every available nook and cranny.

Apart from the natural conditions, the fortified wines of Rutherglen have one enormous advantage over other Australian fortifieds: the attitudes of the people who make them. As already indicated, many vineyards are run by families who have owned the land virtually since it was first settled – while others, relative newcomers, have been influenced by that dedication. People such as Bill Chambers of Chambers Rosewood or Mick Morris of the Morris winery, or Norman Killeen of Stanton & Killeen, besides being great – and charming – characters, show an awareness of the quality of their fortifieds and of their special place in Australian winemaking which means that, although production of fortifieds may have fallen dramatically since the 1950s, the place of the top quality wines seems to be assured.

About 30 miles (19 km) south of Rutherglen is the smaller area of Glenrowan, also famous for its fortifieds. This is on the west side of the Warby Range of hills and presents another baking hot landscape, with the same red loam soil. Here the Baileys winery is located, one of the oldest in Australia, set up in the 1850s, and, like the wineries of Rutherglen, now producing both fortified and table wines. Close by, in the Ovens River Valley at Milawa, Brown Brothers has developed a range of Muscat-based dessert wines as well as making port-style wines and fortified Muscats.

Styles of Northeast Victoria Fortified Wine

Sherry-style wine This style was popular in the early days of Rutherglen, and *flor* yeast sent from Spain was used by Dr John Harris in 1916 to seed the wines made from Palomino grapes grown in Rutherglen. Some of the dry sherry styles (known in Australia as 'dry flor') are among the driest to be found in the country. The *amontillados*, many made from wine laid down in old *soleras*, have an authentically nutty quality about them and not too much sweetness.

Port-style wine Rutherglen port-style wine tends to be sweeter and heavier than other Australian port styles. The tawny also seems to have a greater ability to age in cask, and there are considerable *soleras* of old port-style wines in the cellars of Rutherglen. The increased plantings of Portuguese grape varieties – particularly Bastardo and Touriga Nacional – have upped the quality of vintage port-style wines in recent years, and these wines are now drier and less vegetal than those made exclusively from Shiraz. The Durif can give some dryness and extra tannin to port-style wines – as well as making good, beefy red table wines.

Fortified Muscat Every fortified Muscat producer in Rutherglen and Glenrowan/Milawa will have an immense *solera* of old wines on which to base his blends. And this accounts for a good part of the success of Rutherglen's fortifieds. A small drop of a 19th-century fortified wine added to a modern blend is enough to give it greater character, depth and intensity.

Fortified Tokays Again, as with the Muscats, it is the age of the wines used in the blends that makes this wine a success. To my mind, it is one of Australia's most complex fortifieds. The Rutherglen style is one of intense, honeyed concentration, turning chocolatey with age.

Rutherglen Producers

All Saints Estate   ★★→
All Saints Road, Wahgunyah. Additional brand: Museum Release series.
All Saints is a remarkable place. Driving up to the imposing castellated red-brick castle, with its flag flapping lazily in the breeze, it seems more like Bordeaux than northeast Victoria. The building was created by George Sutherland Smith in the 1860s. He had

previously worked at the Castle of May in northern Scotland and castles were obviously in his thoughts as he set to work on a winery. Today the building stands much as he left it, although in 1988 it left the Sutherland Smith family and is now owned by BROWN BROTHERS of Milawa. Hopefully the new owners, with their considerable resources and investment in fortified wines, will be able to raise the reputation of the winery, which seems to have lost its direction in recent years.

It is only, it seems, with the reserve wines – the Museum Release series – that the winery comes to life. Here, when I last tasted the wines, the stars were the sherry styles (especially a very fine dry *amontillado*). The vintage tawny port styles appeared to age well and to develop an attractive, somewhat burnt quality. The Muscats and Tokays used to suffer from a lightness in the house style and a lack of real intensity.

R L Buller & Son
(Bullers Calliope Vineyard)   ★★→★★★
Three Chain Road, Rutherglen, Victoria 3685. Tel (60) 329960. Founded 1921. V'yds: 23 ha. Additional brands: Black Label range; Ceramic Jar Collection; Classic Liqueur Muscat; Museum Release; Red Cross Tawny Port; Victoria range. Visits: daily 9–5.

This is a relative newcomer among the great names of Rutherglen. The firm was founded in 1921 by Reginald Buller, who took up land in a soldier resettlement scheme. He planted the Calliope vineyard, which had been abandoned since before phylloxera struck, and developed it for fortified winemaking with plantings of Shiraz, Brown Muscat, Frontignac, Grenache, Cinsuat and Muscadelle. Like all the best fortified wine vineyards in the area, it is not irrigated. There are two generations in the business, and one of the most interesting aspects of the way they work is that Andrew Buller, one of the two family winemakers, pays regular visits to Taylor, Fladgate & Yeatman in Portugal. Apart from the fortifieds, the firm also makes table wines at the Beverford Vineyard, which is much larger than Bullers Calliope.

The standard of the Black Label range is good, of a high commercial standard, and I have particularly enjoyed the Victoria range of tawny port styles (as might be expected of wines that have benefited from Portuguese experience). The Museum range consists of sherry styles and port styles. Liqueur Muscat and liqueur Frontignac are the other two fortifieds that Bullers does well.

Campbells of Rutherglen ★★★→
PO Box 44, Murray Valley Highway, Rutherglen, Victoria 3685. Tel (60) 329458. Founded 1870. V'yds: 18 ha. Additional brands: Collector's series; Isabella Tokay; Merchant Prince Muscat; Old Rutherglen Tokay, Muscat and Port; Quary Hill Tawny Port, Tokay, Muscat. Visits: Mon–Sat 9–5, Sun 10–5.

John Campbell, the founder of Campbells, arrived in Rutherglen in 1859 to prospect for gold. He worked the Bobbie Burns field, and once the gold dwindled, purchased land next door to the gold workings, which he named, again, Bobbie Burns. This 32 hectares of land still forms the heart of the Campbell vineyards, and has been added to by purchases of land in 1943 and 1952. The winery and vineyards are now run by Malcolm and Colin Campbell. Shiraz, Touriga, Alvarello, Muscadelle and Brown Muscat are used for the fortifieds.

Under half the land is now devoted to fortified wines. Campbells seems to be one of the Rutherglen companies that has managed to steer a course successfully in both fortified and table wine production. Modern winery stainless steel is much to the fore here, but the stocks of old fortifieds are large enough to give considerable quality to the wines. Like other Rutherglen producers, Colin Campbell, the winemaker, uses a type of *solera* system for his fortifieds, giving the commercial range at least four years in *solera*, and the older wines about seven. He has been experimenting with techniques for rapidly ageing fortifieds using heating processes, to replace the need for long maturation – so far, from the samples I have tasted, with only mixed success.

Quarry Hill is the basic range, and has a light and fruity Muscat. The Old Rutherglen range is the top commercial release; both the Muscat and the Tokay exhibit good intensity of fruit, with the Tokay especially full of caramel flavours streaked with orange. None of the wines is cloying. Merchant Prince is released in smaller quantities: a luscious wine, with nut and raisin flavours. The Collector's series of vintage Tokays is of a particularly high quality. The port styles are in typical Rutherglen style, with the tawnies the most successful.

Chambers Rosewood ★★★★
PO Box 8, Rutherglen, Victoria 3685. Tel (60) 329641. Founded 1858. V'yds: 28 ha. Additional brands: Dry Flor Sherry; Old Liqueur Muscat and Tokay; Special Liqueur Muscat and Tokay; Rutherglen Liqueur Muscat. Visits: Mon–Sat 10–5, Sun 11–5..

Here is one of the great originals in Rutherglen. There has been a Chambers at Rosewood for over 100 years, and present incumbent Bill Chambers, quietly-spoken, widely-read and utterly charming, makes some of the finest fortifieds in Australia. To a casual observer, used to the stainless steel and high tech of other Australian wineries, the chaos and the dark corrugated sheds which make up the Rosewood winery must seem disconcerting – but of course this is just the atmosphere in which fortifieds can excel.

The vineyard at Rosewood was originally owned by a German settler, Anthony Ruche, whose wines reached unheard of prices in Melbourne and who established the reputation of Rutherglen as a wine-producing area. When the Chambers purchased this vineyard, the Rutherglen area was booming. After phylloxera devastated the land, the vineyard was replanted and many of those vines survive to this day. The main Rosewood vineyard is unirrigated and, with its small yields, resulting from low moisture levels and old vines, produces modest quantities of just the right fruit for fortifieds.

Like many small Australian wineries, Chambers makes a bewildering variety of wines, especially in the realm of fortifieds. There are some excellent sherry styles, including a really dry *fino*, made with Palomino, and an *amontillado* that is blessed with a considerable quantity of old *finos* in the blend. The most interesting port style is a late-bottled vintage that includes Touriga Nacional, giving good dryness, but the tawnies are rather too sweet. The Muscats and Tokays come in three ranges – the Special, the Old Liqueur, and a standard commercial range. Inevitably, the Old Liqueurs are superb, based on huge stocks of old wines, with style and surprising elegance, neither of them too sweet. But the advantages of old wines in a blend are also apparent in the less expensive Special wines, particularly in the Special Liqueur Tokay, while the standard range is never cloying and has excellent acidity. All in all, these are Australian fortifieds at their best.

Fairfield   ★★→
Murray Valley Highway, Browns Plains via Rutherglen, Victoria 3685. Tel (60) 329381.

This is but the remnant of what was once the foremost vineyard in Rutherglen. It was established in the 1870s by George Frederick Morris, ancestor of the present Mick Morris of the MORRIS winery, for it was George Frederick's son who established what is now the Morris winery while his father's Fairfield estate was still flourishing. But phylloxera and family quarrels put paid to Fairfield. It was sold in 1910 and thereafter was virtually abandoned until a current member of the Morris family decided to revive it in a small way in the 1970s – 100 years after Fairfield was started up. Steve Morris, the winemaker at Fairfield, is first cousin to Mick Morris.

Today, small quantities of table and fortified wines are produced in the firm's huge stone *lagares* (wine presses), with their amazing gravity systems, which seem to have been designed to produce enough wine to quench the thirst of the whole British Empire. For people in the area, the preservation of the Fairfield name is almost as important as the wines produced – but the wine being made here is nothing to be ashamed of.

Gehrig   ★★→
Murray Valley Highway, Barnawartha, Victoria 3685. Tel (60) 267296. Founded 1858. V'yds: 10 ha. Visits: Mon–Sat 9–5, Sun 10–5.

One of the family-owned wineries that still survives in a modern age that might seem to have passed it by. The Gehrig family arrived from Germany in the 1850s, settling in Barnawartha in 1858. The current, brick house, with its prominent bell tower and large winery, dates from 1870, but the family's original small cottage still stands across the courtyard, an indication – reinforced by the friendly clutter of the winery – that little is thrown away here. Today, Bernard and winemaker son Brian are in charge.

Morris's extensive cellars and vineyards in Rutherglen

There has been a considerable improvement in the Gehrig wines in recent years, and the table wines have started to pick up trophies. The fortifieds include port styles and liqueur wines, a good vintage port style, light and fruity, and some liqueur Muscat that is very much in the local tradition.

Morris ★★★★
Mia Mia Vineyard, Rutherglen, Victoria 3685. Tel (60) 267303. Founded 1859. V'yds: 50 ha. Brands: Old Premium range. Visits: Mon–Sat 9–5, Sun 10–5.

The history of the Morris family in Rutherglen is a long one. G F Morris arrived in nearby Ovens River Valley in 1852, where he prospected for gold. He then set up as a trader and made enough money eventually to buy a 100-acre property at Browns Plain, which became the core of the FAIRFIELD vineyard. His son, C H Morris, set up the Mia Mia Vineyard in 1887 as a separate operation, and, while Fairfield disappeared, Mia Mia survived. The current generation of the Morris family is represented by Mick Morris, and, although the firm is now owned by the Orlando/ Wyndham group (one of the largest wine producers in Australia), he is still very much in charge of his family's empire. His grapes come from three main vineyards in the area: the original Mia Mia land, Mount Prior vineyard (under contract) and Buckland Valley (also under contract).

In recent years, Morris has branched widely into the field of table wines and established a considerable reputation for its whites from Sémillon and Chardonnay as well as for its red made from the local Durif grape. But Morris's greatness still rests with fortified wines, especially the liqueur Muscats and Tokays. As with the other top producers in the area, it is the stocks of old wines that give the Morris fortifieds their quality. Mick Morris still has small casks of pre-phylloxera wines which can be added to the blend of wines sold today – just tiny amounts of these are sufficient to change the whole character of a blend.

Choose any of the Morris wines and it will be great by any standards. The *amontillado* sherry style, made from Palomino, has considerable dryness and a nutty character, while the vintage port styles, when young, exhibit immense amounts of tannin (from the use of Durif in the blend) which suggests a potential for long ageing. The Old Premium range, with an average age of 12 years, is the firm's glory in both the Muscat and the Tokay versions; and the quality of the four-year old liqueur Muscat and liqueur Tokay is high, with all the right character and style in evidence.

Pfeiffer ★★★
Distillery Road, Wahgunyah, Victoria 3687. Tel (60) 332805. Founded 1984. V'yds: 4 ha. Additional brand: Old Distillery. Visits: Mon–Sat 9–5, Sun 11–4.

Chris Pfeiffer, former fortified winemaker at SEPPELT, bought his vineyard from that giant firm when it moved out of the area in 1984, and included in his purchase both the lovely stone distillery that now forms the winery, and his family house, an elegant colonial-style building quite close to the banks of Lake Moodemere. The vineyards are across a branch of the creek that flows past his winery.

The creation and acquisition of good stocks of older blending material has meant that the Pfeiffer fortifieds are showing great promise and character. The vintage port style is full of fruit, but has good tannic structure, the liqueur Muscat is a classic, lovely, rich wine with slightly burnt, marmalade fruit, while the liqueur Tokay is more delicate.

Stanton & Killeen ★★★→
PO Box 15, Rutherglen, Victoria 3685. Tel (60) 329457.
Founded 1875. V'yds: 10 ha. Additional brands: Special
Old Muscat; Show Muscat. Visits: Mon–Sat 9–5, Sun 10–5.

This is another of the original wineries of Rutherglen, founded by
the Stanton family in the 1850s. It flourished through the period of
phylloxera, but was sold to the CAMPBELL family in the 1940s.
Meanwhile, another member of the family had started the
Gracerray vineyard in 1925, and this now forms the core of the
family estate. The Killeen element arrived in 1953, when Norman
Killeen, married to Joan Stanton, joined his father-in-law in the
family firm. Now, Norman, his wife, and son Chris run the business.

There are three vineyards in the estate, plus over 300 hectares of
farm land. Two vineyards are near Lake Moodemere, to the west
of Rutherglen, while the third surrounds the Gracerray winery.
The operation is a judicious mix of ancient and modern, with
open, stone fermentation tanks still being used alongside temperature-controlled stainless steel. Nearly 80 percent of production is of
fortified wines, one of the highest proportions in Rutherglen.

The Stanton & Killeen style produces lighter wines than the
blockbusters of MORRIS and CHAMBERS ROSEWOOD, but is consistently good right across the firm's range of vintage port styles,
Muscats and Tokays. The Portuguese variety Touriga Nacional has
been planted as a contributing grape for the port styles, and this
gives a drier wine than those made wholly from Shiraz by some
other producers. Durif is also used and this supplies extra tannin. A
range of vintage port styles is sold and an excellent tawny, made
from 50 percent Touriga. The small quantity of Tokay is light and
fresh in style, the Muscats – especially the vintage Muscats – are top
class. The liqueur Muscat has an average age of 6–8 years, while
the Special Old Muscat, with lovely, light, fresh, honeyed acidity,
averages 20 years of age. There is more acidity and more old wines
in the Show Muscat.

The firm has built up considerable stocks of old wines for
blending, so, although to say that this is one of the up-and-coming
companies in Rutherglen would be to overlook its history, it does
seem that production here is currently getting better and better.

Milawa/Glenrowan Producers

Baileys of Glenrowan ★★★→★★★★
Taminick Gap Road, Glenrowan, Victoria 3675. Tel (57)
662392. Founded 1870. V'yds: 36 ha. Additional brands:
Fine Liqueur Port; Founders Tawny Port, Liqueur Muscat,
Liqueur Tokay; Gold Label Liqueur Muscat; Old Liqueur
range; Warby Range Port, Muscat, Tokay; Winemaker's
Selection Old Liqueur Muscat, Old Liqueur Tokay. Visits:
weekdays 9–5, weekends 10–5.

The Baileys vineyard is on the western face of the Warby Range,
a low, dusty row of hills which lies near shallow Lake Mokoan.
The Bailey family was one of the first to come to this region of
Victoria, in the 1840s, looking for gold, and when the gold ran out
it bought this property. The vineyard and winery remained in
family control for over 100 years, until, in 1972, it was sold to the
massive Goodman Fielder Wattie company. Recently, it has
changed hands again, and the firm is owned once more by people
with wine interests – as part of the Rothbury group, from New
South Wales.

Luckily, changes of ownership and winemaker (now Steve
Goodwin, who was born in Manchester, England, the original
home of the Bailey family) have done little to change the Baileys
operation apart from bringing useful improvements such as the
introduction of stainless steel, and an increase in the production of
table wines. The fortifieds continue to be as fine as they ever were.

The stars of the Baileys show are the Muscats. On the whole,
they tend to be even more concentrated than Rutherglen fortifieds. The Warby Range is the basic label: the wines are concentrated and the Muscat has good, rosehip flavours. The Founders
Liqueur Muscat, honeyed but again with sufficient acidity, is a top
rate commercial wine. The Founders Tokay is luscious, full of ripe
fruit, and the Old Liqueur Tokay is really huge, with delicious,
mature, fruit flavours. The vintage port styles are made from Shiraz
and are rather too sweet.

Brown Brothers Milawa Vineyard ★★★
Milawa, Victoria 3678. Founded 1889. V'yds: 20 ha. Visits:
Mon–Sat 9–5, Sun 10–5.

The Brown Brothers dynasty is one of the most remarkable families in Australian winemaking. From the early 1850s, when George Harry Brown arrived in the area and started a small vineyard at Hurdle Creek, to the present, with John Brown Senior as the patriarch and his four sons running different areas of the company, it has been a story of steady growth, with an enormous spurt in the last 30 years which has made Brown Brothers one of the largest of Australia's middle-sized wine companies.

The main part of Brown Brothers' production is table wines. The firm's own vineyards in Ovens Valley, King Valley and Hurdle Creek, and a new vineyard at Whitlands (which, at 770 m, is the highest in Australia), provide 40 percent of its grapes. But fortified wines play their part here too. The classically correct liqueur Muscats and Tokays do not quite exhibit the inspired genius of some Rutherglen wines, but with the vintage port styles, now made using a proportion of Portuguese grape varieties, there is considerable intensity of fruit, and a good, dry, tannic structure. The tawnies are light in colour and show considerable elegance. The best port style is a perfumed, not too sweet vintage from the Hurdle Creek vineyard. The Tokays – especially the older styles – have the typical orange marmalade flavours of this wine. But the best of the fortifieds (inevitably given the firm's success with Muscat dessert wines) are the liqueur Muscats, which show lovely, orange and other citrus fruit character, which balances with honey and acidity very well.

Fortified Wines
from Other Countries

South Africa

The history of winemaking in the Cape dates back to Jan van Riebeeck, the first Dutch commander, who landed in 1652. He quickly realized the potential of the Cape peninsula as a vineyard area, likening it in climate to parts of Spain and Portugal. The first vines he planted were Muscat d'Alexandrie (the Muscat of Alexandria, which he called Spanish grapes – *Spaanse druyfen* – and which later became known in the Cape as 'Hanepoot') and Chenin Blanc (known as 'Steen').

It was Hanepoot that became one of the principal constituents of what was probably the Cape's first fortified wine and was certainly one of the wine world's most famous wines: Constantia. This happened less than half a century after the first plantations were laid out when Simon van de Stel, the Cape's first governor, created the Constantia estate on the eastern slopes of the Constantiaberg mountains, facing the Indian Ocean. He planted Palomino, Hanepoot and Pontac (which Jancis Robinson says in *Vines Grapes and Wines*, Mitchell Beazley, 1986, may have been the Petit Verdot of Bordeaux), and produced some table wines that were considered far superior to anything else made in the Cape's, by then, extensive vineyards.

Governor van de Stel grew ambitious and decided to make a fortified dessert wine (he probably wished to fortify it for export purposes). To make this, it is likely that he used red and white Muscadelle plus some Frontignac (the Muscat Blanc à Petits Grains, known in France as Muscat de Frontignan). He named the wine Constantia, and it became a legend. As the wine's fame spread, so the technique for making it improved, and by the end of the 18th century it was being made from grapes that had been allowed to shrivel on the vine and become raisin-like.

Constantia was probably made on the estate right up to the advent of phylloxera, in 1885, when the Cloete family, who owned the farm, sold it to the government (although there are no records of its existence for some time before that). There is always speculation, and a certain mysteriousness, about a wine that attracted so much fame and comment but apparently left no imitators. It is possible that the closest equivalents are the fortified

Muscats of Australia, although currently an argument is raging as to whether Constantia was in fact a fortified wine at all. At Klein Constantia vineyard, once part of van de Stel's property, they now produce an unfortified dessert wine, Vin de Constance, made from Frontignac, which winemaker Ross Gower believes is in the style of the old Constantia.

But if the original Constantia died, fortified winemaking in the Cape did not. Indeed it boomed. With the arrival of the British in South Africa in 1806, and the development of an imperial market, there came a demand for fortified wines – especially those made in a port style – which lasted up to the Second World War. Sherry styles appeared later, in the 20th century, when sherry swept the British wine-drinking world after the First World War, and South African winemakers developed a cheaper alternative to the pricey (and at that time often less reliable) Spanish sherry. Cyprus sherry and Australian sherry were developed at the same time. Unlike Cyprus – but like Australia – South Africa lost its right to call these wines 'sherry' when Spain entered the EC in 1987.

Today, however, although South African sherry-style wine is still made, port-style fortifieds are equally important (especially the tawny wines). And there is a small amount of fortified Muscadel and fortified Hanepoot (both wines are known locally as Jerepigo).

Styles of South African Fortified Wine

Port-style wine A fair mixture of grapes is used in port-style wines. One of the more interesting aspects of South African fortifieds is the use of a wide range of Portuguese varieties in the port styles. In the early years of this century, Alvarelhão, Bastardo, Dozelinho do Castello and Tourigo (the local name for Touriga Nacional) were all planted. Later came Mourisco Tinto, Tinta Barroca, Cornifesto, Tinta Francisca, Tinta Roriz, Malvasia Rei and Souzão. Of this bewildering variety, Souzão and Tinta Barroca seem to be the most widely used.

Of the non-Portuguese varieties, Grenache and Cinsaut (previously known in South Africa as Hermitage) are the most widely used for port-style wines. There are also smaller plantings of California's Zinfandel and the local Pontac. Steen is used for white port-style wines.

Port-style wines are made in most of the hotter vine-growing areas, but there is a concentration of production in Stellenbosch, Paarl, the Tulbagh Valley and Robertson. The wines are made in a similar way to port proper, with fermentation being stopped with grape alcohol before it is complete. Tawny styles are aged for up to ten years in wood, ruby styles for five years. Vintage port styles are bottled after two years in wood – as in Portugal.

Sherry-style wine The Spanish Palomino grape figures in the roster of grapes used for South African sherry style wines. In addition, Steen, Sémillon (known locally as the Green Grape, from the colour of its leaves) and Pedro (not the Pedro Ximénez of Spain, but a lesser variety called Pedro Luis) are all employed in the blend.

Most grapes for sherry-style wines are grown in Boberg (for *finos*) and Klein-Karoo (for *finos* and *olorosos*). The making of sherry-style wines follows a modified form of the Spanish *solera* system. For dry styles, the wine is inoculated with yeasts to produce *flor*, and fermented dry. Fortification is carried out with wine brandy before final maturation in wood. Sweeter, *oloroso*, styles are fortified with spirit to stop any *flor* growth and then matured for up to ten years in wood.

Red and white Muscadel (or Muskadel) is made by a few producers, mainly in the Stellenbosch area, as well as Hanepoot.

Producers

Allesverloren Estate

This 180-hectare vineyard in Swartland makes what is often considered to be the best South African port-style wine (★★→★★★). It is a blend of Tinta Barroca, Pontac and Souzão.

Backsberg Estate

Sydney Back, one of the grand old men of South African wine, continues to make a Hanepoot (★★→) on his estate. Its production may be small, but it is still very much part of the South African wine scene.

The Bergkelder

This firm acts as a marketing company for a number of independent estates as well as making wines itself. It sells fortifieds under a variety of different brand names, including Drostdy sherry-style wines (made by the cooperative at Drostdy in the Tulbagh Valley), of which the Full Cream is the most attractive (★→), and the ALLESVERLOREN port-style wine .

Blaauwklippen

This producer in Stellenbosch makes a vintage port-style wine (★→) from Zinfandel and Pontac, which suffers from the usual somewhat vegetal taste that the Zinfandel produces in fortifieds.

Boplaas Estate

While fortifieds only form ten percent of production at this estate in the Klein-Karoo, they are seen as its flagship. All styles are made – dessert wines such as Muscadel and Hanepoot, and a red dessert wine from Tinta Barroca and Muscadel. Most important of all, however, are the port-style wines (★★→) in ruby, vintage, vintage reserve (only made in exceptional years) and white versions. The red port styles are made entirely from Portuguese grape varieties, the white from Steen – both styles are processed in traditional, open, stone *lagares* (wine presses).

Douglas Green Bellingham

This firm does not make wines, but uses the facilities of KWV for bottling. It sells a range of sherry-style wines under the Flor Range label, of which the Extra Dry has a definite *flor* taste (★★), as well as ruby and white port styles.

Gilbeys

Although this Stellenbosch-based firm was founded by the British company of W & A Gilbey, it is now South African-owned. Labels it sells under include Bertrams table wines and the Twee Jongegezellen estate. The firm's port-style wines go under the brand names of Malamed (a range of kosher wines) and Santys. None of the wines is very impressive (★).

Goue Vallei Wines
The Citrusdal Cooperative Winecellar (★) in the Olifants River Valley makes Jerepigo – from Pinotage, Hanepoot and Frontignac – and a red port style from Tinta Barroca and Pinotage.

KWV
The Kooperatieve Wijnbouwers Vereniging, based in Paarl, is by far the largest producer of wine in South Africa. Its purpose when it started was to enable farmers to get a better price for their grapes in the years immediately after the First World War, but it is now responsible for 95 percent of South African fortified wine exports and for a small percentage of table wines (it is not allowed to sell wine on the home market). Its sherry styles come the closest to Spanish sherry of any South African sherry-style wine. These include: Cavendish Cape (→★★★); Meymering (★★), a pale dry sherry style with a touch of *flor*, and Renasans (★★), a pale cream which benefits from a nutty aftertaste. Old Vintage (★★★), a port-style wine, is another famous product, and widely sought after.

Landskroon Estate
A vintage port style is made on this Paarl estate using Tinta Barroca, Souzão, Tinta Roriz, Cinsaut and Alicante Bouschet. It tends to be quite dry and firm, with a good measure of tannin (★★→).

Mons Ruber Estate
Unusually, for the modern South African wine industry, here is a wine producer for whom fortifieds account for the majority of production (★). The estate uses Cabernet Sauvignon to make red Elegantia Jerepigo and a port–style wine, white Muscadel to make Regalis Jerepigo, and Muscat d'Alexandrie to make a sweet, white port style and Bonitas Jerepigo.

Muratie Estate
Ruby port-style wine, called Special Old Port, is made at this

50-hectare Stellenbosch farm. The grapes used include Cinsaut plus a number of Portuguese varieties (★★).

Overgaauw Estate

A small quantity of Portuguese varieties – Touriga Nacional, Tinta Barroca, Tinta Francisca, Tinta Roriz, Cornifesto and Souzão – are the source for the port-style wines at this 71-hectare Stellenbosch estate. The first Touriga was planted in South Africa here. The range includes a vintage and a dry port style, of which the former is by far the better (★★).

Rustenberg Estate

This Stellenbosch estate is highly regarded for its table wines and, locally, for its vintage port style made from Souzão and Cabernet Sauvignon, which is only produced in dry years. It is certainly one of the best in South Africa (→★★★).

Spier Estate

This is another of the old wine farms of Stellenbosch. It started in 1692 and is now owned by the Joubert family. A vintage port-style wine (★→) is produced here as well as Mistelle, a fortified wine made from a blend of Hanepoot and Steen.

Stellenbosch Farmers' Winery

The producer of some of South Africa's biggest-selling fortifieds: wines of sound quality, including Monis sherry styles, Very Old Port, and Collector's Port (★★), which is the best of the range. Under the Sidgwick label it produces an amazingly sweet Old Brown Sherry as well as the, less complex, Ship Sherry, fortified Muscadels and Hanepoot and Government House Port.

Worcester cooperatives

A number of cooperatives in Worcester make fortified wines. Grapes grown in this hot region used mainly to be processed into raisins, so the production of fortifieds follows logically on from a local tradition. Although some port-style wines are made, the bulk of the fortifieds use Hanepoot. The best wines come from the De Doorns and the Du Toit cooperatives.

New Zealand

New Zealand's wine industry has come of age in the last 10–15 years. Although vines arrived in the country in the 1840s, wine production was never as much a part of the New Zealand scene as it was in Australia. The only people to take any interest in wine-making were Dalmatian immigrants, who, at the turn of the century, started to produce some fairly rough stuff for their own needs. It was usually fortified and made from hybrid vines rather than true *vitis vinifera*.

There are still producers who concentrate on bulk fortifieds for this market, but in the past 15 years New Zealand has followed the worldwide move to light table wines, achieving considerable success with its Sauvignon Blanc and Chardonnay and, increasingly, through the good quality of its Cabernet Sauvignon. Some wine-makers have pulled out of fortified wine production altogether, while those that remain find it is a part of their business that is increasingly in decline.

As in Australia, where fortified wine producers while losing the bulk market have developed a quality market, so in New Zealand wine producers have begun to investigate the possibilities of making top range fortifieds, especially port-style wines.

Styles of New Zealand Fortified Wine

New Zealand's fortified wine styles follow a similar pattern to Australia's, although they never achieve the same outstanding quality. There are dry and sweet sherry styles, and vintage and ruby port styles. Sweeter sherry styles will occasionally be labelled 'madeira'. The tendency in traditional fortifieds was towards sweetness, but there seems to be a move now in favour of greater elegance and dryness – in the vintage port-style wines at least. I have encountered a few tawny port styles, but have seen more *flor* sherry styles, none of which, alas, seems to have benefited from being kept under this mysterious yeast (*see* Sherry, page 88).

Port-style wine For port styles, the traditional grapes are hybrids such as Tintara and Plantet, but, with the move towards making quality port styles, these are being superseded by Cabernet Sauvignon, Pinot Noir and Merlot.

Sherry-style wine For sherry styles, the Palomino is usually used for dry wines, while sweeter wines can be made with any number of grapes (sometimes including hybrids such as Seibel and Baco 22A) although Palomino generally appears somewhere in the blend.

Producers

While few New Zealand fortified wines are exported, a number of brands are distributed nationally.

Port-style wine
Babich, a high-quality family firm, makes Reserve Port (★★→), a rich, full style of wine. Both **Cooks** and **Corbans** make port styles; Cooks' offering is a vintage style (★★), while Corbans' is the more basic Cellarman's Port (★). **Montana**, the country's largest wine producer, makes a full range of port styles. **Collards** produces one of the few not too sweet tawnies (★→). Another family company, **Glenvale**, in Hawkes Bay, makes use of a good stock of older wines when blending its port style (★→). **Matua Valley** makes one of the best vintage wines (★★→★★★), while its Hunting Lodge is a cheaper, but reliable, blended wine (★→★★).

Of the smaller wineries (often originally Dalmatian) which still specialize in fortifieds, the **Ozich** family makes a number of branded port styles, including Physicians' and St Jerome vintage (★★). **Pacific** in Henderson, makes a tawny (→★) which stays in wood for ten years, and a vintage wine (★→). **Pleasant Valley**, also in Henderson, continues to make Family Tawny, which is an enjoyable wine of its class (★). Again in Henderson, **West Brook** makes Panorama fortifieds, which they describe as 'great value for money'; they are however a declining part of the business. **Lincoln** (★) also continues to make vintage, tawny and ruby port styles, based on Pinotage, Shiraz, Seibel and Cabernet Sauvignon, but its heart lies much more with table wines. **Soljans**' Founder's Tawny is good, if rather too sweet (★→).

Sherry-style wine

There is less to recommend among the sherry style wines. Of the large companies, **Montana** makes a Flor Fino and a Pale Dry Fino (★), neither of which shows much character. Among the specialist fortified wine producers, some of the best wines come from **Lincoln** in Henderson, whose Reserve Dry Sherry (★★) has something of an *amontillado* style, and whose Palomino Dry (→★★) does exhibit some *flor* character. **Ozich** sherry styles are fairly basic, although at least well made and containing some Palomino (★). **Soljans** makes a full range of sherry styles, of which the best is the nutty medium (→★★).

Cyprus

Cyprus has a wine industry that dates back to biblical times. It did, however, virtually disappear during the occupation by the Muslim Turks, and was only revived by the arrival of the British at the end of the last century. The British created the market for Cyprus sherry, and it is Cyprus sherry which still dominates this country's wine export market.

Although these wines do not approach the quality of true Spanish sherry, Cyprus sherry can be quite acceptable. The dry style is made using specially-cultured *flor* (*see* Sherry, page 88), while the sweeter styles are left in casks in the sun to oxidize, as are the *olorosos* in Jerez. The four companies which dominate the Cyprus wine trade – **Etko**, **Keo**, **Loel** and the **Sodap** cooperative – each make a brand of Cyprus sherry using the local Xynisteri grape and Muscat of Alexandria.

Of the four brands, I find Mosaic from Keo the most consistent and attractive. The firm makes a particularly good dry style (★★). The most familiar brand is Emva, made by Etko; the Emva Cream is a major brand in the British market (★). Emva Dry is rather unpleasant (→★).

The brand from Loel is called Command. The dry style of this wine seems to have less *flor* character than the other Cyprus sherries on the market (★). Sodap's offering goes under the brand name of Lysander; the sweeter version (★) is better, to my mind, than the dry.

When Spain entered the EC, it was widely assumed that the word 'sherry' would have to be dropped by Cypriot producers. However, a special derogation (which also applied to British sherry) allowed the use of the term to continue in the UK and the Irish Republic, provided it was preceded by the name 'Cyprus'. This derogation will be phased out in 1995.

Portugal

Not only port is made in Portugal, two other fortified wines are also made here.

Producers

Moscatel de Setúbal

Just south of Lisbon, across the Tagus estuary, lie the vineyards of Setúbal. Apart from producing good, local table wines, they are famous for the Moscatel de Setúbal. This wine is bred of long-standing and honourable traditions; the first records of it date back to the 18th century, although Moscatel grapes had been planted around the town of Azeitão, north of Setúbal, for some time before that. The region was demarcated in 1907, but only for the Moscatel wines, not for table wines. Two grapes are planted: the Moscatel de Setúbal and the Moscatel Roxo.

The wine is rich and unctuous, with the flavour of caramelized oranges, and has some similarity to Málaga. It can, it seems, age in wood for an enormous length of time.

There are three producers of Moscatel de Setúbal (although there are about 900 growers). By far the largest and most important is **J M da Fonseca**, whose old winery at Azeitão is a source of pilgrimage to those wishing to taste ancient vintages of the wine. The other two producers are the **Adega Co-operativa de Palmela** and the small estate of **Quinta de São Francisco**.

Carcavelos

This is a wine that has almost disappeared from the wine scene completely. It is produced from a tiny area of vineyard that has survived in the urban sprawl between Estoril and Lisbon, along the north bank of the Tagus estuary. Created by the Marquês de Pombal, Portugal's famous 18th-century Prime Minister, who had an estate in the area, it was, like many fortifieds, made famous by the British — in this case, officers in Wellington's army during the Peninsular War.

Carcavelos is generally found (when it is found at all) in the form of a dry wine, with what some commentators have called a nutty taste, which – on the one occasion I tasted the wine – I found to be rather unpleasant. It is fortified by the addition of grape must after fermentation, to bring it up to 20 percent alcohol. The grapes used include Arinto, Boais, Espadeiro and Galego Dourado – a formidable array for such a tiny amount of wine being made.

Until recently there was only one producer left: **Quinta do Barão**, owned by Raul Ferreira, which makes about 200 hectolitres a year. However, in 1987, Manuel Bulhosa of **Quinta dos Pesos**, a retired oil executive, began producing small quantities of Carcavelos under the supervision of Australian winemaker, Peter Bright, who works for J P Vinhos in nearby Setúbal, and the results do in fact suggest that this wine could be more than simply a historical curiosity.

Argentina

Considerable quantities of sherry-style wines are made in the region around Mendoza and (principally) San Juan, on the flat, irrigated plain to the east of the Andes, in the centre of Argentina. Pedro Ximénez and Palomino are the grapes used. I have not had a chance to taste any of the wines.